Henry Wadsworth Longfellow
Selected Poems

Henry Wadsworth Longfellow
Selected Poems

Edited by
Johanna Brownell and Lisa Lipkin

CASTLE BOOKS

This edition published by
CASTLE BOOKS
a division of Book Sales, Inc.
114 Northfield Avenue
Edison, NJ 08837

Designed by Tony Meisel
Printed in the United States of America

ISBN 0-7858-1285-7

CONTENTS

Introduction

The poems of Henry Wadsworth Longfellow have earned him an unshakable place in American literary history, recalled through popular nursery rhymes and songs or in unforgettable lines, such as "On the shores of Gitche Gumee," or "Listen my children and you shall hear of the midnight ride of Paul Revere." So many of his poems are known to us that Longfellow may well qualify as America's best loved poet.

Born in 1807 to Stephen and Zilpah Longfellow, Henry grew up in the seaport town of Portland, Maine, along with seven brothers and sisters. He began school at age three and his love of words soon became apparent. "Master Henry Longfellow is one of the best boys we have in school," his elementary teacher wrote in a report to his parents. "He spells and reads very well." His mother helped cultivate his love of literature by reading aloud to him and his brothers classics like *Don Quixote*, by Cervantes and traditional Gaelic folktales. But it was the "Sketch Book," by Washington Irving, which was most influential to Longfellow, engendering a lifetime fascination with the Native-American legend and landscape.

At 19, while still a senior at Bowdoin College, Longfellow was invited to become a professor of the college's newly established department of modern languages. Here, Longfellow created an innovative curricula, introducing his students to the literature of Spain, France, Italy and Germany. Five years later, in 1834, he left Bowdoin for a professorship at Harvard. In preparation for his new position, Longfellow and his wife of three years, Mary Storer Potter, traveled to Europe. But tragedy struck in Rotterdam, when his wife died. Longfellow returned to America where he took up his position at Harvard. He remained a lone romantic figure in Cambridge, sporting yellow gloves and dramatic waistcoasts while producing a plethora of books of verse, such as *Voices of the Night* (1839), and *Ballads* (1841), which includes "The Wreck of the Hesperus," and "The Village Blacksmith."

Longfellow married Fanny Appleton in 1843 and soon began work on "Evangeline," based on a story outline given to him by his good friend, Nathaniel Hawthorne. The poem achieved critical success and prompted Longfellow to devote his energies full-time to writing. He resigned his position at Harvard in 1854, and began work on one his greatest poems : "The Song of Hiawatha." Soon followed "The Courtship of Miles Standish" which sold thousands of copies within its first day of publication.

Longfellow had become a literary giant but, despite Longfellow's fortune and success in the literary world, his personal life again faced tragedy when, in 1861, his second wife, Francis, was burnt to death in a freak household accident in which her dress caught fire. Longfellow memorialized her just before his own death in 1879 with "The Cross of Snow."

Perhaps Longfellow's life is best illuminated by a letter he once wrote to his father as young man, explaining why he couldn't pursue a career as lawyer. "I most eagerly aspire after future eminence in literature; my whole soul burns ardently for it, and every earthly thought centers in it. Whatever I do study ought to be engaged in with all my soul, —for I will be eminent in something." And indeed he was.

The Builders

All are architects of Fate,
    Working in these walls of Time;
Some with massive deeds and great,
    Some with ornaments and rhyme.

Nothing useless is, or low;
    Each thing in its place is best;
And what seems is idle show
    Strengthens and supports the rest.

For the structure that we raise,
    Time is with materials filled;
Our to-days and yesterdays
    Are the blocks with which we build.

The Arrow and the Song

I shot an arrow into the air,
It fell to earth, I knew not where;
For, so swiftly it flew, the sight
Could not follow it in its flight.

I breathed a song into the air,
It fell to earth, I knew not where;
For who has sight so keen and strong,
That it can follow the flight of song?

Long, long afterward, in an oak
I found the arrow, still unbroke;
And the song, from beginning to end,
I found again in the heart of a friend.

The Old Clock on the Stairs

Somewhat back from the village street
Stands the old-fashioned country-seat.
Across its antique portico
Tall poplar-trees their shadows throw;
And from its station in the hall
An ancient timepiece says to all, –
    "Forever – never!
    Never – forever!"

Halfway up the stairs it stands,
And points and beckons with its hands
From its case of massive oak,
Like a monk, who, under his cloak,
Crosses himself, and sighs, alas!
With sorrowful voice to all who pass, –
    "Forever – never!
    Never – forever!"

By day its voice is low and light;
But in the silent dead of night,
Distinct as a passing footstep's fall,
It echoes along the vacant hall,
Along the ceiling, along the floor,
And seems to say, at each chamber-door, –
    "Forever – never!
    Never – forever!"

Through days of sorrow and of mirth,
Through days of death and days of birth,
Through every swift vicissitude
Of changeful time, unchanged it has stood,
And as if, like God, it all things saw,
It calmly repeats those words of awe, –
    "Forever – never!
    Never – forever!"

In that mansion used to be
Free-hearted Hospitality;
His great fires up the chimney roared;
The stranger feasted at his board;
But, like the skeleton at the feast,
That warning timepiece never ceased, –
     "Forever – never!
     Never – forever!"

There groups of merry children played,
There youths and maidens dreaming strayed;
O precious hours! O golden prime,
And affluence of love and time!
Even as a miser counts his gold,
Those hours the ancient timepiece told, –
     "Forever – never!
     Never – forever!"

From that chamber, clothed in white,
The bride came forth on her wedding night;
There, in that silent room below,
The dead lay in his shroud of snow;
And in the hush that followed the prayer,
Was heard the old clock on the stair, –
     "Forever – never!
     Never – forever!"

All are scattered now and fled,
Some are married, some are dead;
And when I ask, with throbs of pain,
"Ah! when shall they all meet again?"
As in the days long since gone by,
The ancient timepiece makes reply, –
     "Forever – never!
     Never – forever!"

Never here, forever there,
Where all parting, pain, and care,
And death, and time shall disappear, –
Forever there, but never here!
The horologe of Eternity
Sayeth this incessantly, –
        "Forever – never!
        Never – forever!"

The Day is Done

The day is done, and the darkness
    Falls from the wings of Night,
As a feather is wafted downward
    From an eagle in his flight.

I see the lights of the village
    Gleam through the rain and the mist,
And a feeling of sadness comes o'er me,
    That my soul cannot resist:

A feeling of sadness and longing,
    That is not akin to pain,
And resembles sorrow only
    As the mist resembles the rain.

Come, read to me some poem,
    Some simple and heartfelt lay,
That shall soothe this restless feeling,
    And banish the thoughts of day.

Not from the grand old masters,
    Not from the bards sublime,
Whose distant footsteps echo
    Through the corridors of Time.

For, like strains of martial music,
    Their mighty thoughts suggest
Life's endless toil and endeavor;
And to-night I long for rest.

Read from some humbler poet,
    Whose songs gushed from his heart,
As showers from the clouds of summer,
    Or tears from the eyelids start;

Who, through long days of labor,
    And nights devoid of ease,
Still heard in his soul the music
    Of wonderful melodies.

Such songs have power to quiet
    The restless pulse of care,
And come like the benediction
    That follows after prayer.

Then read from the treasured volume
    The poem of thy choice,
And lend to the rhyme of the poet
    The beauty of thy voice.

And the night shall be filled with music,
    And the cares that infest the day,
Shall fold their tents, like the Arabs,
    And as silently steal away.

My Lost Youth

Often I think of the beautiful town
    That is seated by the sea;
Often in thought go up and down
The pleasant streets of that dear old town,
    And my youth comes back to me.
       And a verse of a Lapland song
       Is haunting my memory still:
"A boy's will is the wind's will,
And the thoughts of youth are long, long thoughts."

I can see the shadowy lines of its trees,
    And catch, in sudden gleams,
The sheen of the far-surrounding seas,
And islands that were the Hesperides
    Of all my boyish dreams.
       And the burden of that old song,
       It murmurs and whispers still:
"A boy's will is the wind's will,
And the thoughts of youth are long, long thoughts."

I remember the black wharves and the slips,
    And the sea-tides tossing free;
And Spanish sailors with bearded lips,
And the beauty and mystery of the ships,
    And the magic of the sea.
       And the voice of that wayward song
       Is singing and saying still:
"A boy's will is the wind's will,
And the thoughts of youth are long, long thoughts."

I remember the bulwarks by the shore,
    And the fort upon the hill;
The sunrise gun, with its hollow roar,
The drum-beat repeated o'er and o'er,
    And the bugle wild and shrill.
       And the music of that old song
       Throbs in my memory still:
"A boy's will is the wind's will,
And the thoughts of youth are long, long thoughts."

I remember the sea-fight far away,
    How it thundered o'er the tide!
And the dead captains, as they lay
In their graves, o'erlooking the tranquil bay,
    Where they in battle died.
        And the sound of that mournful song
        Goes through me with a thrill:
"A boy's will is the wind's will,
And the thoughts of youth are long, long thoughts."

I can see the breezy dome of groves,
    The shadows of Deering's Woods;
And the friendships old and the early loves
Come back with a Sabbath sound, as of doves
    In quiet neighborhoods.
        And the verse of that sweet old song,
        It flutters and murmurs still:
"A boy's will is the wind's will,
And the thoughts of youth are long, long thoughts."

I remember the gleams and glooms that dart
    Across the school-boy's brain;
The song and the silence in the heart,
That in part are prophecies, and in part
    Are longings wild and vain.
        And the voice of that fitful song
        Sings on, and is never still:
"A boy's will is the wind's will,
And the thoughts of youth are long, long thoughts."

There are things of which I may not speak;
    There are dreams that cannot die;
There are thoughts that make the strong heart weak,
And bring a pallor into the cheek,
    And a mist before the eye.
        And the words of that fatal song
        Come over me like a chill:
"A boy's will is the wind's will,
And the thoughts of youth are long, long thoughts."

Strange to me now are the forms I meet
 When I visit the dear old town;
But the native air is pure and sweet,
And the trees that o'ershadow each well-known street,
 As they balance up and down, .
  Are singing the beautiful song,
  Are sighing and whispering still:
"A boy's will is the wind's will,
And the thoughts of youth are long, long thoughts."

And Deering's Woods are fresh and fair,
 And with joy that is almost pain
My heart goes back to wander there,
And among the dreams of the days that were,
 I find my lost youth again.
  And the strange and beautiful song,
  The groves are repeating it still:
"A boy's will is the wind's will,
And the thoughts of youth are long, long thoughts."

Paul Revere's Ride

Listen my children and you shall hear
Of the midnight ride of Paul Revere,
On the eighteenth of April, in Seventy-five;
Hardly a man is now alive
Who remembers that famous day and year.

He said to his friend, "If the British march
By land or sea from the town to-night,
Hang a lantern aloft in the belfry arch
Of the North Church tower as a signal light,—
One if by land, and two if by sea;
And I on the opposite shore will be,
Ready to ride and spread the alarm
Through every Middlesex village and farm,
For the country folk to be up and to arm."

Then he said "Good-night!" and with muffled oar
Silently rowed to the Charlestown shore,
Just as the moon rose over the bay,
Where swinging wide at her moorings lay
The Somerset, British man-of-war;
A phantom ship, with each mast and spar
Across the moon like a prison bar,
And a huge black hulk, that was magnified
By its own reflection in the tide.

Meanwhile, his friend through alley and street
Wanders and watches, with eager ears,
Till in the silence around him he hears
The muster of men at the barrack door,
The sound of arms, and the tramp of feet,
And the measured tread of the grenadiers,
Marching down to their boats on the shore.

Then he climbed the tower of the Old North Church,
By the wooden stairs, with stealthy tread,
To the belfry chamber overhead,
And startled the pigeons from their perch
On the sombre rafters, that round him made
Masses and moving shapes of shade,—
By the trembling ladder, steep and tall,
To the highest window in the wall,
Where he paused to listen and look down
A moment on the roofs of the town
And the moonlight flowing over all.

Beneath, in the churchyard, lay the dead,
In their night-encampment on the hill,
Wrapped in silence so deep and still
That he could hear, like a sentinel's tread
The watchful night-wind, as it went
Creeping along from tent to tent,
And seeming to whisper, "All is well!"
A moment only he feels the spell
Of the place and the hour, and the secret dread
Of the lonely belfry and the dead;
For suddenly all his thoughts are bent

On a shadowy something far away,
Where the river widens to meet the bay,–
A line of black that bends and floats
On the rising tide, like a bridge of boats.

Meanwhile, impatient to mount and ride,
Booted and spurred, with a heavy stride
On the opposite shore walked Paul Revere.
Now he patted his horse's side,
Now he gazed at the landscape far and near,
Then, impetuous, stamped the earth,
And turned and tightened his saddle-girth;
But mostly he watched with eager search
The belfry tower of the Old North Church,
As it rose above the graves on the hill,
Lonely and spectral and sombre and still.
And lo! as he looks, on the belfry's height
A glimmer, and then a gleam of light!
He springs to the saddle, the bridle he turns,
But lingers and gazes, till full on his sight
A second lamp in the belfry burns!

A hurry of hoofs in a village street,
A shape in the moonlight, a bulk in the dark,
And beneath, from the pebbles, in passing, a spark
Struck out by a steed flying fearless and fleet:
That was all! And yet, through the gloom and the light,
The fate of a nation was riding that night;
And the spark struck out by that steed, in his flight,
Kindled the land into flame with its heat.

He has left the village and mounted the steep,
And beneath him, tranquil and broad and deep,
Is the Mystic, meeting the ocean tides;
And under the alders that skirt its edge,
Now soft on the sand, now loud on the ledge,
Is heard the tramp of his steed as he rides.

It was twelve by the village clock,
When he crossed the bridge into Medford town.
He heard the crowing of the cock,

And the barking of the farmer's dog,
And felt the damp of the river fog,
That rises after the sun goes down.

It was one by the village clock,
When he galloped into Lexington.
He saw the gilded weathercock
Swim in the moonlight as he passed,
And the meeting-house windows, black and bare,
Gaze at him with a spectral glare,
As if they already stood aghast
At the bloody work they would look upon.

It was two by the village clock,
When he came to the bridge in Concord town.
He heard the bleating of the flock,
And the twitter of birds among the trees,
And felt the breath of the morning breeze
Blowing over the meadow brown.
And one was safe and asleep in his bed
Who at the bridge would be first to fall,
Who that day would be lying dead,
Pierced by a British musket-ball.

You know the rest. In the books you have read
How the British Regulars fired and fled, –
How the farmers gave them ball for ball,
From behind each fence and farmyard wall,
Chasing the red-coats down the lane,
Then crossing the fields to emerge again
Under the trees at the turn of the road,
And only pausing to fire and load.

So through the night rode Paul Revere;
And so through the night went his cry of alarm
To every Middlesex village and farm, –
A cry of defiance, and not of fear,
A voice in the darkness, a knock at the door,
And a word that shall echo forevermore!
For, borne on the night-wind of the Past,
Through all our history, to the last,

In the hour of darkness and peril and need,
The people will waken and listen to hear
The hurrying hoof-beats of that steed,
And the midnight message of Paul Revere.

The Building of the Ship

"Build me straight, O worthy Master!
    Stanch and strong, a goodly vessel,
That shall laugh at all disaster,
    And with wave and whirlwind wrestle!"

The merchant's word
Delighted the Master heard;
For his heart was in his work, and the heart
Giveth grace unto every Art.
A quiet smile played round his lips,
As the eddies and dimples of the tide
Play round the bows of ships,
That steadily at anchor ride.
And with a voice that was full of glee,
He answered, "Erelong we will launch
A vessel as goodly, and strong, and stanch,
As ever weathered a wintry sea!"
And first with nicest skill and art,
Perfect and finished in every part,
A little model the Master wrought,
Which should be to the larger plan
What the child is to the man,
Its counterpart in miniature;
That with a hand more swift and sure
The greater labor might be brought
To answer to his inward thought.
And as he labored, his mind ran o'er
The various ships that were built of yore,
And above them all, and strangest of all
Towered the Great Harry, crank and tall,
Whose picture was hanging on the wall,

With bows and stern raised high in air,
And balconies hanging here and there,
And signal lanterns and flags afloat,
And eight round towers, like those that frown
From some old castle, looking down
Upon the drawbridge and the moat.
And he said with a smile, "Our ship, I wis,
Shall be of another form than this!"
It was of another form, indeed;
Built for freight, and yet for speed,
A beautiful and gallant craft;
Broad in the beam, that the stress of the blast,
Pressing down upon sail and mast,
Might not the sharp bows overwhelm;
Broad in the beam, but sloping aft
With graceful curve and slow degrees,
That she might be docile to the helm,
And that the currents of parted seas,
Closing behind, with mighty force,
Might aid and not impede her course.

In the ship-yard stood the Master,
With the model of the vessel,
That should laugh at all disaster,
And with wave and whirlwind wrestle!

Covering many a rood of ground,
Lay the timber piled around;
Timber of chestnut, and elm, and oak,
And scattered here and there, with these,
The knarred and crooked cedar knees;
Brought from regions far away,
From Pascagoula's sunny bay,
And the banks of the roaring Roanoke!
Ah! what a wondrous thing it is
To note how many wheels of toil
One thought, one word, can set in motion!
There 's not a ship that sails the ocean,
But every climate, every soil,
Must bring its tribute, great or small,
And help to build the wooden wall!

The sun was rising o'er the sea,
And long the level shadows lay,
As if they, too, the beams would be
Of some great, airy argosy,
Framed and launched in a single day.
That silent architect, the sun,
Had hewn and laid them every one,
Ere the work of man was yet begun.
Beside the Master, when he spoke,
A youth, against an anchor leaning,
Listened, to catch his slightest meaning.
Only the long waves, as they broke
In ripples on the pebbly beach,
Interrupted the old man's speech.

Beautiful they were, in sooth,
The old man and the fiery youth!
The old man, in whose busy brain
Many a ship that sailed the main
Was modelled o'er and o'er again; —
The fiery youth, who was to be
The heir of his dexterity,
The heir of his house, and his daughter's hand,
When he had built and launched from land
What the elder head had planned.

"Thus," said he, "will we build this ship!
Lay square the blocks upon the slip,
And follow well this plan of mine.
Choose the timbers with greatest care;
Of all that is unsound beware;
For only what is sound and strong
To this vessel shall belong.
Cedar of Maine and Georgia pine
Here together shall combine.
A goodly frame, and a goodly fame,
And the Union be her name!
For the day that gives her to the sea
Shall give my daughter unto thee!"

The Master's word
Enraptured the young man heard;
And as he turned his face aside,
With a look of joy and a thrill of pride
Standing before
Her father's door,
He saw the form of his promised bride.
The sun shone on her golden hair,
And her cheek was glowing fresh and fair,
With the breath of morn and the soft sea air.
Like a beauteous barge was she,
Still at rest on the sandy beach,
Just beyond the billow's reach;
But he
Was the restless, seething, stormy sea!
Ah, how skilful grows the hand
That obeyeth Love's command!
It is the heart, and not the brain,
That to the highest doth attain,
And he who followeth Love's behest
Far excelleth all the rest!

Thus with the rising of the sun
Was the noble task begun,
And soon throughout the shipyard's bounds
Were heard the intermingled sounds
Of axes and of mallets, plied
With vigorous arms on every side;
Plied so deftly and so well,
That, ere the shadows of evening fell,
The keel of oak for a noble ship,
Scarfed and bolted, straight and strong,
Was lying ready, and stretched along
The blocks, well placed upon the slip.
Happy, thrice happy, every one
Who sees his labor well begun,
And not perplexed and multiplied,
By idly waiting for time and tide!

And when the hot, long day was o'er,
The young man at the Master's door

Sat with the maiden calm and still,
And within the porch, a little more
Removed beyond the evening chill,
The father sat, and told them tales
Of wrecks in the great September gales,
Of pirates coasting the Spanish Main,
And ships that never came back again,
The chance and change of a sailor's life,
Want and plenty, rest and strife,
His roving fancy, like the wind,
That nothing can stay and nothing can bind,
And the magic charm of foreign lands,
With shadows of palms, and shining sands,
Where the tumbling surf,
O'er the coral reefs of Madagascar,
Washes the feet of the swarthy Lascar,
As he lies alone and asleep on the turf.
And the trembling maiden held her breath
At the tales of that awful, pitiless sea,
With all its terror and mystery,
The dim, dark sea, so like unto Death,
That divides and yet unites mankind!
And whenever the old man paused, a gleam
From the bowl of his pipe would awhile illume
The silent group in the twilight gloom,
And thoughtful faces, as in a dream;
And for a moment one might mark
What had been hidden by the dark,
That the head of the maiden lay at rest,
Tenderly, on the young man's breast!

Day by day the vessel grew,
With timbers fashioned strong and true,
Stemson and keelson and sternson-knee,
Till, framed with perfect symmetry,
A skeleton ship rose up to view!
And around the bows and along the side
The heavy hammers and mallets plied,
Till after many a week, at length,
Wonderful for form and strength,
Sublime in its enormous bulk,

Loomed aloft the shadowy hulk!
And around it columns of smoke, upwreathing,
Rose from the boiling, bubbling, seething
Caldron, that glowed,
And overflowed
With the black tar, heated for the sheathing.
And amid the clamors
Of clattering hammers,
He who listened heard now and then
The song of the Master and his men:

"Build me straight, O worthy Master,
    Stanch and strong, a goodly vessel,
That shall laugh at all disaster,
    And with wave and whirlwind wrestle!"

With oaken brace and copper band,
Lay the rudder on the sand,
That, like a thought, should have control
Over the movement of the whole;
And near it the anchor, whose giant hand
Would reach down and grapple with the land,
And immovable and fast
Hold the great ship against the bellowing blast!
And at the bows an image stood,
By a cunning artist carved in wood,
With robes of white, that far behind
Seemed to be fluttering in the wind.
It was not shaped in a classic mould,
Not like a Nymph or Goddess of old,
Or Naiad rising from the water,
But modelled from the Master's daughter!
On many a dreary and misty night,
'T will be seen by the rays of the signal light,
Speeding along through the rain and the dark,
Like a ghost in its snow-white sark,
The pilot of some phantom bark,
Guiding the vessel, in its flight,
By a path none other knows aright!
Behold, at last,
Each tall and tapering mast

Is swung into its place;
Shrouds and stays
Holding it firm and fast!

Long ago,
In the deer-haunted forests of Maine,
When upon mountain and plain
Lay the snow,
They fell, – those lordly pines!
Those grand, majestic pines!
'Mid shouts and cheers
The jaded steers,
Panting beneath the goad,
Dragged down the weary, winding road
Those captive kings so straight and tall,
To be shorn of their streaming hair,
And naked and bare,
To feel the stress and the strain
Of the wind and the reeling main,
Whose roar
Would remind them forevermore
Of their native forests they should not see again.

And everywhere
The slender, graceful spars
Poise aloft in the air,
And at the masthead,
White, blue, and red,
A flag unrolls the stripes and stars.
Ah! when the wanderer, lonely, friendless,
In foreign harbors shall behold
That flag unrolled,
'T will be as a friendly hand
Stretched out from his native land,
Filling his heart with memories sweet and endless!

All is finished! and at length
Has come the bridal day
Of beauty and of strength.
To-day the vessel shall be launched!
With fleecy clouds the sky is blanched,

And o'er the bay,
Slowly, in all his splendors dight,
The great sun rises to behold the sight.

The ocean old,
Centuries old,
Strong as youth, and as uncontrolled,
Paces restless to and fro,
Up and down the sands of gold.
His beating heart is not at rest;
And far and wide,
With ceaseless flow,
His beard of snow
Heaves with the heaving of his breast.
He waits impatient for his bride.
There she stands,
With her foot upon the sands,
Decked with flags and streamers gay,
In honor of her marriage day,
Her snow-white signals fluttering, blending,
Round her like a veil descending,
Ready to be
The bride of the gray old sea.

On the deck another bride
Is standing by her lover's side.
Shadows from the flags and shrouds,
Like the shadows cast by clouds,
Broken by many a sunny fleck,
Fall around them on the deck.

The prayer is said,
The service read,
The joyous bridegroom bows his head;
And in tears the good old Master
Shakes the brown hand of his son,
Kisses his daughter's glowing cheek
In silence, for he cannot speak,
And ever faster
Down his own the tears begin to run.

The worthy pastor —
The shepherd of that wandering flock,
That has the ocean for its wold,
That has the vessel for its fold,
Leaping ever from rock to rock —
Spake, with accents mild and clear,
Words of warning, words of cheer,
But tedious to the bridegroom's ear.
He knew the chart
Of the sailor's heart,
All its pleasures and its griefs,
All its shallows and rocky reefs,
All those secret currents, that flow
With such resistless undertow,
And lift and drift, with terrible force,
The will from its moorings and its course.
Therefore he spake, and thus said he:

"Like unto ships far off at sea,
Outward or homeward bound, are we.
Before, behind, and all around,
Floats and swings the horizon's bound,
Seems at its distant rim to rise
And climb the crystal wall of the skies,
And then again to turn and sink,
As if we could slide from its outer brink.
Ah! it is not the sea,
It is not the sea that sinks and shelves,
But ourselves
That rock and rise
With endless and uneasy motion,
Now touching the very skies,
Now sinking into the depths of ocean.
Ah! if our souls but poise and swing
Like the compass in its brazen ring,
Ever level and ever true
To the toil and the task we have to do,
We shall sail securely, and safely reach
The Fortunate Isles, on whose shining beach
The sights we see, and the sounds we hear,
Will be those of joy and not of fear!"

Then the Master,
With a gesture of command,
Waved his hand;
And at the word,
Loud and sudden there was heard,
All around them and below,
The sound of hammers, blow on blow,
Knocking away the shores and spurs.
And see! she stirs!
She starts, – she moves, – she seems to feel
The thrill of life along her keel,
And, spurning with her foot the ground,
With one exulting, joyous bound,
She leaps into the ocean's arms!

And lo! from the assembled crowd
There rose a shout, prolonged and loud,
That to the ocean seemed to say,
"Take her, O bridegroom, old and gray,
Take her to thy protecting arms,
With all her youth and all her charms!"

How beautiful she is! How fair
She lies within those arms, that press
Her form with many a soft caress
Of tenderness and watchful care!
Sail forth into the sea, O ship!
Through wind and wave, right onward steer!
The moistened eye, the trembling lip,
Are not the signs of doubt or fear.

Sail forth into the sea of life,
O gentle, loving, trusting wife,
And safe from all adversity
Upon the bosom of that sea
Thy comings and thy goings be!
For gentleness and love and trust
Prevail o'er angry wave and gust;
And in the wreck of noble lives
Something immortal still survives!

Thou, too, sail on, O Ship of State!
Sail on, O Union, strong and great!
Humanity with all its fears,
With all the hopes of future years,
Is hanging breathless on thy fate!
We know what Master laid thy keel,
What Workmen wrought thy ribs of steel,
Who made each mast, and sail, and rope,
What anvils rang, what hammers beat,
In what a forge and what a heat
Were shaped the anchors of thy hope!
Fear not each sudden sound and shock,
'T is of the wave and not the rock;
'T is but the flapping of the sail,
And not a rent made by the gale!
In spite of rock and tempest's roar,
In spite of false lights on the shore,
Sail on, nor fear to breast the sea!
Our hearts, our hopes, are all with thee,
Our hearts, our hopes, our prayers, our tears,
Our faith triumphant o'er our fears,
Are all with thee, – are all with thee!

Seaweed

When descends on the Atlantic
 The gigantic
Storm-wind of the equinox,
Landward in his wrath he scourges
 The toiling surges,
Laden with seaweed from the rocks:

From Bermuda's reefs; from edges
 Of sunken ledges,
In some far-off, bright Azore;
From Bahama, and the dashing,
 Silver-flashing
Surges of San Salvador;

From the tumbling surf, that buries
    The Orkneyan skerries,
Answering the hoarse Hebrides;
And from wrecks of ships, and drifting
    Spars, uplifting
On the desolate, rainy seas; —

Ever drifting, drifting, drifting,
    On the shifting
Currents of the restless main;
Till in sheltered coves, and reaches
    Of sandy beaches,
All have found repose again.

So when storms of wild emotion
    Strike the ocean
Of the poet's soul, ere long
From each cave and rocky fastness,
    In its vastness,
Floats some fragment of a song:

From the far-off isles enchanted,
    Heaven has planted
With the golden fruit of Truth;
From the flashing surf, whose vision
    Gleams Elysian
In the tropic clime of Youth;

From the strong Will, and the Endeavor
    That forever
Wrestle with the tides of Fate;
From the wreck of Hopes far-scattered,
    Tempest-shattered,
Floating waste and desolate; —

Ever drifting, drifting, drifting
    On the shifting
Currents of the restless heart;
Till at length in books recorded,
    They, like hoarded
Household words, no more depart.

The Fire of Drift-Wood

Devereux Farm, near Marblehead

*After a visit to Marblehead, described in the following excerpt from a
letter, Longfellow was inspired to write The Fire of Drift-Wood.*

"September 29, 1846. A delicious drive with F. through Malden
and Lynn to Marblehead, to visit E.W. at the Devereux Farm by the
sea-side. Drove across the beautiful sand. What a delicious scene!
The ocean in the sunshine changing from the silvery hue of the
thin waves upon the beach, through the lighter and the deeper green,
to a rich purple in the horizon. We recalled the times past, and the
days when we were at Nahant. The Devereux Farm is by the sea,
some miles from Lynn. An old-fashioned farm-hourse, with low
rooms, and narrow windows rattling in the sea-breeze."

We sat within the farm-house old,
  Whose windows, looking o'er the bay,
Gave to the sea-breeze damp and cold,
  An easy entrance, night and day.

Not far away we saw the port,
  The strange, old-fashioned, silent town,
The lighthouse, the dismantled fort,
  The wooden houses, quaint and brown.

We sat and talked until the night,
  Descending, filled the little room;
Our faces faded from the sight,
  Our voices only broke the gloom.

We spake of many a vanished scene,
  Of what we once had thought and said,
Of what had been, and might have been,
  And who was changed, and who was dead;

And all that fills the hearts of friends,
    When first they feel, with secret pain,
Their lives thenceforth have separate ends,
    And never can be one again;

The first slight swerving of the heart,
    That words are powerless to express,
And leave it still unsaid in part,
    Or say it in too great excess.

The very tones in which we spake
    Had something strange, I could but mark;
The leaves of memory seemed to make
    A mournful rustling in the dark.

Oft died the words upon our lips,
    As suddenly, from out the fire
Built of the wreck of stranded ships,
    The flames would leap and then expire.

And, as their splendor flashed and failed,
    We thought of wrecks upon the main,
Of ships dismasted, that were hailed
    And sent no answer back again.

The windows, rattling in their frames,
    The ocean, roaring up the beach,
The gusty blast, the bickering flames,
    All mingled vaguely in our speech;

Until they made themselves a part
    Of fancies floating through the brain,
The long-lost ventures of the heart,
    That send no answers back again.

O flames that glowed! O hearts that yearned!
    They were indeed too much akin,
The drift-wood fire without that burned,
    The thoughts that burned and glowed within.

Dante

Tuscan, that wandereth through the realms of gloom
    With thoughtful pace, and sad, majestic eyes,
    Stern thoughts and awful from thy soul arise,
    Like Farinata from his fiery tomb.
Thy sacred song is like the trump of doom;
    Yet in thy heart what human sympathies,
    What soft compassion glows, as in the skies
    The tender stars their clouded lamps relume!
Methinks I see thee stand with pallid cheeks
    By Fra Hilario in his diocese,
    As up the convent-walls, in golden streaks,
The ascending sunbeams mark the day's decrease;
    And, as he asks what there the stranger seeks,
    Thy voice along the cloister whispers "Peace!"

Divina Commedia

The six sonnets which follow were written during the progress of
Mr. Longfellow's work in translating *The Divina Commedia*, and
were published as poetical flyleaves to the three parts. The first was
written just after he had put the first two cantos of *Inferno* into the
hands of the printer. This, with the second, prefaced *Inferno;* the
third and fourth introduced *Purgatorio*, and the fifth and the sixth
Paradiso.

Oft have I seen at some cathedral door
    A laborer, pausing in the dust and heat,
    Lay down his burden, and with reverent feet
    Enter, and cross himself, and on the floor
Kneel to repeat his paternoster o'er;
    Far off the noises of the world retreat;
    The loud vociferations of the street
    Become an undistinguishable roar.
So, as I enter here from day to day,
    And leave my burden at this minster gate,
    Kneeling in prayer, and not ashamed to pray,

The tumult of the time disconsolate
     To inarticulate murmurs dies away,
     While the eternal ages watch and wait.

II.

How strange the sculptures that adorn these towers!
     This crowd of statues, in whose folded sleeves
     Birds build their nests; while canopied with leaves
     Parvis and portal bloom like trellised bowers,
And the vast minster seems a cross of flowers!
     But fiends and dragons on the gargoyled eaves
     Watch the dead Christ between the living thieves,
     And, underneath, the traitor Judas lowers!
Ah! from what agonies of heart and brain,
     What exultations trampling on despair,
     What tenderness, what tears, what hate of wrong,
What passionate outcry of a soul in pain,
     Uprose this poem of the earth and air,
     This mediæval miracle of song!

III.

I enter, and I see thee in the gloom
     Of the long aisles, O poet saturnine!
     And strive to make my steps keep pace with thine.
     The air is filled with some unknown perfume;
The congregation of the dead make room
     For thee to pass; the votive tapers shine;
     Like rooks that haunt Ravenna's groves of pine
     The hovering echoes fly from tomb to tomb.
From the confessionals I hear arise
     Rehearsals of forgotten tragedies,
     And lamentations from the crypts below;
And then a voice celestial that begins
     With the pathetic words, "Although your sins
     As scarlet be," and ends with "as the snow."

IV

With snow–white veil and garments as of flame,
    She stands before thee, who so long ago
    Filled thy young heart with passion and the woe
    From which thy song and all its splendors came;
And while with stern rebuke she speaks thy name,
    The ice about thy heart melts as the snow
    On mountain heights, and in swift overflow
    Comes gushing from thy lips in sobs of shame.
Thou makest full confession; and a gleam,
    As of the dawn on some dark forest cast,
    Seems on thy lifted forehead to increase;
Lethe and Eunoë – the remembered dream
    And the forgotten sorrow – bring at last
    That perfect pardon which is perfect peace.

I lift mine eyes, and all the windows blaze
    With forms of Saints and holy men who died,
    Here martyred and hereafter glorified;
    And the great Rose upon its leaves displays
Christ's Triumph, and the angelic roundelays,
    With splendor upon splendor multiplied;
    And Beatrice again at Dante's side
    No more rebukes, but smiles her words of praise.
And then the organ sounds, and unseen choirs
    Sing the old Latin hymns of peace and love
    And benedictions of the Holy Ghost;
And the melodious bells among the spires
    O'er all the house-tops and through heaven above
    Proclaim the elevation of the Host!

O star of morning and of liberty!
    O bringer of the light, whose splendor shines
    Above the darkness of the Apennines,
    Forerunner of the day that is to be!

The voices of the city and the sea,
 The voices of the mountains and the pines,
 Repeat thy song, till the familiar lines
 Are footpaths for the thought of Italy!
Thy fame is blown abroad from all the heights,
 Through all the nations, and a sound is heard,
 As of a mighty wind, and men devout,
Strangers of Rome, and the new proselytes,
 In their own language hear thy wondrous word,
 And many are amazed and many doubt.

Chaucer

An old man in a lodge within a park;
 The chamber walls depicted all around
 With portraitures of huntsman, hawk, and hound,
 And the hurt deer. He listeneth to the lark,
Whose song comes with the sunshine through the dark
 Of painted glass in leaden lattice bound;
 He listeneth and he laugheth at the sound,
 Then writeth in a book like any clerk.
He is the poet of the dawn, who wrote
 The Canterbury Tales, and his old age
 Made beautiful with song; and as I read
I hear the crowing cock, I hear the note
 Of lark and linnet, and from every page
 Rise odors of ploughed field or flowery mead.

Keats

The young Endymion sleeps Endymion's sleep;
 The shepherd-boy whose tale was left half told!
 The solemn grove uplifts its shield of gold
 To the red rising moon, and loud and deep
The nightingale is singing from the steep;
 It is midsummer, but the air is cold;

Can it be death? Alas, beside the fold
A shepherd's pipe lies shattered near his sheep.
Lo! in the moonlight gleams a marble white,
On which I read: "Here lieth one whose name
Was writ in water." And was this the meed
Of his sweet singing? Rather let me write:
"The smoking flax before it burst to flame
Was quenched by death, and broken the bruised
reed."

Milton

I pace the sounding sea-beach and behold
How the voluminous billows roll and run,
Upheaving and subsiding, while the sun
Shines through their sheeted emerald far unrolled,
And the ninth wave, slow gathering fold by fold
All its loose-flowing garments into one,
Plunges upon the shore, and floods the dun
Pale reach of sands, and changes them to gold.
So in majestic cadence rise and fall
The mighty undulations of thy song,
O sightless bard, England's Mæonides!
And ever and anon, high over all
Uplifted, a ninth wave superb and strong,
Floods all the soul with its melodious seas.

Shakespeare

A vision as of crowded city streets,
With human life in endless overflow;
Thunder of thoroughfares; trumpets that blow
To battle; clamor, in obscure retreats,
Of sailors landed from their anchored fleets;
Tolling of bells in turrets, and below
Voices of children, and bright flowers that throw
O'er garden walls their intermingled sweets!

This vision comes to me when I unfold
    The volume of the Poet paramount,
    Whom all the Muses loved, not one alone; –
Into his hands they put the lyre of gold,
    And, crowned with sacred laurel at their fount,
    Placed him as Musagetes on their throne.

Morituri Salutamus

Poem for the Fiftieth Anniversary of the Class of 1825 in Bowdoin College

"O Cæsar, we who are about to die
Salute you!" was the gladiators' cry
In the arena, standing face to face
With death and with the Roman populace.

O ye familiar scenes,– ye groves of pine,
That once were mine and are no longer mine,–
Thou river, widening through the meadows green
To the vast sea, so near and yet unseen, –
Ye halls, in whose seclusion and repose
Phantoms of fame, like exhalations, rose
And vanished,– we who are about to die,
Salute you; earth and air and sea and sky,
And the Imperial Sun that scatters down
His sovereign splendors upon grove and town.

Ye do not answer us! ye do not hear!
We are forgotten; and in your austere
And calm indifference, ye little care
Whether we come or go, or whence or where.
What passing generations fill these halls,
What passing voices echo from these walls,
Ye heed not; we are only as the blast,
A moment heard, and then forever past.

Not so the teachers who in earlier days
Led our bewildered feet through learning's maze;
They answer us – alas! what have I said?
What greetings come there from the voiceless dead?
What salutation, welcome, or reply?
What pressure from the hands that lifeless lie?
They are no longer here; they all are gone
Into the land of shadows,– all save one.
Honor and reverence, and the good repute
That follows faithful service as its fruit,
Be unto him, whom living we salute.

The great Italian poet, when he made
His dreadful journey to the realms of shade,
Met there the old instructor of his youth,
And cried in tones of pity and of ruth:
"Oh, never from the memory of my heart
Your dear, paternal image shall depart,
Who while on earth, ere yet by death surprised,
Taught me how mortals are immortalized;
How grateful am I for that patient care
All my life long my language shall declare."

To-day we make the poet's words our own,
And utter them in plaintive undertone;
Nor to the living only be they said,
But to the other living called the dead,
Whose dear, paternal images appear
Not wrapped in gloom, but robed in sunshine here;
Whose simple lives, complete and without flaw,
Were part and parcel of great Nature's law;
Who said not to their Lord, as if afraid,
"Here is thy talent in a napkin laid,"
But labored in their sphere, as men who live
In the delight that work alone can give.
Peace be to them; eternal peace and rest,
And the fulfillment of the great behest:
"Ye have been faithful over a few things,
Over ten cities shall ye reign as kings."

And ye who fill the places we once filled,
And follow in the furrows that we tilled,
Young men, whose generous hearts are beating high,
We who are old, and are about to die,
Salute you; hail you; take your hands in ours,
And crown you with our welcome as with flowers!

How beautiful is youth! how bright it gleams
With its illusions, aspirations, dreams!
Book of Beginnings, Story without End,
Each maid a heroine, and each man a friend!
Aladdin's Lamp, and Fortunatus' Purse,
That holds the treasures of the universe!
All possibilities are in its hands,
No danger daunts it, and no foe withstands;
In its sublime audacity of faith,
"Be thou removed!" it to the mountain saith,
And with ambitious feet, secure and proud,
Ascends the ladder leaning on the cloud!

As ancient Priam at the Scæan gate
Sat on the walls of Troy in regal state
With the old men, too old and weak to fight,
Chirping like grasshoppers in their delight
To see the embattled hosts, with spear and shield,
Of Trojans and Achaians in the field;
So from the snowy summits of our years
We see you in the plain, as each appears,
And question of you; asking, "Who is he
That towers above the others? Which may be
Atreides, Menelaus, Odysseus,
Ajax the great, or bold Idomeneus?"

Let him not boast who puts his armor on
As he who puts it off, the battle done.
Study yourselves; and most of all note well
Wherein kind Nature meant you to excel.
Not every blossom ripens into fruit;
Minerva, the inventress of the flute,
Flung it aside, when she her face surveyed
Distorted in a fountain as she played;

The unlucky Marsyas found it, and his fate
Was one to make the bravest hesitate.
Write on your doors the saying wise and old,
"Be bold! be bold!" and everywhere, "Be bold;
Be not too bold!" Yet better the excess
Than the defect; better the more than less;
Better like Hector in the field to die,
Than like a perfumed Paris turn and fly.

And now, my classmates; ye remaining few
That number not the half of those we knew,
Ye, against whose familiar names not yet
The fatal asterisk of death is set,
Ye I salute! The horologe of Time
Strikes the half-century with a solemn chime,
And summons us together once again,
The joy of meeting not unmixed with pain.

Where are the others? Voices from the deep
Caverns of darkness answer me: "They sleep!"
I name no names; instinctively I feel
Each at some well-remembered grave will kneel,
And from the inscription wipe the weeds and moss,
For every heart best knoweth its own loss.
I see their scattered gravestones gleaming white
Through the pale dusk of the impending night;
O'er all alike the impartial sunset throws
Its golden lilies mingled with the rose;
We give to each a tender thought, and pass
Out of the graveyards with their tangled grass,
Unto these scenes frequented by our feet
When we were young, and life was fresh and sweet.

What shall I say to you? What can I say
Better than silence is? When I survey
This throng of faces turned to meet my own,
Friendly and fair, and yet to me unknown,
Transformed the very landscape seems to be;
It is the same, yet not the same to me.
So many memories crowd upon my brain,
So many ghosts are in the wooded plain,

I fain would steal away, with noiseless tread,
As from a house where some one lieth dead.
I cannot go; – I pause;– I hesitate;
My feet reluctant linger at the gate;
As one who struggles in a troubled dream
To speak and cannot, to myself I seem.

Vanish the dream! Vanish the idle fears!
Vanish the rolling mists of fifty years!
Whatever time or space may intervene,
I will not be a stranger in this scene.
Here every doubt, all indecision, ends;
Hail, my companions, comrades, classmates, friends!

Ah me! the fifty years since last we met
Seem to me fifty folios bound and set
By Time, the great transcriber, on his shelves,
Wherein are written the histories of ourselves.
What tragedies, what comedies, are there;
What joy and grief, what rapture and despair!
What chronicles of triumph and defeat,
Of struggle, and temptation, and retreat!
What records of regrets, and doubts, and fears!
What pages blotted, blistered by our tears!
What lovely landscapes on the margin shine,
What sweet, angelic faces, what divine
And holy images of love and trust,
Undimmed by age, unsoiled by damp or dust!

Whose hand shall dare to open and explore
These volumes, closed and clasped forevermore?
Not mine. With reverential feet I pass;
I hear a voice that cries, "Alas! alas!
Whatever hath been written shall remain,
Nor be erased nor written o'er again;
The unwritten only still belongs to thee:
Take heed, and ponder well what that shall be."

As children frightened by a thunder-cloud
Are reassured if some one reads aloud
A tale of wonder, with enchantment fraught,

Or wild adventure, that diverts their thought,
Let me endeavor with a tale to chase
The gathering shadows of the time and place,
And banish what we all too deeply feel
Wholly to say, or wholly to conceal.

In mediæval Rome, I know not where,
There stood an image with its arm in air,
And on its lifted finger, shining clear,
A golden ring with the device, "Strike here!"
Greatly the people wondered, though none guessed
The meaning that these words but half expressed,
Until a learned clerk, who at noonday
With downcast eyes was passing on his way,
Paused, and observed the spot, and marked it well,
Whereon the shadow of the finger fell;
And, coming back at midnight, delved, and found
A secret stairway leading underground.
Down this he passed into a spacious hall,
Lit by a flaming jewel on the wall;
And opposite, in threatening attitude,
With bow and shaft a brazen statue stood.
Upon its forehead, like a coronet,
Were these mysterious words of menace set:
"That which I am, I am; my fatal aim
None can escape, not even yon luminous flame!"

Midway the hall was a fair table placed,
With cloth of gold, and golden cups enchased
With rubies, and the plates and knives were gold,
And gold the bread and viands manifold.
Around it, silent, motionless, and sad,
Were seated gallant knights in armor clad,
And ladies beautiful with plume and zone,
But they were stone, their hearts within were stone;
And the vast hall was filled in every part
With silent crowds, stony in face and heart.

Long at the scene, bewildered and amazed
The trembling clerk in speechless wonder gazed;
Then from the table, by his greed made bold,

He seized a goblet and a knife of gold,
And suddenly from their seats the guests upsprang,
The vaulted ceiling with loud clamors rang,
The archer sped his arrow, at their call,
Shattering the lambent jewel on the wall,
And all was dark around and overhead; –
Stark on the floor the luckless clerk lay dead!

The writer of this legend then records
Its ghostly application in these words:
The image is the Adversary old,
Whose beckoning finger points to realms of gold;
Our lusts and passions are the downward stair
That leads the soul from a diviner air;
The archer, Death; the flaming jewel, Life;
Terrestrial goods, the goblet and the knife;
The knights and ladies, all whose flesh and bone
By avarice have been hardened into stone;
The clerk, the scholar whom the love of pelf
Tempts from his books and from his nobler self.

The scholar and the world! The endless strife,
The discord in the harmonies of life!
The love of learning, the sequestered nooks,
And all the sweet serenity of books;
The market-place, the eager love of gain,
Whose aim is vanity, and whose end is pain!

But why, you ask me, should this tale be told
To men grown old, or who are growing old?
It is too late! Ah, nothing is too late
Till the tired heart shall cease to palpitate.
Cato learned Greek at eighty; Sophocles
Wrote his grand Oedipus, and Simonides
Bore off the prize of verse from his compeers,
When each had numbered more than fourscore years,
And Theophrastus, at fourscore and ten,
Had but begun his Characters of Men.
Chaucer, at Woodstock with the nightingales,
At sixty wrote the Canterbury Tales;
Goethe at Weimar, toiling to the last,

Completed Faust when eighty years were past.
These are indeed exceptions; but they show
How far the gulf-stream of our youth may flow
Into the arctic regions of our lives,
Where little else than life itself survives.

As the barometer foretells the storm
While still the skies are clear, the weather warm
So something in us, as old age draws near,
Betrays the pressure of the atmosphere.
The nimble mercury, ere we are aware,
Descends the elastic ladder of the air;
The telltale blood in artery and vein
Sinks from its higher levels in the brain;
Whatever poet, orator, or sage
May say of it, old age is still old age.
It is the waning, not the crescent moon;
The dusk of evening, not the blaze of noon;
It is not strength, but weakness; not desire,
But its surcease; not the fierce heat of fire,
The burning and consuming element,
But that of ashes and of embers spent,
In which some living sparks we still discern,
Enough to warm, but not enough to burn.

What then? Shall we sit idly down and say
The night hath come; it is no longer day?
The night hath not yet come; we are not quite
Cut off from labor by the failing light;
Something remains for us to do or dare;
Even the oldest tree some fruit may bear;
Not Oedipus Coloneus, or Greek Ode,
Or tales of pilgrims that one morning rode
Out of the gateway of the Tabard Inn,
But other something, would we but begin;
For age is opportunity no less
Than youth itself, though in another dress,
And as the evening twilight fades away
The sky is filled with stars, invisible by day.

The Evening Star

Lo! in the painted oriel of the West,
    Whose panes the sunken sun incarnadines,
    Like a fair lady at her casement, shines
    The evening star, the star of love and rest!
And then anon she doth herself divest
    Of all her radiant garments, and reclines
    Behind the sombre screen of yonder pines,
    With slumber and soft dreams of love oppressed.
O my beloved, my sweet Hesperus!
    My morning and my evening star of love!
    My best and gentlest lady! even thus,
As that fair planet in the sky above,
    Dost thou retire unto thy rest at night,
    And from thy darkened window fades the light.

Mezzo Cammin

Half of my life is gone, and I have let
    The years slip from me and have not fulfilled
    The aspiration of my youth, to build
    Some tower of song with lofty parapet.
Not indolence, nor pleasure, nor the fret
    Of restless passions that would not be stilled,
    But sorrow, and a care that almost killed,
    Kept me from what I may accomplish yet;
Though, half-way up the hill, I see the Past
    Lying beneath me with its sounds and sights, –
    A city in the twilight dim and vast,
With smoking roofs, soft bells, and gleaming lights, –
    And hear above me on the autumnal blast
    The cataract of Death far thundering from the
heights.

The Children's Hour

Between the dark and the daylight,
    When the night is beginning to lower,
Comes a pause in the day's occupations,
    That is known as the Children's Hour.

I hear in the chamber above me
    The patter of little feet,
The sound of a door that is opened,
    And voices soft and sweet.

From my study I see in the lamplight,
    Descending the broad hall stair,
Grave Alice, and laughing Allegra,
    And Edith with golden hair.

A whisper, and then a silence:
    Yet I know by their merry eyes
They are plotting and planning together
    To take me by surprise.

A sudden rush from the stairway,
    A sudden raid from the hall!
By three doors left unguarded
    They enter my castle wall!

They climb up into my turret
    O'er the arms and back of my chair;
If I try to escape, they surround me;
    They seem to be everywhere.

They almost devour me with kisses,
    Their arms about me entwine,
Till I think of the Bishop of Bingen
    In his Mouse-Tower on the Rhine!

Do you think, O blue-eyed banditti,
    Because you have scaled the wall,
Such an old mustache as I am
    Is not a match for you all!

I have you fast in my fortress,
    And will not let you depart,
But put you down into the dungeon
    In the round-tower of my heart.

And there will I keep you forever,
    Yes, forever and a day,
Till the walls shall crumble to ruin,
    And moulder in dust away!

There Was a Little Girl

There was a little girl,
Who had a little curl,
Right in the middle of her forehead.
When she was good,
She was very good indeed,
But when she was bad she was horrid.

Hymn to the Night

Aspasie, trillistos.

I heard the trailing garments of the Night
    Sweep through her marble halls!
I saw her sable skirts all fringed with light
    From the celestial walls!

I felt her presence, by its spell of might,
    Stoop o'er me from above;
The calm, majestic presence of the Night,
    As of the one I love.

I heard the sounds of sorrow and delight,
    The manifold, soft chimes,
That fill the haunted chambers of the Night,
    Like some old poet's rhymes.

From the cool cisterns of the midnight air
    My spirit drank repose;
The fountain of perpetual peace flows there, –
    From those deep cisterns flows.

O holy Night! from thee I learn to bear
    What man has borne before!
Thou layest thy finger on the lips of Care,
    And they complain no more.

Peace! Peace! Orestes-like I breathe this prayer!
    Descend with broad-winged flight,
The welcome, the thrice-prayed for, the most fair,
    The best-beloved Night!

The Cross of Snow

In the long, sleepless watches of the night,
    A gentle face – the face of one long dead –
    Looks at me from the wall, where round its head
    The night-lamp casts a halo of pale light.
Here in this room she died; and soul more white
    Never through martyrdom of fire was led
    To its repose; nor can in books be read
    The legend of a life more benedight.
There is a mountain in the distant West
    That, sun-defying, in its deep ravines
    Displays a cross of snow upon its side.
Such is the cross I wear upon my breast
    These eighteen years, through all the changing
        scenes
    And seasons, changeless since the day she died.

Nature

As a fond mother, when the day is o'er,
    Leads by the hand her little child to bed,
    Half willing, half reluctant to be led,
    And leave his broken playthings on the floor,
Still gazing at them through the open door,
    Nor wholly reassured and comforted
    By promises of others in their stead,
    Which, though more splendid, may not please him
    more;
So Nature deals with us, and takes away
    Our playthings one by one, and by the hand
    Leads us to rest so gently, that we go
Scarce knowing if we wish to go or stay,
    Being too full of sleep to understand
    How far the unknown transcends what we know.

Snow-flakes

Out of the bosom of the Air,
    Out of the cloud-folds of her garments shaken,
Over the woodlands brown and bare,
    Over the harvest-fields forsaken,
        Silent, and soft, and slow
        Descends the snow.

Even as our cloudy fancies take
    Suddenly shape in some divine expression,
Even as the troubled heart doth make
    In the white countenance confession,
        The troubled sky reveals
        The grief it feels.

This is the poem of the air,
    Slowly in silent syllables recorded;
This is the secret of despair,
    Long in its cloudy bosom hoarded,
        Now whispered and revealed
        To wood and field.

The Sound of the Sea

The sea awoke at midnight from its sleep,
And round the pebbly beaches far and wide
I heard the first wave of the rising tide
Rush onward with uninterrupted sweep;
A voice out of the silence of the deep,
A sound mysteriously multiplied
As of a cataract from the mountain's side,
Or roar of winds upon a wooded steep.
So comes to us at times, from the unknown
And inaccessible solitudes of being,
The rushing of the sea-tides of the soul;
And inspirations, that we deem our own,
Are some divine foreshadowing and foreseeing
Of things beyond our reason or control.

A Psalm of Life

WHAT THE HEART OF THE YOUNG MAN SAID TO THE PSALMIST

Longfellow said of this poem: "I kept it some time in manuscript, unwilling to show it to any one, it being a voice from my innermost heart, at a time when I was rallying from depression." Before it was published in the "Knickerbocker Magazine," October 1838, it was read by the poet to his college class at the close of a lecture on Goethe. Its title, though used now exclusively for this poem, was originally, in the poet's mind, a generic one. He notes from time to time that he has written a psalm, a psalm of death, or another psalm of life. The "psalmist" is thus the poet himself. When printed in the "Knickerbocker" it bore as a motto the lines from Crashaw:

> Life that shall send
> A challenge to its end,
> And when it comes say, Welcome, friend.

Tell me not, in mournful numbers,
    Life is but an empty dream! –
For the soul is dead that slumbers,
    And things are not what they seem.

Life is real! Life is earnest!
    And the grave is not its goal;
Dust thou art, to dust returnest,
    Was not spoken of the soul.

Not enjoyment, and not sorrow,
    Is our destined end or way;
But to act, that each to-morrow
    Find us farther than to-day.

Art is long, and Time is fleeting,
    And our hearts, though stout and brave,
Still, like muffled drums, are beating
    Funeral marches to the grave.

In the world's broad field of battle,
    In the bivouac of Life,
Be not like dumb, driven cattle!
    Be a hero in the strife!

Trust no Future, howe'er pleasant!
    Let the dead Past bury its dead!
Act, – act in the living Present!
    Heart within, and God o'erhead!

Lives of great men all remind us
    We can make our lives sublime,
And, departing, leave behind us
    Footprints on the sands of time;

Footprints, that perhaps another,
    Sailing o'er life's solemn main,
A forlorn and shipwrecked brother,
    Seeing, shall take heart again.

Let us, then, be up and doing,
    With a heart for any fate;
Still achieving, still pursuing,
    Learn to labor and to wait.

The Reaper and the Flowers

There is a Reaper, whose name is Death,
    And, with his sickle keen,
He reaps the bearded grain at a breath,
    And the flowers that grow between.

"Shall I have naught that is fair?" saith he;
    "Have naught but the bearded grain?
Though the breath of these flowers is sweet to me,
    I will give them all back again."

He gazed at the flowers with tearful eyes,
    He kissed their drooping leaves;
It was for the Lord of Paradise
    He bound them in his sheaves.

"My Lord has need of these flowerets gay,"
    The Reaper said, and smiled;
"Dear tokens of the earth are they,
    Where He was once a child."

"They shall all bloom in fields of light,
    Transplanted by my care,
And saints, upon their garments white,
    These sacred blossoms wear."

And the mother gave, in tears and pain,
    The flowers she most did love;
She knew she should find them all again
    In the fields of light above.

O, not in cruelty, not in wrath,
    The Reaper came that day;
'T was an angel visited the green earth,
    And took the flowers away.

Footsteps of Angels

When the hours of Day are numbered,
    And the voices of the Night
Wake the better soul that slumbered,
    To a holy, calm delight;

Ere the evening lamps are lighted,
    And, like phantoms grim and tall,
Shadows from the fitful firelight
    Dance upon the parlor wall;

Then the forms of the departed
    Enter at the open door;
The beloved, the true-hearted
    Come to visit me once more;

He, the young and strong, who cherished
    Noble longings for the strife,
By the roadside, fell and perished,
    Weary with the march of life!

They, the holy ones and weakly,
    Who the cross of suffering bore,
Folded their pale hands so meekly,
    Spake with us on earth no more!

And with them the Being Beauteous,
    Who unto my youth was given,
More than all things else to love me
    And is now a saint in heaven.

With a slow and noiseless footstep
    Comes that messenger divine
Takes the vacant chair beside me,
    Lays her gentle hand in mine.

And she sits and gazes at me
    With those deep and tender eyes
Like the stars, so still and saint-like,
    Looking downward from the skies.

Uttered not, yet comprehended
    In the spirit's voiceless prayer,
Soft rebukes, in blessings ended,
    Breathing from her lips of air.

Oh though oft depressed and lonely
    All my fears are laid aside
If I but remember only
    Such as these have lived and died!

The Skeleton in Armor

Speak! speak! thou fearful guest,
Who, with thy hollow breast
Still in rude armor drest,
    Comest to daunt me!
Wrapt not in Eastern balms,
But with thy fleshless palms
Stretched, as if asking alms,
    Why dost thou haunt me?"

Then, from those cavernous eyes
Pale flashes seemed to rise,
As when the Northern skies
    Gleam in December;
And, like the water's flow
Under December's snow,
Came a dull voice of woe
    From the heart's chamber.

"I was a Viking old!
My deeds, though manifold,
No Skald in song has told,
    No Saga taught thee!
Take heed, that in thy verse
Thou dost the tale rehearse,
Else dread a dead man's curse
    For this I sought thee.

"Far in the Northern Land,
By the wild Baltic's strand,
I, with my childish hand,
    Tamed the gerfalcon;
And, with my skates fast-bound,
Skimmed the half-frozen Sound,
That the poor whimpering hound
    Trembled to walk on.

"Oft to his frozen lair
Tracked I the grisly bear,
While from my path the hare
    Fled like a shadow;
Oft through the forest dark
Followed the were-wolf's bark,
Until the soaring lark
    Sang from the meadow.

"But when I older grew,
Joining a corsair's crew,
O'er the dark sea I flew
    With the marauders.
Wild was the life we led;
Many the souls that sped,
Many the hearts that bled
    By our stern orders.

"Many a wassail-bout
Wore the long Winter out;
Often our midnight shout
    Set the cocks crowing,
As we the Berserk's tale
Measured in cups of ale,
Draining the oaken pail,
    Filled to o'erflowing.

"Once as I told in glee
Tales of the stormy sea,
Soft eyes did gaze on me,
    Burning yet tender;
And as the white stars shine
On the dark Norway pine,
On that dark heart of mine
    Fell their soft splendor.

"I wooed the blue-eyed maid,
Yielding, yet half afraid,
And in the forest's shade
    Our vows were plighted.

Under its loosened vest
Fluttered her little breast,
Like birds within their nest
    By the hawk frighted.

"Bright in her father's hall
Shields gleamed upon the wall,
Loud sang the minstrels all,
    Chaunting his glory;
When of old Hildebrand
I asked his daughter's hand,
Mute did the minstrels stand
    To hear my story.

"While the brown ale he quaffed,
Loud then the champion laughed.
And as the wind gusts waft
    The sea-foam brightly,
So the loud laugh of scorn,
Out of those lips unshorn,
From the deep drinking-horn
    Blew the foam lightly.

"She was a Prince's child,
I but a Viking wild,
And though she blushed and smiled,
    I was discarded!
Should not the dove so white
Follow the sea-mew's flight
Why did they leave that night
    Her nest unguarded?

"Scarce had I put to sea,
Bearing the maid with me, –
Fairest of all was she
    Among the Norsemen!
When on the white sea-strand,
Waving his armed hand,
Saw we old Hildebrand,
    With twenty horsemen.

"Then launched they to the blast,
Bent like a reed each mast,
Yet we were gaining fast,
    When the wind failed us;
And with a sudden flaw
Came round the gusty Skaw,
So that our foe we saw
    Laugh as he hailed us.

"And as to catch the gale
Round veered the flapping sail,
'Death!' was the helmsman's hail,
    'Death without quarter!'
Mid-ships with iron keel
Struck we her ribs of steel;
Down her black hulk did reel
    Through the black water!

"As with his wings aslant,
Sails the fierce cormorant,
Seeking some rocky haunt,
    With his prey laden,–
So toward the open main,
Beating to sea again,
Through the wild hurricane
    Bore I the maiden.

"Three weeks we westward bore,
And when the storm was o'er,
Cloud-like we saw the shore
    Stretching to leeward;
There for my lady's bower
Built I the lofty tower,
Which, to this very hour,
    Stands looking seaward.

"There lived we many years;
Time dried the maiden's tears;
She had forgot her fears,
    She was a mother;
Death closed her mild blue eyes,
Under that tower she lies;
Ne'er shall the sun arise
    On such another!

"Still grew my bosom then,
Still as a stagnant fen!
Hateful to me were men
    The sunlight hateful!
In the vast forest here,
Clad in my warlike gear,
Fell I upon my spear,
    O, death was grateful!

"Thus, seamed with many scars
Bursting these prison bars,
Up to its native stars
    My soul ascended!
There from the flowing bowl
Deep drinks the warrior's soul,
Skoal! to the Northland! *skoal!*"
    Thus the tale ended.

The Village Blacksmith

Under a spreading chestnut-tree
    The village smithy stands;
The smith, a mighty man is he,
    With large and sinewy hands;
And the muscles of his brawny arms
    Are strong as iron bands.

His hair is crisp, and black, and long,
    His face is like the tan;
His brow is wet with honest sweat,
    He earns whate'er he can,
And looks the whole world in the face,
    For he owes not any man.

Week in, week out, from morn till night,
    You can hear his bellows blow;
You can hear him swing his heavy sledge,
    With measured beat and slow,
Like a sexton ringing the village bell,
    When the evening sun is low.

And children coming home from school
    Look in at the open door;
They love to see the flaming forge,
    And hear the bellows roar,
And catch the burning sparks that fly
    Like chaff from a threshing-floor.

He goes on Sunday to the church,
    And sits among his boys;
He hears the parson pray and preach,
    He hears his daughter's voice,
Singing in the village choir,
    And it makes his heart rejoice.

It sounds to him like her mother's voice,
    Singing in Paradise!

He needs must think of her once more,
　　How in the grave she lies;
And with his hard, rough hand he wipes
　　A tear out of his eyes.

Toiling,– rejoicing,– sorrowing,
　　Onward through life he goes;
Each morning sees some task begin,
　　Each evening sees it close;
Something attempted, something done,
　　Has earned a night's repose.

Thanks, thanks to thee, my worthy friend,
　　For the lesson thou hast taught!
Thus at the flaming forge of life
　　Our fortunes must be wrought;
Thus on its sounding anvil shaped
　　Each burning deed and thought.

Excelsior

The shades of night were falling fast,
As through an Alpine village passed
A youth, who bore, 'mid snow and ice,
A banner with the strange device,
　　Excelsior!

His brow was sad; his eye beneath,
Flashed like a falchion from its sheath,
And like a silver clarion rung
The accents of that unknown tongue,
　　Excelsior!

In happy homes he saw the light
Of household fires gleam warm and bright;
Above, the spectral glaciers shone,
And from his lips escaped a groan,
　　Excelsior!

"Try not the Pass!" the old man said;
"Dark lowers the tempest overhead,
The roaring torrent is deep and wide!"
And loud that clarion voice replied,
       Excelsior!

"Oh stay," the maiden said, "and rest
Thy weary head upon this breast! "
A tear stood in his bright blue eye,
But still he answered, with a sigh,
       Excelsior!

"Beware the pine-tree's withered branch!
Beware the awful avalanche!"
This was the peasant's last Good-night,
A voice replied, far up the height,
       Excelsior!

At break of day, as heavenward
The pious monks of Saint Bernard
Uttered the oft-repeated prayer,
A voice cried through the startled air,
       Excelsior!

A traveller, by the faithful bound,
Half-buried in the snow was found,
Still grasping in his hand of ice
That banner with the strange device,
       Excelsior!

There in the twilight cold and gray,
Lifeless, but beautiful, he lay,
And from the sky, serene and far,
A voice fell, like a falling star,
       Excelsior!

The Wreck of the Hesperus

It was the schooner Hesperus,
    That sailed the wintry sea;
And the skipper had taken his little daughter,
    To bear him company.

Blue were her eyes as the fairy-flax,
    Her cheeks like the dawn of day,
And her bosom white as the hawthorn buds,
    That ope in the month of May.

The skipper he stood beside the helm,
    His pipe was in his mouth,
And he watched how the veering flaw did blow
    The smoke now West, now South.

Then up spake an old Sailor,
    Had sailed to the Spanish Main,
"I pray thee, put into yonder port,
    For I fear a hurricane.

"Last night, the moon had a golden ring,
    And to-night no moon we see!"
The skipper, he blew a whiff from his pipe,
    And a scornful laugh laughed he.

Colder and louder blew the wind,
    A gale from the Northeast,
T'he snow fell hissing in the brine,
    And the billows frothed like yeast.

Down came the storm, and smote amain
    The vessel in its strength;
She shuddered and paused, like a frighted steed,
    Then leaped her cable's length.

"Come hither! come hither! my little daughter,
    And do not tremble so;
For I can weather the roughest gale
    That ever wind did blow."

He wrapped her warm in his seaman's coat
    Against the stinging blast;
He cut a rope from a broken spar,
    And bound her to the mast.

"O fatherl I hear the church-bells ring,
    Oh say, what may it be?'
"'Tis a fog-bell on a rock-bound coast!"–
    And he steered for the open sea.

"O fathert I hear the sound of guns,
    Oh say, what may it be?"
"Some ship in distress, that cannot live
    In such an angry sea!"

"O fatherl I see a gleaming light,
    Oh say, what may it be?"
But the father answered never a word,
    A frozen corpse was he.

Lashed to the helm, all stiff and stark,
    With his face turned to the skies,
The lantern gleamed through the gleaming snow
    On his fixed and glassy eyes.

Then the maiden clasped her hands and prayed
    That saved she might be;
And she thought of Christ, who stilled the wave,
    On the Lake of Galilee.

And fast through the midnight dark and drear,
    Through the whistling sleet and snow,
Like a sheeted ghost, the vessel swept
    Tow'rds the reef of Norman's Woe.

And ever the fitful gusts between
    A sound came from the land;
It was the sound of the trampling surf
    On the rocks and the hard sea-sand.

The breakers were right beneath her bows,
    She drifted a dreary wreck,
And a whooping billow swept the crew
    Like icicles from her deck.

She struck where the white and fleecy waves
    Looked soft as carded wool,
But the cruel rocks, they gored her side
    Like the horns of an angry bull.

Her rattling shrouds, all sheathed in ice,
    With the masts went by the board;
Like a vessel of glass, she stove and sank,
    Ho! ho! the breakers roared!

At daybreak, on the bleak sea-beach,
    A fisherman stood aghast,
To see the form of a maiden fair,
    Lashed close to a drifting mast.

The salt sea was frozen on her breast,
    The salt tears in her eyes;
And be saw her hair, like the brown sea-weed,
    On the billows fall and rise.

Such was the wreck of the Hesperus,
    In the midnight and the snow!
Christ save us all from a death like this,
    On the reef of Norman's Woe!

The Witnesses

In Ocean's wide domains,
　　Half buried in the sands,
Lie skeletons in chains,
　　With shackled feet and hands.

Beyond the fall of dews,
　　Deeper than plummet lies,
Float ships, with all their crews,
　　No more to sink nor rise.

There the black Slave-ship swims,
　　Freighted with human forms,
Whose fettered, fleshless limbs
　　Are not the sport of storms.

These are the bones of Slaves;
　　They gleam from the abyss;
They cry, from yawning waves,
　　"We are the Witnesses!"

Within Earth's wide domains
　　Are markets for men's lives;
Their necks are galled with chains,
　　Their wrists are cramped with gyves.

Dead bodies, that the kite
　　In deserts makes its prey;
Murders, that with affright
　　Scare school-boys from their play!

All evil thoughts and deeds;
　　Anger, and lust, and pride;
The foulest, rankest weeds,
　　That choke Life's groaning tide!

These are the woes of Slaves;
　　They glare from the abyss;
They cry, from unknown graves,
　　"We are the Witnesses!"

The Jewish Cemetery at Newport

How strange it seems! These Hebrews in their graves!
    Close by the street of this fair seaport town,
Silent beside the never-silent waves,
    At rest in all this moving up and down!

The trees are white with dust, that o'er their sleep
    Wave their broad curtains in the south-wind's
    breath,
While underneath these leafy tents they keep
    The long, mysterious Exodus of Death.

And these sepulchral stones, so old and brown,
    That pave with level flags their burial-place,
Seem like the tablets of the Law, thrown down
    And broken by Moses at the mountain's base.

The very names recorded here are strange,
    Of foreign accent, and of different climes;
Alvares and Rivera interchange
    With Abraham and Jacob of old times.

"Blessed be God! for he created Death!"
    The mourners said, "and Death is rest and peace;"
Then added, in the certainty of faith,
    "And giveth Life that nevermore shall cease."

Closed are the portals of their Synagogue,
    No Psalms of David now the silence break,
No Rabbi reads the ancient Decalogue
    In the grand dialect the Prophets spake.

Gone are the living, but the dead remain,
    And not neglected; for a hand unseen,
Scattering its bounty, like a summer rain,
    Still keeps their graves and their remembrance
    green.

How came they here? What burst of Christian hate,
   What persecution, merciless and blind,
Drove o'er the sea — that desert desolate —
   These Ishmaels and Hagars of mankind?

They lived in narrow streets and lanes obscure,
   Ghetto and Judenstrass, in mirk and mire;
Taught in the school of patience to endure
   The life of anguish and the death of fire.

All their lives long, with the unleavened bread
   And bitter herbs of exile and its fears,
The wasting famine of the heart they fed,
   And slaked its thirst with marah of their tears.

Anathema maranatha! was the cry
   That rang from town to town, from street to street;
At every gate the accursed Mordecai
   Was mocked and jeered, and spurned by Christian
   feet.

Pride and humiliation hand in hand
   Walked with them through the world where'er
   they went;
Trampled and beaten were they as the sand,
   And yet unshaken as the continent.

For in the background figures vague and vast
   Of patriarchs and of prophets rose sublime,
And all the great traditions of the Past
   They saw reflected in the coming time.

And thus forever with reverted look
   The mystic volume of the world they read,
Spelling it backward, like a Hebrew book,
   Till life became a Legend of the Dead.

But ah! what once has been shall be no more!
   The groaning earth in travail and in pain
Brings forth its races, but does not restore,
   And the dead nations never rise again.

The Ladder of St. Augustine

Saint Augustine! well hast thou said,
    That of our vices we can frame
A ladder, if we will but tread
    Beneath our feet each deed of shame!

All common things, each day's events,
    That with the hour begin and end,
Our pleasures and our discontents,
    Are rounds by which we may ascend.

The low desire, the base design,
    That makes another's virtues less;
The revel of the ruddy wine,
    And all occasions of excess;

The longing for ignoble things;
    The strife for triumph more than truth;
The hardening of the heart, that brings
    Irreverence for the dreams of youth;

All thoughts of ill; all evil deeds,
    That have their root in thoughts of ill;
Whatever hinders or impedes
    The action of the nobler will; –

All these must first be trampled down
    Beneath our feet, if we would gain
In the bright fields of fair renown
    The right of eminent domain.

We have not wings, we cannot soar;
    But we have feet to scale and climb
By slow degrees, by more and more,
    The cloudy summits of our time.

The mighty pyramids of stone
    That wedge-like cleave the desert airs,
When nearer seen, and better known,
    Are but gigantic flights of stairs.

The distant mountains, that uprear
    Their solid bastions to the skies,
Are crossed by pathways, that appear
    As we to higher levels rise.

The heights by great men reached and kept
    Were not attained by sudden flight,
But they, while their companions slept,
    Were toiling upward in the night.

Standing on what too long we bore
    With shoulders bent and downcast eyes,
We may discern – unseen before –
    A path to higher destinies,

Nor doom the irrevocable Past
    As wholly wasted, wholly vain,
If, rising on its wrecks, at last
    To something nobler we attain.

Tegner's Drapa

"October 14, 1847. Went to town, after finishing a poem on Tegner's death, in the spirit of the old Norse poetry." In the first edition, this poem bore the title Tegner's Death. The word "drapa" signifies death-song, or dirge.

I heard a voice, that cried,
"Balder the Beautiful
Is dead, is dead!"
And through the misty air
Passed like the mournful cry
Of sunward sailing cranes.

I saw the pallid corpse
Of the dead sun
Borne through the Northern sky.
Blasts from Niffelheim
Lifted the sheeted mists
Around him as he passed.

And the voice forever cried,
"Balder the Beautiful
Is dead, is dead!"
And died away
Through the dreary night,
In accents of despair.

Balder the Beautiful,
God of the summer sun,
Fairest of all the Gods!
Light from his forehead beamed,
Runes were upon his tongue,
As on the warrior's sword.

All things in earth and air
Bound were by magic spell
Never to do him harm;
Even the plants and stones;
All save the mistletoe,
The sacred mistletoe!

Hoeder, the blind old God,
Whose feet are shod with silence,
Pierced through that gentle breast
With his sharp spear, by fraud,
Made of the mistletoe!
The accursed mistletoe!

They laid him in his ship,
With horse and harness,
As on a funeral pyre.
Odin placed
A ring upon his finger,
And whispered in his ear.

They launched the burning ship!
It floated far away
Over the misty sea,
Till like the sun it seemed,
Sinking beneath the waves.
Balder returned no more!

So perish the old Gods!
But out of the sea of Time
Rises a new land of song,
Fairer than the old.
Over its meadows green
Walk the young bards and sing.

Build it again,
O ye bards,
Fairer than before;
Ye fathers of the new race,
Feed upon morning dew,
Sing the new Song of Love!

The law of force is dead!
The law of love prevails!
Thor, the thunderer,
Shall rule the earth no more,
No more, with threats,
Challenge the meek Christ.

Sing no more,
O ye bards of the North,
Of Vikings and of Jarls!
Of the days of Eld
Preserve the freedom only,
Not the deeds of blood!

The Tide Rises, the Tide Falls

The tide rises, the tide falls,
The twilight darkens, the curfew calls;
Along the sea-sands damp and brown
The traveller hastens toward the town,
And the tide rises, the tide falls.

Darkness settles on roofs and walls,
But the sea, the sea in the darkness calls;
The little waves, with their soft, white hands,
Efface the footprints in the sands,
And the tide rises, the tide falls.

The morning breaks; the steeds in their stalls
Stamp and neigh, as the hostler calls;
The day returns, but nevermore
Returns the traveller to the shore,
And the tide rises, the tide falls.

The Courtship of Miles Standish

I

Miles Standish

In the Old Colony days, in Plymouth the land of the Pilgrims,
To and fro in a room of his simple and primitive dwelling,
Clad in doublet and hose, and boots of Cordovan leather,
Strode, with a martial air, Miles Standish the Puritan Captain.
Buried in thought he seemed, with his hands behind him, and
    pausing
Ever and anon to behold his glittering weapons of warfare,
Hanging in shining array along the walls of the chamber, –
Cutlass and corselet of steel, and his trusty sword of Damascus,
Curved at the point and inscribed with its mystical Arabic
    sentence,
While underneath, in a corner, were fowling-piece, musket, and
    matchlock.
Short of stature he was, but strongly built and athletic,
Broad in the shoulders, deep-chested, with muscles and sinews of
    iron;
Brown as a nut was his face, but his russet beard was already
Flaked with patches of snow, as hedges sometimes in November.
Near him was seated John Alden, his friend and household
    companion,
Writing with diligent speed at a table of pine by the window;
Fair-haired, azure-eyed, with delicate Saxon complexion,
Having the dew of his youth, and the beauty thereof, as the
    captives
Whom Saint Gregory saw, and exclaimed, "Not Angles, but
    Angels."
Youngest of all was he of the men who came in the Mayflower.

Suddenly breaking the silence, the diligent scribe interrupting,
Spake, in the pride of his heart, Miles Standish the Captain of
    Plymouth.
"Look at these arms," he said, "the war-like weapons that hang
    here
Burnished and bright and clean, as if for parade or inspection!

This is the sword of Damascus I fought with in Flanders; this
    breastplate,
Well I remember the day! once save my life in a skirmish;
Here in front you can see the very dint of the bullet
Fired point-blank at my heart by a Spanish arcabucero.
Had it not been of sheer steel, the forgotten bones of Miles
    Standish
Would at this moment be mould, in their grave in the Flemish
    morasses."
Thereupon answered John Alden, but looked not up from his
    writing:
"Truly the breath of the Lord hath slackened the speed of the
    bullet;
He in his mercy preserved you, to be our shield and our
    weapon!"
Still the Captain continued, unheeding the words of the stripling:
"See, how bright they are burnished, as if in an arsenal hanging;
That is because I have done it myself, and not left it to others.
Serve yourself, would you be well served, is an excellent adage;
So I take care of my arms, as you of your pens and your inkhorn.
Then, too, there are my soldiers, my great, invincible army,
Twelve men, all equipped, having each his rest and his matchlock,
Eighteen shillings a month, together with diet and pillage,
And, like Caesar, I know the name of each of my soldiers!"
This he said with a smile, that danced in his eyes, as the sunbeams
Dance on the waves of the sea, and vanish again in a moment.
Alden laughed as he wrote, and still the Captain continued:
"Look! you can see from this window my brazen howitzer
    planted
High on the roof of the church, a preacher who speaks to the
    purpose,
Steady, straightforward, and strong, with irresistible logic,
Orthodox, flashing conviction right into the hearts of the
    heathen.
Now we are ready, I think, for any assault of the Indians;
Let them come, if they like, and the sooner they try it the better,
Let them come, if they like, be it sagamore, sachem, or pow-wow,
Aspinet, Samoset, Corbitant, Squanto, or Tokamahamon!"

Long at the window he stood, and wistfully gazed on the
    landscape,

Washed with a cold gray mist, the vapory breath of the east-wind,
Forest and meadow and hill, and the steel-blue rim of the ocean,
Lying silent and sad, in the afternoon shadows and sunshine.
Over his countenance flitted a shadow like those on the
  landscape,
Gloom intermingled with light; and his voice was subdued with
  emotion,
Tenderness, pity, regret, as after a pause he proceeded:
"Yonder there, on the hill by the sea, lies buried Rose Standish;
Beautiful rose of love, that bloomed for me by the wayside!
She was the first to die of all who came in the Mayflower!
Green above her is growing the field of wheat we have sown
  there,
Better to hide from the Indian scouts the graves of our people,
Lest they should count them and see how many already have
  perished!"
Sadly his face he averted, and strode up and down, and was
  thoughtful.

Fixed to the opposite wall was a shelf of books, and among them
Prominent three, distinguished alike for bulk and for binding:
Bariffe's Artillery Guide, and the Commentaries of Caesar
Out of the Latin translated by Arthur Goldinge of London,
And, as if guarded by these, between them was standing the Bible.
Musing a moment before them, Miles Standish paused, as if
  doubtful
Which of the three he should choose for his consolation and
  comfort,
Whether the wars of the Hebrews, the famous campaigns of the
  Romans,
Or the Artillery practice, designed for belligerent Christians.
Finally down from its shelf he dragged the ponderous Roman,
Seated himself at the window, and opened the book and in silence
Turned o'er the well-worn leaves, where thumb-marks thick on
  the margin,
Like the trample of feet, proclaimed the battle was hottest.
Nothing was heard in the room but the hurrying pen of the
  stripling,
Busily writing epistles important, to go by the Mayflower,
Ready to sail on the morrow, or next day at latest, God willing!
Homeward bound with the tidings of all that terrible winter,

Letters written by Alden and full of the name of Priscilla!
Full of the name and the fame of the Puritan maiden Priscilla!

II
LOVE AND FRIENDSHIP

Nothing was heard in the room but the hurrying pen of the
    stripling,
Or an occasional sign from the laboring heart of the Captain,
Reading the marvellous words and achievements of Julius Caesar.
After a while he exclaimed, as he smote with his hand, palm
    downwards,
Heavily on the page: "A wonderful man was this Caesar!
You are a writer, and I am a fighter, but here is a fellow
Who could both write and fight, and in both was equally
    skillful!"
Straightway answered and spake John Alden, the comely, the
    youthful:
"Yes, he was equally skilled, as you say, with his pen and his
    weapons.
Somewhere have I read, but where I forget, he could dictate
Seven letters at once, at the same time writing his memoirs."
"Truly," continued the Captain, not heeding or hearing the other,
"Truly a wonderful man was Caius Julius Caesar!
Better be first, he said, in a little Iberian village,
Than be second in Rome, and I think he was right when he said
    it.
Twice was he married before he was twenty, and many times
    after;
Battles five hundred he fought, and a thousand cities he
    conquered;
He, too, fought in Flanders, as he himself has recorded;
Finally he was stabbed by his friend, the orator Brutus!
Now, do you know what he did on a certain occasion in Flanders,
When the rear-guard of his army retreated, the front giving way
    too,
And the immortal Twelfth Legion was crowded so closely
    together
There was no room for their swords? Why, he seized a shield from
    a soldier,

Put himself straight at the head of his troops, and commanded the
    captains,
Calling on each by his name, to order forward the ensigns;
Then to widen the ranks, and give more room for their weapons;
So he won the day, the battle of something-or-other.
That's what I always say; if you wish a thing to be well done,
You must do it yourself, you must not leave it to others!"

All was silent again; the Captain continued his reading.
Nothing was heard in the room but the hurrying pen of the
    stripling
Writing epistles important to go next day by the Mayflower,
Filled with the name and the fame of the Puritan maiden
    Priscilla;
Every sentence began or closed with the name of Priscilla,
Till the treacherous pen, to which he confided the secret,
Strove to betray it by singing and shouting the name of Priscilla!
Finally closing his book, with a bang of the ponderous cover,
Sudden and loud as the sound of a soldier grounding his musket,
Thus to the young man spake Miles Standish the Captain of
    Plymouth:
"When you have finished your work, I have something important
    to tell you.
Be not, however, in haste; I can wait; I shall not be impatient!"
Straightway Alden replied, as he folded the last of his letters,
Pushing his papers aside, and giving respectful attention:
"Speak; for whenever you speak, I am always ready to listen,
Always ready to hear whatever pertains to Miles Standish."
Thereupon answered the Captain, embarrassed, and culling his
    phrases:
'T is not good for a man to be alone, say the Scriptures.
This I have said before, and again and again I repeat it;
Every hour in the day, I think it, and feel it, and say it.
Since Rose Standish died, my life has been weary and dreary;
Sick at heart have I been, beyond the healing of friendship;
Oft in my lonely hours have I thought of the maiden Priscilla.
She is alone in the world; her father and mother and brother
Died in the winter together; I saw her going and coming,
Now to the grave of the dead, and now to the bed of the dying,
Patient, courageous, and strong, and said to myself, that if ever
There were angels on earth, as there are angels in heaven,

Two have I seen and known; and the angel whose name is
  Priscilla
Holds in my desolate life the place which the other abandoned.
Long have I cherished the thought, but never have dared to
  reveal it,
Being a coward in this though valiant enough for the most part.
Go to the damsel Priscilla, the loveliest maiden of Plymouth,
Say that a blunt old Captain, a man not of words but of actions,
Offers his hand and his heart, the hand and heart of a soldier.
Not in these words, you know, but this in short is my meaning;
I am a maker of war, and not a maker of phrases.
You, who are bred as a scholar, can say it in elegant language,
Such as you read in your books of the pleadings and wooings of
  lovers,
Such as you think best adapted to win the heart of a maiden."

When he had spoken, John Alden, the fair-haired, taciturn
  stripling,
All aghast at his words, surprised, embarrassed, bewildered,
Trying to mask his dismay by treating the subject with lightness,
Trying to smile, and yet feeling his heart stand still in his bosom,
Just as a timepiece stops in a house that is stricken by lightning,
Thus made answer and spake, or rather stammered than answered:
"Such a message as that, I am sure I should mangle and mar it;
If you would have it well done, – I am only repeating your
  maxim, –
You must do it yourself, you must not leave it to others!"
But with the air of a man whom nothing can turn from his
  purpose,
Gravely shaking his head, made answer the Captain of Plymouth:
"Truly the maxim is good, and I do not mean to gainsay it;
But we must use it discreetly, and not waste powder for nothing.
Now, as I said before, I was never a maker of phrases.
I can march up to a fortress and summon the place to surrender,
But march up to a woman with such a proposal, I dare not.
I'm not afraid of bullets, nor shot from the mouth of a cannon,
But of a thundering 'No!' point-blank from the mouth of a
  woman,
That I confess I'm afraid of, nor am I ashamed to confess it!
So you must grant my request, for you are an elegant scholar,
Having the graces of speech, and skill in the turning of phrases."

Taking the hand of his friend, who still was reluctant and
  doubtful,
Holding it long in his own, and pressing kindly, he added:
"Though I have spoken thus lightly, yet deep is the feeling that
  prompts me;
Surely you cannot refuse what I ask in the name of our
  friendship!"
Then made answer John Alden: "The name of friendship is sacred;
What you demand in that name, I have not the power to deny
  you!"
So the strong will prevailed, subduing and moulding the gentler,
Friendship prevailed over love, and Alden went on his errand.

III

THE LOVER'S ERRAND

So the strong will prevailed, and Alden went on his errand,
Out of the street of the village, and into the paths of the forest,
Into the tranquil woods, where bluebirds and robins were building
Towns in the populous trees, with hanging gardens of verdure,
Peaceful, aerial cities of joy and affection and freedom.
All around him was calm, but within him commotion and
  conflict,
Love contending with friendship, and self with each generous
  impulse.
To and fro in his breast his thoughts were heaving and dashing,
As in a foundering ship, with every roll of the vessel,
Washes the bitter sea, the merciless surge of the ocean!
"Must I relinquish it all," he cried with a wild lamentation, —
"Must I relinquish it all, the joy, the hope, the illusion?
Was it for this I have loved, and waited, and worshipped in
  silence?
Was it for this I have followed the flying feet and the shadow
Over the wintry sea, to the desolate shores of New England?
Truly the heart is deceitful, and out of its depths of corruption
Rise, like an exhalation, the misty phantoms of passion;
Angels of light they seem, but are only delusions of Satan.
All is clear to me now; I feel it, I see it distinctly!
This is the hand of the Lord; it is laid upon me in anger,
For I have followed too much the heart's desires and devices,

Worshipping Astaroth blindly, and impious idols of Baal.
This is the cross I must bear; the sin and the swift retribution."

So through the Plymouth woods John Alden went on his errand;
Crossing the brook at the ford, where it brawled over pebble and
    shallow,
Gathering still, as he went, the May-flowers blooming around
    him,
Fragrant, filling the air with a strange and wonderful sweetness,
Children lost in the woods, and covered with leaves in their
    slumber.
"Puritan flowers," he said, "and the type of Puritan maidens,
Modest and simple and sweet, the very type of Priscilla!
So I will take them to her; to Priscilla the May-flower of
    Plymouth,
Modest and simple and sweet, as a parting gift will I take them;
Breathing their silent farewells, as they fade and wither and perish,
Soon to be thrown away as is the heart of the giver,"
So through the Plymouth woods John Alden went on his errand;
Came to an open space, and saw the disk of the ocean,
Sailless, sombre and cold with the comfortless breath of the
    east-wind;
Saw the new-built house, and people at work in a meadow;
Heard, as he drew near the door, the musical voice of Priscilla
Singing the hundredth Psalm, the grand old Puritan anthem,
Music that Luther sang to the sacred words of the Psalmist,
Full of the breath of the Lord, consoling and comforting many.
Then, as he opened the door, he beheld the form of the maiden
Seated beside her wheel, and the carded wool like a snow-drift
Piled at her knee, white hands feeding the ravenous spindle,
While with her foot on the treadle she guided the wheel in its
    motion.
Open wide on her lap lay the well-worn psalm-book of
    Ainsworth,
Printed in Amsterdam, the words and the music together,
Rough-hewn, angular notes, like stones in the wall of a
    churchyard,
Darkened and overhung by the running vine of the verses.
Such was the book from whose pages she sang the old Puritan
    anthem,
She, the Puritan girl, in the solitude of the forest,

Making the humble house and the modest apparel of homespun
Beautiful with her beauty, and rich with the wealth of her being!
Over him rushed, like a wind that is keen and cold and relentless,
Thoughts of what might have been, and the weight and woe of
    his errand:
All the dreams that had faded, and all the hopes that had vanished,
All his life henceforth a dreary and tenant-less mansion,
Haunted by vain regrets, and pallid, sorrowful faces.
Still he said to himself, and almost fiercely he said it,
"Let not him that putteth his hand to the plough look backwards;
Though the ploughshare cut through the flowers of life to its
    fountains,
Though it pass o'er the graves of the dead and the hearths of the
    living,
It is the will of the Lord; and his mercy endureth forever!"

So he entered the house: and the hum of the wheel and the
    singing
Suddenly ceased; for Priscilla, aroused by his step on the
    threshold,
Rose as he entered, and gave him her hand in signal of welcome,
Saying, "I knew it was you, when I heard your step in the passage;
For I was thinking of you, as I sat there singing and spinning."
Awkward and dumb with delight, that a thought of him had been
    mingled
Thus in the sacred psalm, that came from the heart of the maiden,
Silent before her he stood, and gave her the flowers for an answer,
Finding no words for his thought. He remembered that day in the
    winter,
After the first great snow, when he broke a path from the village,
Reeling and plunging along through the drifts that encumbered
    the doorway,
Stamping the snow from his feet as he entered the house, and
    Priscilla
Laughed at his snowy locks, and gave him a seat by the fireside,
Grateful and pleased to know he had thought of her in the
    snow-storm.
Had he but spoken then! perhaps not in vain had he spoken;
Now it was all too late; the golden moment had vanished!
So he stood there abashed, and gave her the flowers for an answer.

Then they sat down and talked of the birds and the beautiful
spring-time,
Talked of their friends at home, and the Mayflower that sailed on
the morrow.
"I have been thinking all day," said gently the Puritan maiden,
"Dreaming all night, and thinking all day, of the hedge-rows of
England, –
They are in blossom now, and the country is all like a garden;
Thinking of lanes and fields, and the song of the lark and the
linnet,
Seeing the village street, and familiar faces of neighbors
Going about as of old, and stopping to gossip together,
And, at the end of the street, the village church, with the ivy
Climbing the old gray tower, and the quiet graves in the
churchyard.
Kind are the people I live with, and dear to me my religion;
Still my heart is so sad, that I wish myself back in Old England.
You will say it is wrong, but I cannot help it: I almost
Wish myself back in Old England, I feel so lonely and wretched."

Thereupon answered the youth: "Indeed I do not condemn you;
Stouter hearts than a woman's have quailed in this terrible winter.
Yours is tender and trusting, and needs a stronger to lean on;
So I have come to you now, with an offer and proffer of marriage
Made by a good man and true, Miles Standish the Captain of
Plymouth!"

Thus he delivered his message, the dexterous writer of letters, —
Did not embellish the theme, nor array it in beautiful phrases,
But came straight to the point, and blurted it out like a
school-boy;
Even the Captain himself could hardly have said it more bluntly.
Mute with amazement and sorrow, Priscilla the Puritan maiden
Looked into Alden's face, her eyes dilated with wonder,
Feeling his words like a blow, that stunned her and rendered her
speechless;
Till at length she exclaimed, interrupting the ominous silence:
"If the great Captain of Plymouth is so very eager to wed me,
Why does he not come himself, and take the trouble to woo me?
If I am not worth the wooing, I surely am not worth the
winning!"

Then John Alden began explaining and smoothing the matter,
Making it worse as he went, by saying the Captain was busy, —
Had no time for such things — such things! the words grating
    harshly
Fell on the ear of Priscilla; and swift as a flash she made answer:
"Has he not time for such things, as you call it, before he is
    married,
Would he be likely to find it, or make it, after the wedding?
That is the way with you men; you don't understand us, you
    cannot.
When you have made up your minds, after thinking of this one
    and that one,
Choosing, selecting, rejecting, comparing one with another,
Then you make known your desire, with abrupt and sudden
    avowal,
And are offended and hurt, and indignant perhaps, that a woman
Does not respond at once to a love that she never suspected,
Does not attain at a bound the height to which you have been
    climbing.
This is not right nor just: for surely a woman's affection
Is not a thing to be asked for, and had for only the asking.
When one is truly in love, one not only says it, but shows it.
Had he but waited awhile, had he only showed that he loved me,
Even this Captain of yours — who knows? — at last might have
    won me,
Old and rough as he is; but now it never can happen."

Still John Alden went on, unheeding the words of Priscilla,
Urging the suit of his friend, explaining, persuading, expanding;
Spoke of his courage and skill, and of all his battles in Flanders,
How with the people of God he had chosen to suffer affliction;
How, in return for his zeal, they had made him Captain of
    Plymouth;
He was a gentleman born, could trace his pedigree plainly
Back to Hugh Standish of Duxbury Hall, in Lancashire, England,
Who was the son of Ralph, and the grandson of Thurston
    de Standish;
Heir unto vast estates of which he was basely defrauded,
Still bore the family arms, and had for his crest a cock argent,
Combed and wattled gules, and all the rest of the blazon.
He was a man of honor, of noble and generous nature;

Thought he was rough, he was kindly; she knew how during the
    winter
He had attended the sick, with a hand as gentle as a woman's;
Somewhat hasty and hot, he could not deny it, and headstrong,
Stern as a soldier might be, but hearty, and placable always,
Not to be laughed at and scorned, because he was little of stature;
For he was great of heart, magnanimous, courtly, courageous;
Any woman in Plymouth, nay, any woman in England,
Might be happy and proud to be called the wife of Miles
    Standish!

But as he warmed and glowed, in his simple and eloquent
    language,
Quite forgetful of self, and full of the praise of his rival,
Archly the maiden smiled, and, with eyes overrunning with
    laughter,
Said, in a tremulous voice, "Why don't you speak for yourself,
    John?"

IV

JOHN ALDEN

Into the open air John Alden, perplexed and bewildered,
Rushed like a man insane, and wandered alone by the seaside;
Paced up and down the sands, and bared his head to the
    east-wind,
Cooling his heated brow, and the fire and fever within him.
Slowly as out of the heavens, with apocalyptical splendors,
Sank the City of God, in the vision of John the Apostle,
So, with its cloudy walls of chrysolite, jasper, and sapphire,
Sank the broad red sun, and over its turrets uplifted
Glimmered the golden reed of the angel who measured the city.

"Welcome, O wind of the East!" he exclaimed in his wild
    exultation,
"Welcome, O wind of the East, from the caves of the misty
    Atlantic!
Blowing o'er fields of dulse, and measureless meadows of
    sea-grass,
Blowing o'er rocky wastes, and the grottos and gardens of ocean!

Lay thy cold, moist hand on my burning forehead, and wrap me
Close in thy garments of mist, to allay the fever within me!"

Like an awakened conscience, the sea was moaning and tossing,
Beating remorseful and loud the mutable sands of the seashore.
Fierce in his soul was the struggle and tumult of passions
    contending;
Love triumphant and crowned, and friendship wounded and
    bleeding,
Passionate cries of desire , and importunate pleadings of duty!
"Is it my fault," he said, "that the maiden has chosen between us?
Is it my fault that he failed, — my fault that I am the victor?"
Then within him there thundered a voice, like the voice of the
    Prophet:
"It hath displeased the Lord!" — and he thought of David's
    transgression,
Bathsheba's beautiful face, and his friend in the front of the battle!
Shame and confusion of guilt, and abasement and self-
    condemnation,
Overwhelmed him at once; and he cried in the deepest
    contrition:
"It hath displeased the Lord! It is the temptation of Satan!"

Then, uplifting his head, he looked at the sea, and beheld there
Dimly the shadowy form of the Mayflower riding at anchor,
Rocked on the rising tide, and ready to sail on the morrow;
Heard the voices of men through the mist, the rattle of cordage
Thrown on the deck, the shouts of the mate, and the sailors'
    "Ay, ay, Sir!"
Clear and distinct, but not loud, in the dripping air of the
    twilight.
Still for a moment he stood and listened, and stared at the vessel,
Then went hurriedly on, as one who, seeing a phantom,
Stops, then quickens his pace, and follows the beckoning shadow.
"Yes, it is plain to me now," he murmured; "the hand of the
    Lord is
Leading me out of the land of darkness, the bondage of error,
Through the sea, that shall lift the walls of its waters around me,
Hiding me, cutting me off, from the cruel thoughts that pursue
    me.
Back will I go o'er the ocean, this dreary land will abandon,

Her whom I may not love, and him whom my heart has
    offended.
Better to be in my grave in the green old churchyard in England,
Close by my mother's side, and among the dust of my kindred;
Better be dead and forgotten, than living in shame and dishonor;
Sacred and safe and unseen, in the dark of the narrow chamber
With me my secret shall lie, like a buried jewel that glimmers
Bright on the hand that is dust, in the chambers of silence and
    darkness, —
Yes, as the marriage-ring of the great espousal hereafter!"

Thus as he spake, he turned, in the strength of his strong
    resolution,
Leaving behind him the shore, and hurried along in the twilight,
Through the congenial gloom of the forest silent and sombre,
Till he beheld the lights in the seven houses of Plymouth,
Shining like seven stars in the dusk and mist of the evening.
Soon he entered his door, and found the redoubtable Captain
Sitting alone, and absorbed in the martial pages of Caesar,
Fighting some great campaign in Hainault of Brabant or Flanders.
"Long have you been on your errand," he said with a cheery
    demeanor,
Even as one who is waiting an answer, and fears not the issue.
"Not far off is the house, although the woods are between us;
But you have lingered so long, that while you were going and
    coming
I have fought ten battles and sacked and demolished a city.
Come, sit down, and in order relate to me all that has happened."

Then John Alden spake, and related the wondrous adventure,
From beginning to end, minutely, just as it happened;
How he had seen Priscilla, and how he had sped in his courtship,
Only smoothing a little, and softening down her refusal.
But when he came at length to the words Priscilla had spoken,
Words so tender and cruel: "Why don't you speak for yourself,
    John?"
Up leaped the Captain of Plymouth, and stamped on the floor, till
    his armor
Clanged on the wall, where it hung, with a sound of sinister
    omen.
All his pent-up wrath burst forth in a sudden explosion,

E'en as a hand-grenade, that scatters destruction around it.
Wildly he shouted, and loud: "John Alden! you have betrayed me!
Me, Miles Standish, your friend! have supplanted, defrauded,
    betrayed me!
One of my ancestors ran his sword through the heart of Wat Tyler;
Who shall prevent me from running my own through the heart of
    a traitor?
Yours is the greater treason, for yours is a treason to friendship!
You, who lived under my roof, whom I cherished and loved as a
    brother;
You, who have fed at my board, and drunk at my cup, to whose
    keeping
I have intrusted my honor, my thoughts the most sacred and
    secret, —
You too, Brutus! as woe to the name of friendship hereafter!
Brutus was Caesar's friend, and you were mine, but, henceforward
Let there be nothing between us save war, and implacable hatred!"

So spake the Captain of Plymouth, and strode about in the
    chamber,
Chafing and choking with rage; like cords were the veins on his
    temples.
But in the midst of his anger a man appeared at the doorway,
Bringing in uttermost haste a message of urgent importance,
Rumors of danger and war and hostile incursions of Indians!
Straightway the Captain paused, and, without further question or
    parley,
Took from the nail on the wall his sword with its scabbard of iron,
Buckled the belt round his waist, and, frowning fiercely, departed.
Alden was left alone. He heard the clank of the scabbard
Growing fainter and fainter, and dying away in the distance.
Then he arose from his seat, and looked forth into the darkness,
Felt the cool air blow on his cheek, that was hot with the insult,
Lifted his eyes to the heavens, and, folding his hands as in
    childhood,
Prayed in the silence of night to the Father who seeth in secret.

Meanwhile the choleric Captain strode wrathful away to the
    council,
Found it already assembled, impatiently waiting his coming;
Men in the middle of life, austere and grave in deportment,

Only one of them old, the hill that was nearest to heaven,
Covered with snow, but erect, the excellent Elder of Plymouth.
God had sifted three kingdoms to find the wheat for this planting,
Then had sifted the wheat, as the living seed of a nation;
So say the chronicles old, and such is the faith of the people!
Near them was standing an Indian, in attitude stern and defiant;
Naked down to the waist, and grim and ferocious in aspect;
While on the table before them was lying unopened a Bible,
Ponderous, bound in leather, brass-studded, printed in Holland,
And beside it outstretched the skin of a rattlesnake glittered,
Filled, like a quiver, with arrows; a signal and challenge of warfare,
Brought by the Indian, and speaking with arrowy tongues of
	defiance.
This Miles Standish beheld, as he entered, and heard them
	debating
What were an answer befitting the hostile message and menace,
Talking of this and of that, contriving, suggesting, objecting;
One voice only for peace, and that the voice of the Elder,
Judging it wise and well that some at least were converted,
Rather than any were slain, for this was but Christian behavior!
Then out spake Miles Standish, the stalwart Captain of Plymouth,
Muttering deep in his throat, for his voice was husky with anger,
"What! do you mean to make war with milk and the water of
	roses?
Is it to shoot red squirrels you have your howitzer planted
There on the roof of the church, or is it to shoot red devils?
Truly the only tongue that is understood by a savage
Must be the tongue of fire that speaks from the mouth of the
	cannon!"
Thereupon answered and said the excellent Elder of Plymouth,
Somewhat amazed and alarmed at this irreverent language:
"Not so thought St. Paul, nor yet the other Apostles;
Not from the cannon's mouth were the tongues of fire they spake
	with!"
But unheeded fell this mild rebuke on the Captain,
Who had advanced to the table, and thus continued discoursing:
"Leave this matter to me, for to me by right it pertaineth.
War is a terrible trade; but in the cause that is righteous,
Sweet is the smell of powder; and thus I answer the challenge!"

Then from the rattlesnake's skin, with a sudden, contemptuous
    gesture,
Jerking the Indian arrows, he filled it with powder and bullets
Full to the very jaws, and handed it back to the savage,
Saying, in thundering tones: "Here, take it! this is your answer!"
Silently out of the room then glided the glistening savage,
Bearing the serpent's skin, and seeming himself like a serpent,
Winding his sinuous way in the dark to the depths of the forest.

V

THE SAILING OF THE MAYFLOWER

Just in the gray of the dawn, as the mists uprose from the
    meadows,
There was a stir and a sound in the slumbering village of
    Plymouth;
Clanging and clicking of arms, and the order imperative,
    "Forward!"
Given in tone suppressed, a tramp of feet, and then silence.
Figures ten, in the mist, marched slowly out of the village.
Standish the stalwart it was, with eight of his valorous army,
Led by their Indian guide, by Hobomok, friend of the white men,
Northward marching to quell the sudden revolt of the savage.
Giants they seemed in the mist, or the mighty men of King
    David;
Giants in heart they were, who believed in God and the Bible, –
Ay, who believed in the smiting of Midianites and Philistines.
Over them gleamed far off the crimson banners of morning;
Under them loud on the sands, the serried billows, advancing,
Fired along the line, and in regular order retreated.

Many a mile had they marched, when at length the village of
    Plymouth
Woke from its sleep and arose, intent on its manifold labors.
Sweet was the air and soft; and slowly the smoke from the
    chimneys
Rose over roofs of thatch, and pointed steadily eastward;
Men came forth from the doors, and paused and talked of the
    weather,

Said that the wind had changed, and was blowing fair for the
    Mayflower;
Talked of their Captain's departure, and all the dangers that
    menaced,
He being gone, the town, and what should be done in his
    absence.
Merrily sang the birds, and the tender voices of women
Consecrated with hymns the common cares of the household.
Out of the sea rose the sun, and the billows rejoiced at his
    coming;
Beautiful were his feet on the purple tops of the mountains;
Beautiful on the sails of the Mayflower riding at anchor,
Battered and blackened and worn by all the storms of the winter.
Loosely against her masts was hanging and flapping her canvas,
Rent by so many gales, and patched by the hands of the sailors.
Suddenly from her side, as the sun rose over the ocean,
Darted a puff of smoke, and floated seaward; anon rang
Loud over field and forest the cannon's roar, and the echoes
Heard and repeated the sound, the signal-gun of departure!
Ah! but with louder echoes replied the hearts of the people!
Meekly, in voices subdued, the chapter was read from the Bible,
Meekly the prayer was begun, but ended in fervent entreaty!
Then from their houses in haste came forth the Pilgrims of
    Plymouth,
Men and women and children, all hurrying down to the seashore,
Eager, with tearful eyes, to say farewell to the Mayflower,
Homeward bound o'er the sea, and leaving them here in the
    desert.

Foremost among them was Alden. All night he had lain without
    slumber,
Turning and tossing about in the heat and unrest of his fever.
He had beheld Miles Standish, who came back late from the
    council,
Stalking into the room, and heard him mutter and murmur,
Sometimes it seemed a prayer, and sometimes it sounded like
    swearing.
Once he had come to the bed, and stood there a moment in
    silence;
Then he had turned away, and said: "I will not awake him;
Let him sleep on, it is best; for what is the use of more talking!"

Then he extinguished the light, and threw himself down on his
   pallet,
Dressed as he was, and ready to start at the break of the
   morning,–
Covered himself with the cloak he had worn in his campaigns in
   Flanders, –
Slept as a soldier sleeps in his bivouac, ready for action.
But with the dawn he arose; in the twilight Alden beheld him
Put on his corselet of steel, and all the rest of his armor,
Buckle about his waist his trusty blade of Damascus,
Take from the corner his musket, and so stride out of the
   chamber.
Often the heart of the youth had burned and yearned to embrace
   him,
Often his lips had essayed to speak, imploring for pardon;
All the old friendship came back, with its tender and grateful
   emotions;
But his pride overmastered the nobler nature within him, –
Pride, and the sense of his wrong, and the burning fire of the
   insult.
So he beheld his friend departing in anger, but spake not,
Saw him go forth to danger, perhaps to death, and he spake not!
Then he arose from his bed, and heard what the people were
   saying.
Joined in the talk at the door, with Stephen and Richard and
   Gilbert,
Joined in the morning prayer, and in the reading of Scripture,
And, with the others, in haste went hurrying down to the
   sea-shore,
Down to the Plymouth Rock, that had been to their feet as a
   doorstep
Into a world unknown, – the corner-stone of a nation!
There with his boat was the Master, already a little impatient
Lest he should lose the tide, or the wind might shift to the
   eastward,
Square-built, hearty, and strong, with an odor of ocean about him,
Speaking with this one and that, and cramming letters and parcels
Into his pockets capacious, and messages mingled together
Into his narrow brain, till at last he was wholly bewildered.
Nearer the boat stood Alden, with one foot placed on the
   gunwale,

One still firm on the rock, and talking at times with the sailors,
Seated erect on the thwarts, all ready and eager for starting.
He too was eager to go, and thus put an end to his anguish,
Thinking to fly from despair, that swifter than keel is or canvas,
Thinking to drown in the sea the ghost that would rise and
    pursue him.
But as he gazed on the crowd, he beheld the form of Priscilla
Standing dejected among them, unconscious of all that was
    passing.
Fixed were her eyes upon his, as if she divined his intention,
Fixed with a look so sad, so reproachful, imploring, and patient,
That with a sudden revulsion his heart recoiled from its purpose,
As from the verge of a crag, where one step more is destruction.
Strange is the heart of man, with its quick, mysterious instincts!
Strange is the life of man, and fatal or fated are moments,
Whereupon turn, as on hinges, the gates of the wall adamantine!
"Here I remain!" he exclaimed, as he looked at the heavens above
    him,
Thanking the Lord whose breath had scattered the mist and the
    madness,
Wherein, blind and lost, to death he was staggering headlong.
"Yonder snow-white cloud, that floats in the ether above me,
Seems like a hand that is pointing and beckoning over the ocean.
There is another hand, that is not so spectral and ghost-like,
Holding me, drawing me back, and clasping mine for protection.
Float, O hand of cloud, and vanish away in the ether!
Roll thyself up like a fist, to threaten and daunt me; I heed not
Either your warning or menace, or any omen of evil!
There is no land so sacred, no air so pure and so wholesome
As is the air she breathes, and the soil that is pressed by her
    footsteps.
Here for her sake will I stay, and like an invisible presence
Hover around her forever, protecting, supporting her weakness;
Yes! as my foot was the first that stepped on this rock at the
    landing,
So, with the blessing of God, shall it be the last at the leaving!"

Meanwhile the Master alert, but with dignified air and important,
Scanning with watchful eye the tide and the wind and the
    weather,
Walked about on the sands, and the people crowded around him

Saying a few last words, and enforcing his careful remembrance.
Then, taking each by the hand, as if he were gripping a tiller,
Into the boat he sprang, and in haste shoved off to his vessel,
Glad in his heart to get rid of all this worry and flurry,
Glad to be gone from a land of sand and sickness and sorrow,
Short allowance of victual, and plenty of nothing but Gospel!
Lost in the sound of the oars was the last farewell of the Pilgrims.
O strong hearts and true! not one went back in the Mayflower!
No, not one looked back, who had set his hand to this ploughing!

Soon were heard on board the shouts and songs of the sailors
Heaving the windlass round, and hoisting the ponderous anchor.
Then the yards were braced, and all sails set to the west-wind,
Blowing steady and strong; and the Mayflower sailed from the
     harbor,
Rounded the point of the Gurnet, and leaving far to the
     southward
Island and cape of sand, and the Field of the First Encounter,
Took the wind on her quarter, and stood for the open Atlantic,
Borne on the send of the sea, and the swelling hearts of the
     Pilgrims.

Long in silence they watched the receding sail of the vessel,
Much endeared to them all, as something living and human;
Then, as if filled with the spirit, and wrapt in a vision prophetic,
Baring his hoary head, the excellent Elder of Plymouth
Said, "Let us pray!' and they prayed, and thanked the Lord and
     took courage.
Mournfully sobbed the waves at the base of the rock, and above
     them
Bowed and whispered the wheat on the hill of death, and their
     kindred
Seemed to awake in their graves, and to join in the prayer that
     they uttered.
Sun-illumined and white, on the eastern verge of the ocean
Gleamed the departing sail, like a marble slab in a graveyard;
Buried beneath it lay forever all hope of escaping.
Lo! as they turned to depart, they saw the form of an Indian,
Watching them from the hill; but while they spake with each
     other,

Pointing with outstretched hands, and saying, "Look!" he had
   vanished.
So they returned to their homes; but Alden lingered a little,
Musing alone on the shore, and watching the wash of the billows
Round the base of the rock, and the sparkle and flash of the
   sunshine,
Like the spirit of God, moving visibly over the waters.

VI

PRISCILLA

Thus for a while he stood, and mused by the shore of the ocean,
Thinking of many things, and most of all of Priscilla;
And as if thought had the power to draw to itself, like the
   loadstone,
Whatsoever it touches, by subtile laws of its nature,
Lo! as he turned to depart, Priscilla was standing beside him.

"Are you so much offended, you will not speak to me?" said she.
"Am I so much to blame, that yesterday, when you were pleading
Warmly the cause of another, my heart, impulsive and wayward,
Pleaded your own, and spake out, forgetful perhaps of decorum?
Certainly you can forgive me for speaking so frankly, for saying
What I ought not to have said, yet now I can never unsay it;
For there are moments in life, when the heart is so full of
   emotion,
That if by chance it be shaken, or into its depths like a pebble
Drops some careless word, it overflows, and its secret,
Spilt on the ground like water, can never be gathered together.
Yesterday I was shocked, when I heard you speak of Miles
   Standish,
Praising his virtues, transforming his very defects into virtues,
Praising his courage and strength, and even his fighting in
   Flanders,
As if by fighting alone you could win the heart of a woman,
Quite overlooking yourself and the rest, in exalting your hero.
Therefore I spake as I did, by an irresistible impulse.
You will forgive me, I hope, for the sake of the friendship
   between us,
Which is too true and too sacred to be so easily broken!"

Thereupon answered John Alden, the scholar, the friend of Miles
  Standish
"I was not angry with you, with myself alone I was angry.
Seeing how badly I managed the matter I had in my keeping."
"No!" interrupted the maiden, with answer prompt and decisive;
"No; you were angry with me, for speaking so frankly and freely.
It was wrong, I acknowledge; for it is the fate of a woman
Long to be patient and silent, to wait like a ghost that is
  speechless,
Till some questioning voice dissolves the spell of its silence.
Hence is the inner life of so many suffering women
Sunless and silent and deep, like subterranean rivers
Running through caverns of darkness, unheard, unseen, and
  unfruitful,
Chafing their channels of stone, with endless and profitless
  murmurs."
Thereupon answered John Alden, the young man, the lover of
  women:
"Heaven forbid it, Priscilla; and truly they seem to me always
More like the beautiful rivers that watered the garden of Eden,
More like the river Euphrates, through deserts of Havilah flowing,
Filling the land with delight, and memories sweet of the garden!"
"Ah, by these words, I can see," again interrupted the maiden,
"How very little you prize me, or care for what I am saying.
When from the depths of my heart, in pain and with secret
  misgiving,
Frankly I speak to you, asking for sympathy only and kindness,
Straightway you take up my words, that are plain and direct and in
  earnest,
Turn them away from their meaning, and answer with flattering
  phrases.
This is not right, is not just, is not true to the best that is in you;
For I know and esteem you, and feel that your nature is noble,
Lifting mine up to a higher, a more ethereal level.
Therefore I value your friendship, and feel it perhaps the more
  keenly
If you say aught that implies I am only as one among many,
If you make use of those common and complimentary phrases
Most men think so fine, in dealing and speaking with women,
But which women reject as insipid, if not as insulting."

Mute and amazed was Alden; and listened and looked at Priscilla,
Thinking he never had seen her more fair, more divine in her
    beauty.
He who but yesterday pleaded so glibly the cause of another,
Stood there embarrassed and silent, and seeking in vain for an
    answer.
So the maiden went on, and little divined or imagined
What was at work in his heart, that made him so awkward and
    speechless.
"Let us, then, be what we are, and speak what we think, and in all
    things
Keep ourselves loyal to truth, and the sacred professions of
    friendship.
It is no secret I tell you, nor am I ashamed to declare it:
I have liked to be with you, to see you, to speak with you always.
So I was hurt at your words, and a little affronted to hear you
Urge me to marry your friend, though he were the Captain Miles
    Standish.
For I must tell you the truth: much more to me is your friendship
Than all the love he could give, were he twice the hero you think
    him."
Then she extended her hand, and Alden, who eagerly grasped it,
Felt all the wounds in his heart, that were aching and bleeding so
    sorely,
Healed by the touch of that hand, and he said, with a voice full of
    feeling:
"Yes, we must ever be friends; and of all who offer you friendship
Let me be ever the first, the truest, the nearest and dearest!"
Casting a farewell look at the glimmering sail of the Mayflower,
Distant, but still in sight, and sinking below the horizon,
Homeward together they walked, with a strange, indefinite
    feeling,
That all the rest had departed and left them alone in the desert.
But, as they went through the fields in the blessing and smile of
    the sunshine,
Lighter grew their hearts, and Priscilla said very archly:
"Now that our terrible Captain has gone in pursuit of the
    Indians,
Where he is happier far than he would be commanding a house
    hold,

You may speak boldly, and tell me of all that happened between
    you,
When you returned last night, and said how ungrateful you found
    me."
Thereupon answered John Alden, and told her the whole of the
    story, —
Told her his own despair, and the direful wrath of Miles Standish.
Whereat the maiden smiled, and said between laughing and
    earnest,
"He is a little chimney, and heated hot in a moment!"
But as he gently rebuked her, and told her how he had suffered, —
How he had even determined to sail that day in the Mayflower,
And had remained for her sake, on hearing the dangers that
    threatened, —
All her manner was changed, and she said with a faltering accent,
"Truly I thank you for this: how good you have been to me
    always!"

Thus, as a pilgrim devout, who toward Jerusalem journeys,
Taking three steps in advance, and one reluctantly backward,
Urged by importunate zeal, and withheld by pangs of contrition;
Slowly but steadily onward, receding yet ever advancing,
Journeyed this Puritan youth to the Holy Land of his longings,
Urged by the fervor of love, and withheld by remorseful
    misgivings.

VII
The March of Miles Standish

Meanwhile the stalwart Miles Standish was marching steadily
    northward,
Winding through forest and swamp, and along the trend of the
    seashore,
All day long, with hardly a halt, the fire of his anger
Burning and crackling within, and the sulphurous odor of powder
Seeming more sweet to his nostrils than all the scents of the
    forest.
Silent and moody he went, and much he revolved his discomfort;
He who was used to success, and to easy victories always,
Thus to be flouted, rejected, and laughed to scorn by a maiden,

Thus to be mocked and betrayed by the friend whom most he
  had trusted!
Ah! 't was too much to be borne, and he fretted and chafed in his
  armor!

"I alone am to blame," he muttered, "for mine was the folly.
What has a rough old soldier, grown grim and gray in the harness,
Used to the camp and its ways, to do with the wooing of
  maidens?
'T was but a dream, – let it pass, – let it vanish like so many
  others!
What I thought was a flower, is only a weed, and is worthless;
Out of my heart will I pluck it, and throw it away, and hence
  forward
Be but a fighter of battles, a lover and wooer of dangers!"
Thus he revolved in his mind his sorry defeat and discomfort,
While he was marching by day or lying at night in the forest,
Looking up at the trees, and the constellations beyond them.

After a three days' march he came to an Indian encampment
Pitched on the edge of a meadow, between the sea and the forest;
Women at work by the tents, and warriors, horrid with war-paint,
Seated about a fire, and smoking and talking together;
Who, when they saw from afar the sudden approach of the white
  men,
Saw the flash of the sun on breastplate and sabre and musket,
Straightway leaped to their feet, and two, from among them
  advancing,
Came to parley with Standish, and offer him furs as a present;
Friendship was in their looks, but in their hearts there was hatred.
Braves of the tribe were these, and brothers, gigantic in stature,
Huge as Goliath of Gath, or the terrible Og, king of Bashan;
One was Pecksuot named, and the other was called Wattwamat.
Round their necks were suspended their knives in scabbards of
  wampum,
Two-edged, trenchant knives, with points as sharp as a needle.
Other arms had they none, for they were cunning and crafty.
"Welcome, English!" they said, – these words they had learned
  from the traders
Touching at times on the coast, to barter and chaffer for peltries.
Then in their native tongue they began to parley with Standish,

Through his guide and interpreter, Hobomok, friend of the white
    man,
Begging for blankets and knives, but mostly for muskets and
    powder,
Kept by the white man, they said, concealed, with the plague, in
    his cellars,
Ready to be let loose, and destroy his brother the red man!
But when Standish refused, and said he would give them the
    Bible,
Suddenly changing their tone, they began to boast and to bluster.
Then Wattawamat advanced with a stride in front of the other,
And, with a lofty demeanor, thus vauntingly spake to the Captain:
"Now Wattawamat can see, by the fiery eyes of the Captain,
Angry is he in his heart; but the heart of the brave Wattawamat
Is not afraid at the sight. He was not born of a woman,
But on a mountain at night, from an oak-tree riven by lightning,
Forth he sprang at a bound, with all his weapons about him,
Shouting, 'Who is there here to fight with the brave
    Wattawamat?'"
Then he unsheathed his knife, and, whetting the blade on his left
    hand,
Held it aloft and displayed a woman's face on the handle;
Saying, with bitter expression and look of sinister meaning:
"I have another at home, with the face of a man on the handle;
By and by they shall marry; and there will be plenty of children!"
Then stood Pecksuot forth, self-vaunting, insulting Miles
    Standish:
While with his fingers he patted the knife that hung at his bosom,
Drawing it half from its sheath, and plunging it back, as he
    muttered,
"By and by it shall see; it shall eat; ah, ha! but shall speak not!
This is the mighty Captain the white men have sent to destroy us!
He is a little man; let him go and work with the women!"

Meanwhile Standish had noted the faces and figures of Indians
Peeping and creeping about from bush to tree in the forest,
Feigning to look for game, with arrows set on their bow-strings,
Drawing about him still closer and closer the net of their ambush.
But undaunted he stood, and dissembled and treated them
    smoothly;
So the old chronicles say, that were writ in the days of the fathers.

But when he heard their defiance, the boast, the taunt, and the
    insult,
All the hot blood of his race, of Sir Hugh and of Thurston de
    Standish,
Boiled and beat in his heart, and swelled in the veins of his
    temples.
Headlong he leaped on the boaster, and, snatching his knife from
    its scabbard,
Plunged it into his heart, and, reeling backward, the savage
Fell with his face to the sky and a fiendlike fierceness upon it.
Straight there arose from the forest the awful sound of the war-
    whoop.
And, like a flurry of snow on the whistling wind of December,
Swift and sudden and keen came a flight of feathery arrows.
Then came a cloud of smoke, and out of the cloud came the
    lightning,
Out of the lightning thunder; and death unseen ran before it.
Frightened the savages fled for shelter in swamp and in thicket,
Hotly pursued and beset; but their sachem, the brave Wattawamat,
Fled not; he was dead. Unswerving and swift had a bullet
Passed through his brain, and he fell with both hands clutching
    the greensward,
Seeming in death to hold back from his foe the land of his
    fathers.
There on the flowers of the meadow the warriors lay, and above
    them
Silent, with folded arms, stood Hobomok, friend of the white
    man.
Smiling at length he exclaimed to the stalwart Captain of
    Plymouth:
"Pecksuot bragged very loud, of his courage, his strength, and his
    stature, —
Mocked the great Captain, and called him a little man; but I see
    now
Be enough have you been to lay him speechless before you!"

Thus the first battle was fought and won by the stalwart Miles
    Standish.
When the tidings thereof were brought to the village of Ply
    mouth,
And as a trophy of war the head of the brave Wattawamat

Scowled from the roof of the fort, which at once was a church and a fortress,
All who beheld it rejoiced, and praised the Lord, and took courage.
Only Priscilla averted her face from this spectre of terror,
Thanking God in her heart that she had not married Miles Standish;
Shrinking, fearing almost, lest, coming home from his battles,
He should lay claim to her hand, as the prize and reward of his valor.

VIII
THE SPINNING-WHEEL

Month after month passed away, and in autumn the ships of the merchants
Came with kindred and friends, with cattle and corn for the Pilgrims.
All in the village was peace; the men were intent on their labors,
Busy with hewing and building, with garden-plot and with merestead,
Busy with breaking the glebe, and mowing the grass in the meadows,
Searching the sea for its fish, and hunting the deer in the forest.
All in the village was peace; but at times the rumor of warfare
Filled the air with alarm, and the apprehension of danger.
Bravely the stalwart Standish was scouring the land with his forces,
Waxing valiant in fight and defeating the alien armies,
Till his name had become a sound of fear to the nations.
Anger was still in his heart, but at times the remorse and contrition
Which in all noble natures succeed the passionate outbreak,
Came like a rising tide, that encounters the rush of a river,
Staying its current awhile, but making it bitter and brackish.

Meanwhile Alden at home had built him a new habitation,
Solid, substantial, of timber rough-hewn from the firs of the forest.
Wooden-barred was the door, and the roof was covered with

rushes;
Latticed the windows were, and the window-panes were of paper,
Oiled to admit the light, while wind and rain were excluded.
There too he dug a well, and around it planted an orchard:
Still may be seen to this day some trace of the well and the
    orchard:
Close to the house was the stall, where, safe and secure from
    annoyance,
Raghorn, the snow-white bull, that had fallen to Alden's
    allotment
In the division of cattle, might ruminate in the night-time
Over the pastures he cropped, made fragrant by sweet pennyroyal.

Oft when his labor was finished, with eager feet would the
    dreamer
Follow the pathway that ran through the woods to the house of
    Priscilla,
Led by illusions romantic and subtile deceptions of fancy,
Pleasure disguised as duty, and love in the semblance of friendship.
Ever of her he thought, when he fashioned the walls of his
    dwelling;
Ever of her he thought, when he delved in the soil of his garden;
Ever of her he thought, when he read in his Bible on Sunday
Praise of the virtuous woman, as she is described in the Proverbs,
How the heart of her husband doth safely trust in her always,
How all the days of her life she will do him good, and not evil,
How she seeketh the wool and the flax and worketh with
    gladness,
How she layeth her hand to the spindle and holdeth the distaff,
How she is not afraid of the snow for herself or her household,
Knowing her household are clothed with the scarlet cloth of her
    weaving!

So as she sat at her wheel one afternoon in the autumn,
Alden, who opposite sat, and was watching her dexterous fingers,
As if the thread she was spinning were that of his life and his
    fortune,
After a pause in their talk, thus spake to the sound of the spindle.
"Truly, Priscilla," he said, "when I see you spinning and spinning,
Never idle a moment, but thrifty and thoughtful of others,
Suddenly you are transformed, are visibly changed in a moment;

You are no longer Priscilla, but Bertha the Beautiful Spinner."
Here the light foot on the treadle grew swifter and swifter; the spindle
Uttered an angry snarl, and the thread snapped short in her fingers;
While the impetuous speaker, not heeding the mischief, continued:
"You are the beautiful Bertha, the spinner, the queen of Helvetia;
She whose story I read at a stall in the streets of Southampton,
Who, as she rode on her palfrey, o'er valley and meadow and mountain,
Ever was spinning her thread from a distaff fixed to her saddle.
She was so thrifty and good, that her name passed into a proverb.
So shall it be with your own, when the spinning-wheel shall no longer
Hum in the house of the farmer, and fill its chambers with music.
Then shall the mothers, reproving, relate how it was in their childhood,
Praising the good old times, and the days of Priscilla the spinner!"
Straight uprose from her wheel the beautiful Puritan maiden,
Pleased with the praise of her thrift from him whose praise was the sweetest,
Drew from the reel on the table a snowy skein of her spinning,
Thus making answer, meanwhile, to the flattering phrases of Alden:
"Come, you must not be idle; if I am a pattern for housewives,
Show yourself equally worthy of being the model of husbands.
Hold this skein on your hands, while I wind it, ready for knitting;
Then who knows but hereafter, when fashions have changed and the manners,
Fathers may talk to their sons of the good old times of John Alden!"
Thus, with a jest and a laugh, the skein on his hands she adjusted,
He sitting awkwardly there, with his arms extended before him,
She standing graceful, erect, and winding the thread from his fingers,
Sometimes chiding a little his clumsy manner of holding,
Sometimes touching his hands, as she disentangled expertly
Twist or knot in the yarn, unawares — for how could she help it?
Sending electrical thrills through every nerve in his body.

Lo! in the midst of this scene, a breathless messenger entered,
Bringing in hurry and heat the terrible news from the village.
Yes; Miles Standish was dead! – an Indian had brought them the
    tidings, –
Slain by a poisoned arrow, shot down in the front of the battle,
Into an ambush beguiled, cut off with the whole of his forces;
All the town would be burned, and all the people be murdered!
Such were the tidings of evil that burst on the hearts of the
    hearers.
Silent and statue-like stood Priscilla, her face looking backward
Still at the face of the speaker, her arms uplifted in horror;
But John Alden, upstarting, as if the barb of the arrow
Piercing the heart of his friend had struck his own, and had
    sundered
Once and forever the bonds that held him bound as a captive,
Wild with excess of sensation, the awful delight of his freedom,
Mingled with pain and regret, unconscious of what he was doing,
Clasped, almost with a groan, the motionless form of Priscilla,
Pressing her close to his heart, as forever his own, and exclaiming:
"Those whom the Lord hath united, let no man put them
    asunder!"

Even as rivulets twain, from distant and separate sources,
Seeing each other afar, as they leap from the rocks, and pursuing
Each one its devious path, but drawing nearer and nearer,
Rush together at last, at their trysting-place in the forest;
So these lives that had run thus far in separate channels,
Coming in sight of each other, then swerving and flowing
    asunder,
Parted by barriers strong, but drawing nearer and nearer,
Rushed together at last, and one was lost in the other.

IX
THE WEDDING DAY

Forth from the curtain of clouds, from the tent of purple and
    scarlet,
Issued the sun, the great High Priest, in his garments resplendent,
Holiness unto the Lord, in letters of light, on his forehead,
Round the hem of his robe the golden bells and pomegranates.

Blessing the world he came, and the bars of vapor beneath him
Gleamed like a grate of brass, and the sea at his feet was a laver!

This was the wedding-morn of Priscilla the Puritan maiden.
Friends were assembled together; the Elder and Magistrate also
Graced the scene with their presence, and stood like the Law and
    the Gospel,
One with the sanction of earth and one with the blessing of
    heaven.
Simple and brief was the wedding, as that of Ruth and of Boaz.
Softly the youth and the maiden repeated the words of betrothal,
Taking each other for husband and wife in the Magistrate's
    presence,
After the Puritan way, and the laudable custom of Holland.
Fervently then, and devoutly, the excellent Elder of Plymouth
Prayed for the hearth and the home, that were founded that day
    in affection,
Speaking of life and of death, and imploring Divine benedictions.

Lo! when the service was ended, a form appeared on the
    threshold,
Clad in armor of steel, a sombre and sorrowful figure!
Why does the bridegroom start and stare at the strange
    apparition?
Why does the bride turn pale, and hide her face on his shoulder?
Is it a phantom of air, – a bodiless, spectral illusion?
Is it a ghost from the grave, that has come to forbid the betrothal?
Long had it stood there unseen, a guest uninvited, unwelcomed;
Over its clouded eyes there had passed at times an expression
Softening the gloom and revealing the warm heart hidden
    beneath them,
As when across the sky the driving rack of the rain-cloud
Grows for a moment thin, and betrays the sun by its brightness.
Once it had lifted its hand, and moved its lips, but was silent,
As if an iron will had mastered the fleeting intention.
But when were ended the troth and the prayer and the last
    benediction,
Into the room it strode, and the people beheld with amazement
Bodily there in his armor Miles Standish, the Captain of
    Plymouth!
Grasping the bridegroom's hand, he said with emotion,

"Forgive me!
I have been angry and hurt, – too long have I cherished the
    feeling;
I have been cruel and hard, but now, thank God! it is ended.
Mine is the same hot blood that leaped in the veins of Hugh
    Standish,
Sensitive, swift to resent, but as swift in atoning for error.
Never so much as now was Miles Standish the friend of John
    Alden."
Thereupon answered the bridegroom: "Let all be forgotten
    between us, –
All save the dear old friendship, and that shall grow older and
    dearer!"
Then the Captain advanced, and bowing, saluted Priscilla,
Gravely, and after the manner of old-fashioned gentry in England,
Something of camp and of court, of town and of country, com
    mingled,
Wishing her joy of her wedding, and loudly lauding her husband.
Then he said with a smile: "I should have remembered the adage,
If you would be well served, you must serve yourself; and
    moreover,
No man can gather cherries in Kent at the season of Christmas!"

Great was the people's amazement, and greater yet their rejoicing,
Thus to behold once more the sunburnt face of their Captain,
Whom they had mourned as dead; and they gathered and
    crowded about him,
Eager to see him and hear him, forgetful of bride and of
    bridegroom,
Questioning, answering, laughing, and each interrupting the
    other,
Till the good Captain declared, being quite overpowered and
    bewildered,
He had rather by far break into an Indian encampment,
Than come again to a wedding to which he had not been invited.

Meanwhile the bridegroom went forth and stood with the bride
    at the doorway,
Breathing the perfumed air of that warm and beautiful morning.
Touched with autumnal tints, but lonely and sad in the sunshine.
Lay extended before them the land of toil and privation;

There were the graves of the dead, and the barren waste of the
    seashore,
There the familiar fields, the groves of pine, and the meadows;
But to their eyes transfigured, it seemed as the Garden of Eden,
Filled with the presence of God, whose voice was the sound of
    the ocean.

Soon was their vision disturbed by the noise and stir of departure,
Friends coming forth from the house, and impatient of longer
    delaying,
Each with his plan for the day, and the work that was left
    uncompleted.
Then from a stall near at hand, amid exclamations of wonder,
Alden the thoughtful, the careful, so happy, so proud of Priscilla,
Brought out his snow-white bull, obeying the hand of its master,
Led by a cord that was tied to an iron ring in its nostrils,
Covered with crimson cloth, and a cushion placed for a saddle.
She should not walk, he said, through the dust and heat of the
    noonday;
Nay, she should ride like a queen, not plod along like a peasant.
Somewhat alarmed at first, but reassured by the others,
Placing her hand on the cushion, her foot in the hand of her
    husband,
Gayly, with joyous laugh, Priscilla mounted her palfrey.
"Nothing is wanting now," he said with a smile, "but the distaff;
Then you would be in truth my queen, my beautiful Bertha!"

Onward the bridal procession now moved to their new
    habitation,
Happy husband and wife, and friends conversing together.
Pleasantly murmured the brook, as they crossed the ford in the
    forest,
Pleased with the image that passed, like a dream of love, through
    its bosom,
Tremulous, floating in air, o'er the depths of the azure abysses.
Down through the golden leaves the sun was pouring his
    splendors,
Gleaming on purple grapes, that, from branches above them
    suspended,
Mingled their odorous breath with the balm of the pine and the
    fir-tree,

Evangeline

A Tale of Acadie

This is the forest primeval. The murmuring pines and the
    hemlocks,
Bearded with moss, and in garments green, indistinct in the
    twilight,
Stand like Druids of eld, with voices sad and prophetic,
Stand like harpers hoar, with beards that rest on their bosoms.
Loud from its rocky caverns, the deep-voiced neighboring ocean
Speaks, and in accents disconsolate answers the wail of the forest.

This is the forest primeval; but where are the hearts that beneath
    it
Leaped like the roe, when he hears in the woodland the voice of
    the huntsman?
Where is the thatch-roofed village, the home of Acadian farmers—
Men whose lives glided on like rivers that water the woodlands,
Darkened by shadows of earth, but reflecting an image of heaven?
Waste are those pleasant farms, and the farmers forever departed!
Scattered like dust and leaves, when the mighty blasts of October
Seize them, and whirl them aloft, and sprinkle them far o'er the
    ocean.
Naught but tradition remains of the beautiful village of Grand-
Pre.

Ye who believe in affection that hopes, and endures, and is patient,
Ye who believe in the beauty and strength of woman's devotion,
List to the mournful tradition still sung by the pines of the forest;
List to a Tale of Love in Acadie, home of the happy.

PART THE FIRST

I

In the Acadian land, on the shores of the Basin of Minas,
Distant, secluded, still, the little village of Grand-Pre
Lay in the fruitful valley. Vast meadows stretched to the eastward,

Giving the village its name, and pasture to flocks without number.
Dikes, that the hands of the farmers had raised with labor
    incessant,
Shut out the turbulent tides; but at stated seasons the flood-gates
Opened, and welcomed the sea to wander at will o'er the
    meadows.
West and south there were fields of flax, and orchards and corn-
    fields
Spreading afar and unfenced o'er the plain; and away to the
    northward
Blomidon rose, and the forests old, and aloft on the mountains
Sea-fogs pitched their tents, and mists from the mighty Atlantic
Looked on the happy valley, but ne'er from their station
    descended.
There, in the midst of its farms, reposed the Acadian village.
Strongly built were the houses, with frames of oak and of
    chestnut,
Such as the peasants of Normandy built in the reign of the
    Henries.
Thatched were the roofs, with dormer-windows; and gables
    projecting
Over the basement below protected and shaded the doorway.
There in the tranquil evenings of summer, when brightly the
    sunset
Lighted the village street, and gilded the vanes on the chimneys,
Matrons and maidens sat in snow-white caps and in kirtles
Scarlet and blue and green, with distaffs spinning the golden
Flax for the gossiping looms, whose noisy shuttles within doors
Mingled their sound with the whir of the wheels and the songs of
    the maidens.
Solemnly down the street came the parish priest, and the children
Paused in their play to kiss the hand he extended to bless them.
Reverend walked he among them; and up rose matrons and
    maidens,
Hailing his slow approach with words of affectionate welcome.
Then came the laborers home from the field, and serenely the sun
    sank
Down to his rest, and twilight prevailed. Anon from the belfry
Softly the Angelus sounded, and over the roofs of the village
Columns of pale blue smoke, like clouds of incense ascending,

Rose from a hundred hearths, the homes of peace and
    contentment.
Thus dwelt together in love these simple Acadian farmers —
Dwelt in the love of God and of man. Alike were they free from
Fear, that reigns with the tyrant, and envy, the vice of republics.
Neither locks had they to their doors, nor bars to their windows;
But their dwellings were open as day and the hearts of the
    owners;
There the richest was poor, and the poorest lived in abundance.

Somewhat apart from the village, and nearer the Basin of Minas,
Benedict Bellefontaine, the wealthiest farmer of Grand-Pre,
Dwelt on his goodly acres; and with him, directing his household,
Gentle Evangeline lived, his child, and the pride of the village.
Stalworth and stately in form was the man of seventy winters;
Hearty and hale was he, an oak that is covered with snow-flakes;
White as the snow were his locks, and his cheeks as brown as the
    oak-leaves.
Fair was she to behold, that maiden of seventeen summers.
Black were her eyes as the berry that grows on the thorn by the
    way-side,
Black, yet how softly they gleamed beneath the brown shade of
    her tresses!
Sweet was her breath as the breath of kine that feed in the
    meadows.
When in the harvest heat she bore to the reapers at noontide
Flagons of home-brewed ale, ah! fair in sooth was the maiden.
Fairer was she when, on Sunday morn, while the bell from its
    turret
Sprinkled with holy sounds the air, as the priest with his hysop
Sprinkles the congregation, and scatters blessings upon them,
Down the long street she passed, with her chaplet of beads and
    her missal,
Wearing her Norman cap, and her kirtle of blue, and the
    ear-rings,
Brought in the olden time from France, and since, as an heirloom,
Handed down from mother to child, through long generations.
But a celestial brightness — a more ethereal beauty —
Shone on her face and encircled her form, when, after confession,
Homeward serenely she walked with God's benediction upon her.

When she had passed, it seemed like the ceasing of exquisite
    music.

Firmly builded with rafters of oak, the house of the farmer
Stood on the side of a hill commanding the sea; and a shady
Sycamore grew by the door, with a woodbine wreathing around
    it.
Rudely carved was the porch, with seats beneath; and a footpath
Led through an orchard wide, and disappeared in the meadow.
Under the sycamore-tree were hives overhung by a pent-house,
Such as the traveler sees in regions remote by the roadside,
Built o'er a box for the poor, or the blessed image of Mary.
Farther down, on the slope of the hill, was the well with its moss-
    grown
Bucket, fastened with iron, and near it a trough for the horses.
Shielding the house from storms, on the north, were the barns
    and the farm-yard.
There stood the broad-wheeled wains and the antique plows and
    the harrows;
There were the folds for the sheep; and there, in his feathered
    seraglio,
Strutted the lordly turkey, and crowed the cock, with the selfsame
Voice that in ages of old had startled the penitent Peter.
Bursting with hay were the barns, themselves a village. In each
    one
Far o'er the gable projected a roof of thatch; and a staircase,
Under the sheltering eaves, led up to the odorous corn-loft.
There too the dove-cot stood, with its meek and innocent
    inmates
Murmuring ever of love; while above in the variant breezes
Numberless noisy weathercocks rattled and sang of mutation.

Thus, at peace with God and the world, the farmer of Grand-Pre
Lived on his sunny farm, and Evangeline governed his household.
Many a youth, as he knelt in the church and opened his missal,
Fixed his eyes upon her, as the saint of his deepest devotion;
Happy was he who might touch her hand or the hem of her
    garment!
Many a suitor came to her door, by the darkness befriended,
And as he knocked and waited to hear the sound of her footsteps,
Knew not which beat the louder, his heart or the knocker of iron;

Or at the joyous feast of the Patron Saint of the village,
Bolder grew, and pressed her hand in the dance as he whispered
Hurried words of love, that seemed a part of the music.
But, among all who came, young Gabriel only was welcome;
Gabriel Lajeunesse, the son of Basil the blacksmith,
Who was a mighty man in the village, and honored of all men;
For since the birth of time, throughout all ages and nations,
Has the craft of the smith been held in repute by the people.
Basil was Benedict's friend. Their children from earliest childhood
Grew up together as brother and sister, and Father Felician,
Priest and pedagogue both in the village, had taught them their
    letters
Out of the selfsame book, with the hymns of the church and the
    plain-song.
But when the hymn was sung, and the daily lesson completed,
Swiftly they hurried away to the forge of Basil the blacksmith.
There at the door they stood, with wondering eyes to behold him
Take in his leathern lap the hoof of the horse as a plaything,
Nailing the shoe in its place; while near him the tire of the cart-
    wheel
Lay like a fiery snake, coiled round in a circle of cinders.
Oft on autumnal eves, when without in the gathering darkness
Bursting with light seemed the smithy, through every cranny and
    crevice,
Warm by the forge within they watched the laboring bellows,
And as its panting ceased, and the sparks expired in the ashes,
Merrily laughed, and said they were nuns going into the chapel.
Oft on sledges in winter, as swift as the swoop of the eagle,
Down the hill-side bounding, they glided away o'er the meadow.
Oft in the barns they climbed to the populous nests on the rafters,
Seeking with eager eyes that wondrous stone, which the swallow
Brings from the shore of the sea to restore the sight of its
    fledglings
Lucky was he who found that stone in the nest of the swallow!
Thus passed a few swift years, and they no longer were children.
He was a valiant youth, and his face, like the face of the morning,
Gladdened the earth with its light and ripened through into
    action.
She was a woman now, with the heart and hopes of a woman.
"Sunshine of Saint Eulalie" was she called; for that was the
    sunshine

Which, as the farmers believed, would load their orchards with
    apples;
She, too, would bring to her husband's house delight and
    abundance,
Filling it full of love and the ruddy faces of children.

II

Now had the season returned, when the nights grow colder and l
    longer,
And the retreating sun the sign of the Scorpion enters.
Birds of passage sailed through the leaden air, from the ice-bound,
Desolate northern bays to the shores of tropical islands.
Harvests were gathered in; and wild with the winds of September
Wrestled the trees of the forests, as Jacob of old with the angel.
All the signs foretold a winter long and inclement.
Bees, with prophetic instinct of want, had hoarded their honey
Till the hives overflowed; and the Indian hunters asserted
Cold would the winter be, for thick was the fur of the foxes.
Such was the advent of autumn. Then followed that beautiful
    season,
Called by the pious Acadian peasants the Summer of All-Saints!
Filled was the air with a dreamy and magical light; and the
    landscape
Lay as if new created in all the freshness of childhood.
Peace seemed to reign upon earth, and the restless heart of the
    ocean
Was for a moment consoled. All sounds were in harmony blended.
Voices of children at play, the crowing of cocks in the farmyards,
Whir of wings in the drowsy air, and the cooing of pigeons,
All were subdued and low as the murmurs of love, and the great
    sun
Looked with the eye of love through the golden vapors around
    him;
While arrayed in its robes of russet and scarlet and yellow,
Bright with the sheen of the dew, each glittering tree of the forest
Flashed like the plane-tree the Persian adorned with mantles and
    jewels.
Now recommenced the reign of rest and affection and stillness.

Day with its burden and heat had departed, and twilight descending
Brought back the evening star to the sky, and the herds to the homestead.
Pawing the ground they came, and resting their necks on each other,
And with their nostrils distended inhaling the freshness of evening.
Foremost, bearing the bell, Evangeline's beautiful heifer,
Proud of her snow-white hide, and the ribbon that waved from her collar,
Quietly paced and slow, as if conscious of human affection.
Then came the shepherd back with his bleating flocks from the seaside,
Where was their favorite pasture. Behind them followed the watch-dog,
Patient, full of importance, and grand in the pride of his instinct,
Walking from side to side with a lordly air, and superbly
Waving his bushy tail, and urging forward the stragglers;
Regent of flocks was he went the shepherd slept; their protector,
When from the forest at night, through the starry silence, the wolves howled.
Late, with the rising moon, returned the wains from the marshes,
Laden with briny hay, that filled the air with its odor.
Cheerily neighed the steeds, with dew on their manes and their fetlocks,
While aloft on their shoulders the wooden and ponderous saddles,
Painted with brilliant dyes, and adorned with tassels of crimson,
Nodded in bright array, like hollyhocks heavy with blossoms.
Patiently stood the cows meanwhile, and yielded their udders
Unto the milkmaid's hand; whilst loud and in regular cadence
Into the sounding pails the foaming streamlets descended.
Lowing of cattle and peals of laughter were heard in the farmyard,
Echoed back by the barns. Anon they sank into stillness;
Heavily closed, with a jarring sound, the valves of the barn doors,
Rattled the wooden bars, and all for a season was silent.

Indoors, warm by the wide-mouthed fireplace, idly the farmer
Sat in his elbow-chair; and watched how the flames and the smoke-wreaths
Struggled together like foes in a burning city. Behind him,

Nodding and mocking along the wall, with gestures fantastic,
Darted his own huge shadow, and vanished away into darkness.
Faces, clumsily carved in oak, on the back of his arm-chair
Laughed in the flickering light, and the pewter plates on the
     dresser
Caught and reflected the flame, as shields of armies the sunshine.
Fragments of song the old man sang, and carols of Christmas,
Such as at home, in the olden time, his fathers before him
Sang in their Norman orchards and bright Burgundian vineyards.
Close at her father's side was the gentle Evangeline seated,
Spinning flax for the loom, that stood in the corner behind her.
Silent awhile were its treadles, at rest was its diligent shuttle,
While the monotonous drone of the wheel, like the drone of a
     bagpipe,
Followed the old man's song, and united the fragments together.
As in a church, when the chant of the choir at intervals ceases,
Footfalls are heard in the aisles, or words of the priest at the altar,
So, in each pause of the song, with measured motion the clock
     clicked.

Thus as they sat, there were footsteps heard, and, suddenly lifted,
Sounded the wooden latch, and the door swung back on its
     hinges.
Benedict knew by the hob-nailed shoes it was Basil the
     blacksmith,
And by her beating heart Evangeline knew who was with him.
"Welcome!" the farmer exclaimed, as their footsteps paused on
     the threshold,
"Welcome, Basil, my friend! Come, take thy place on the settle
Close by the chimney-side, which is always empty without thee;
Take from the shelf overhead thy pipe and the box of tobacco;
Never so much thyself art thou as when through the curling
Smoke of the pipe or the forge thy friendly and jovial face gleams
Round and red as the harvest moon through the mist of the
     marshes."
Then, with a smile of content, thus answered Basil the blacksmith,
Taking with easy air the accustomed seat by the fireside –
"Benedict Bellefontaine, thou hast ever thy jest and thy ballad!
Ever in cheerfulest mood art thou, when others are filled with
Gloomy forebodings of ill, and see only ruin before them.
Happy art thou, as if every day thou hadst picked up a horseshoe."

Pausing a moment, to take the pipe that Evangeline brought him,
And with a coal from the embers had lighted, he slowly
    continued –
"Four days now are passed since the English ships at their anchors
Ride in the Gaspereau's mouth, with their cannon pointed against
    us.
What their design may be is unknown; but all are commanded
On the morrow to meet in the church, where his Majesty's
    mandate
Will be proclaimed as law in the land. Alas! in the mean time
Many surmises of evil alarm the hearts of the people."
Then made answer the farmer: "Perhaps some friendlier purpose
Brings these ships to our shores. Perhaps the harvests in England
By the untimely rains or untimelier heat have been blighted,
And from our bursting barns they would feed their cattle and
    children."
"Not so thinketh the folk in the village," said, warmly, the
    blacksmith,
Shaking his head, as in doubt; then, heaving a sigh, he continued –
"Louisburg is not forgotten, nor Beau Sejour, nor Port Royal.
Many already have fled to the forest, and lurk on its outskirts,
Waiting with anxious hearts the dubious fate of to-morrow.
Arms have been taken from us, and warlike weapons of all kinds;
Nothing is left but the blacksmith's sledge and the scythe of the
    mower."
Then with a pleasant smile made answer the jovial farmer:
"Safer are we unarmed, in the midst of our flocks and our
    cornfields,
Safer within these peaceful dikes, besieged by the ocean,
Than were our fathers in forts, besieged by the enemy's cannon.
Fear no evil, my friend, and to-night may no shadow of sorrow
Fall on this house and hearth; for this is the night of the contract.
Built are the house and the barn. The merry lads of the village
Strongly have built them and well; and, breaking the glebe round
    about them,
Filled the barn with hay, and the house with food for a
    twelvemonth.
Rene Leblanc will be here anon, with his papers and inkhorn.
Shall we not then be glad, and rejoice in the joy of our children?"
As apart by the window she stood, with her hand in her lover's,

Blushing Evangeline heard the words that her father had spoken,
And as they died on his lips the worthy notary entered.

III

Bent like a laboring oar, that toils in the surf of the ocean,
Bent, but not broken, by age was the form of the notary public;
Shocks of yellow hair, like the silken floss of the maize, hung
Over his shoulders; his forehead was high; and glasses with horn
    bows
Sat astride on his nose, with a look of wisdom supernal.

Father of twenty children was he, and more than a hundred
Children's children rode on his knee, and heard his great watch
    tick.
Four long years in the times of the war had he languished a
    captive,
Suffering much in an old French fort as the friend of the English.
Now, though warier grown, without all guile or suspicion,
Ripe in wisdom was he, but patient, and simple and childlike.
He was beloved by all, and most of all by the children;
For he told them tales of the Loup-garou in the forest,
And of the goblin that came in the night to water the horses,
And of the white Letiche, the ghost of a child who unchristened
Died, and was doomed to haunt unseen the chambers of children;
And how on Christmas eve the oxen talked in the stable,
And how the fever was cured by a spider shut up in a nutshell,
And of the marvelous powers of four-leaved clover and horse
    shoes,
With whatsoever else was writ in the lore of the village.
Then up rose from his seat by the fireside Basil the blacksmith,
Knocked from his pipe the ashes, and slowly extending his right
    hand,
"Father Leblanc," he exclaimed, "thou hast heard the talk in the
    village,
And, perchance, canst tell us some news of these ships and their
    errand."
Then with modest demeanor made answer the notary public —
"Gossip enough have I heard, in sooth, yet am never the wiser;
And what their errand may be I know not better than others.

Yet am I not of those who imagine some evil intention
Brings them here, for we are at peace; and why then molest us?"
"God's name!" shouted the hasty and somewhat irascible
    blacksmith;
"Must we in all things look for the how, and the why, and the
    wherefore?
Daily injustice is done, and might is the right of the strongest!"
But, without heeding his warmth, continued the notary public —
"Man is unjust, but God is just; and finally justice
Triumphs; and well I remember a story, that often consoled me,
When as a captive I lay in the old French fort at Port Royal."
This was the old man's favorite tale, and he loved to repeat it
When his neighbors complained that any injustice was done
    them.
"Once in an ancient city, whose name I no longer remember,
Raised aloft on a column, a brazen statue of Justice
Stood in the public square, upholding the scales in its left hand,
And in its right a sword, as an emblem that justice presided
Over the laws of the land, and the hearts and homes of the people.
Even the birds had built their nests in the scales of the balance,
Having no fear of the sword that flashed in the sunshine above
    them.
But in the course of time the laws of the land were corrupted;
Might took the place of right, and the weak were oppressed, and
    the mighty
Ruled with an iron rod. Then it chanced in a nobleman's palace
That a necklace of pearls was lost, and ere long a suspicion
Fell on an orphan girl who lived as maid in the household.
She, after form of trial condemned to die on the scaffold,
Patiently met her doom at the foot of the statue of Justice.
As to her Father in heaven her innocent spirit ascended,
Lo! o'er the city a tempest rose; and the bolts of the thunder
Smote the statue of bronze, and hurled in wrath from its left hand
Down on the pavement below the clattering scales of the balance,
And in the hollow thereof was found the nest of a magpie,
Into whose clay-built walls the necklace of pearls was inwoven."
Silenced, but not convinced, when the story was ended, the
    blacksmith
Stood like a man who fain would speak, but findeth no language;
All his thoughts were congealed into lines on his face, as the
    vapors

Freeze in fantastic shapes on the window-panes in the winter.

Then Evangeline lighted the brazen lamp on the table,
Filled, till it overflowed, the pewter tankard with home-brewed
Nut-brown ale, that was famed for its strength in the village of
    Grand-Pre;
While from his pocket the notary drew his papers and inkhorn,
Wrote with a steady hand the date and the age of the parties,
Naming the dower of the bride in flocks of sheep and in cattle.
Orderly all things proceeded, and duly and well were completed,
And the great seal of the law was set like a sun on the margin.
Then from his leathern pouch the farmer threw on the table
Three times the old man's fee in solid pieces of silver;
And the notary rising, and blessing the bride and the bridegroom,
Lifted aloft the tankard of ale and drank to their welfare.
Wiping the foam from his lip, he solemnly bowed and departed,
While in silence the others sat and mused by the fire-side,
Till Evangeline brought the draught-board out of its corner.
Soon was the game begun. In friendly contention the old men
Laughed at each lucky hit, or unsuccessful manoeuver,
Laughed when a man was crowned, or a breach was made in the
    king-row.
Meanwhile apart, in the twilight gloom of a window's embrasure,
Sat the lovers, and whispered together, beholding the moon rise
Over the pallid sea and the silvery mist of the meadows.
Silently one by one, in the infinite meadows of heaven,
Blossomed the lovely stars, the forget-me-nots of the angels.

Thus was the evening passed. Anon the bell from the belfry
Rang out the hour of nine, the village curfew, and straightway
Rose the guests and departed; and silence reigned in the
    household.
Many a farewell word and sweet good-night on the doorstep
Lingered long in Evangeline's heart, and filled it with gladness.
Carefully then were covered the embers that glowed on the
    hearthstone,
And on the oaken stairs resounded the tread of the farmer.
Soon with a soundless step the foot of Evangeline followed.
Up the staircase moved a luminous space in the darkness,
Lighted less by the lamp than the shining face of the maiden.

Silent she passed through the hall, and entered the door of her
    chamber.
Simple that chamber was, with its curtains of white, and its
    clothes-press
Ample and high, on whose spacious shelves were carefully folded
Linen and woolen stuffs, by the hand of Evangeline woven.
This was the precious dower she would bring to her husband in
    marriage,
Better than flocks and herds, being proofs of her skill as a house
    wife.
Soon she extinguished her lamp, for the mellow and radiant
    moonlight
Streamed through the windows, and lighted the room, till the
heart of the maiden
Swelled and obeyed its power, like the tremulous tides of the
    ocean.
Ah! she was fair, exceeding fair to behold, as she stood with
Naked snow-white feet on the gleaming floor of her chamber!
Little she dreamed that below, among the trees of the orchard,
Waited her lover and watched for the gleam of her lamp and her
    shadow.
Yet were her thoughts of him, and at times a feeling of sadness
Passed o'er her soul, as the sailing shade of clouds in the
    moonlight
Flitted across the floor and darkened the room for a moment.
And as she gazed from the window she saw serenely the moon
    pass,
Forth from the folds of a cloud, and one star follow her footsteps,
As out of Abraham's tent young Ishmael wandered with Hagar!

IV

Pleasantly rose next morn the sun on the village of Grand-Pre.
Pleasantly gleamed in the soft, sweet air the Basin of Minas,
Where the ships, with their wavering shadows, were riding at
    anchor.
Life had long been astir in the village, and clamorous labor
Knocked with its hundred hands at the golden gates of the
    morning.

Now from the country around, from the farms and the
      neighboring hamlets,
Came in their holiday dresses the blithe Acadian peasants.
Many a glad good-morrow and jocund laugh from the young folk
Made the bright air brighter, as up from the numerous meadows,
Where no path could be seen but the track of wheels in the
      greensward,
Group after group appeared, and joined, or passed on the highway.
Long ere noon, in the village all sounds of labor were silenced.
Thronged were the streets with people; and noisy groups at the
      house-doors
Sat in the cheerful sun, and rejoiced and gossiped together,
Every house was an inn, where all were welcomed and feasted;
For with this simple people, who lived like brothers together,
All things were held in common, and what one had was another's.
Yet under Benedict's roof hospitality seemed more abundant:
For Evangeline stood among the guests of her father;
Bright was her face with smiles, and words of welcome and
      gladness
Fell from her beautiful lips, and blessed the cup as she gave it.

Under the open sky, in the odorous air of the orchard,
Bending with golden fruit, was spread the feast of betrothal.
There in the shade of the porch were the priest and the notary
      seated;
There good Benedict sat, and sturdy Basil the blacksmith.
Not far withdrawn from these, by the cider-press and the
      beehives,
Michael the fiddler was placed, with the gayest of hearts and of
      waistcoats.
Shadow and light from the leaves alternately played on his
      snow-white
Hair, as it waved in the wind; and the jolly face of the fiddler
Glowed like a living coal when the ashes are blown from the
      embers.
Gayly the old man sang to the vibrant sound of his fiddle,
Tous les Bourgeois de Chartres, and *Le Carillon de Dunkerque*,
And anon with his wooden shoes beat time to the music.
Merrily, merrily whirled the wheels of the dizzying dances
Under the orchard-trees and down the path to the meadows;
Old folk and young together, and children mingled among them.

Fairest of all the maids was Evangeline, Benedict's daughter!
Noblest of all the youths was Gabriel, son of the blacksmith!

So passed the morning away. And lo! with a summons sonorous
Sounded the bell from its tower, and over the meadows a
     drum beat.
Thronged ere long was the church with men. Without, in the
     churchyard,
Waited the women. They stood by the graves, and hung on the
     headstones
Garlands of autumn leaves and evergreens fresh from the forest.
Then came the guard from the ships, and marching proudly
     among them
Entered the sacred portal. With loud and dissonant clangor
Echoed the sound of their brazen drums from ceiling and
     casement —
Echoed a moment only, and slowly the ponderous portal,
Closed, and in silence the crowd awaited the will of the soldiers.
Then uprose their commander, and spake from the steps of the
     altar,
Holding aloft in his hands, with its seals, the royal commission.
"You are convened this day," he said, "by his Majesty's orders.
Clement and kind has he been; but how you have answered his
     kindness,
Let your own hearts reply! To my natural make and my temper
Painful the task is I do, which to you I know must be grievous.
Yet must I bow and obey, and deliver the will of our monarch;
Namely, that all your lands, and dwellings, and cattle of all kinds
Forfeited be to the crown; and that you yourselves from this
     province
Be transported to other lands. God grant you may dwell there
Ever as faithful subjects, a happy and peaceable people!
Prisoners now I declare you; for such is his Majesty's pleasure!"
As, when the air is serene in the sultry solstice of summer,
Suddenly gathers a storm, and the deadly sling of the hailstones
Beats down the farmer's corn in the field and shatters his
     windows,
Hiding the sun, and strewing the ground with thatch from the
     house-roofs,
Bellowing fly the herds, and seek to break their inclosures;

So on the hearts of the people descended the words of the
    speaker.
Silent a moment they stood in speechless wonder, and then rose
Louder and ever louder a wail of sorrow and anger,
And, by one impulse moved, they madly rushed to the doorway.
Vain was the hope of escape; and cries and fierce imprecations
Rang through the house of prayer; and high o'er the heads of the
    others
Rose, with his arms uplifted, the figure of Basil the blacksmith,
As, on a stormy sea, a spar is tossed by the billows.
Flushed was his face and distorted with passion, and wildly he
    shouted —
"Down with the tyrants of England! we never have sworn them
allegiance!
Death to these foreign soldiers, who seize on our homes and our
    harvests!"
More he fain would have said, but the merciless hand of a soldier
Smote him upon the mouth, and dragged him down to the
    pavement.

In the midst of the strife and tumult of angry contention,
Lo! the door of the chancel opened, and Father Felician
Entered, with serious mien, and ascended the steps of the altar.
Raising his reverend hand, with a gesture he awed into silence
All that clamorous throng; and thus he spake to his people;
Deep were his tones and solemn; in accents measured and
    mournful
Spake he, as, after the tocsin's alarum, distinctly the clock strikes.
"What is this that ye do, my children? what madness has seized
    you?
Forty years of my life have I labored among you, and taught you,
Not in word alone, but in deed, to love one another!
Is this the fruit of my toils, of my vigils and prayers and
    privations?
Have you so soon forgotten all lessons of love and forgiveness?
This is the house of the Prince of Peace, and would you profane it
Thus with violent deeds and hearts overflowing with hatred?
Lo! where the crucified Christ from His cross is gazing upon you!
See! in those sorrowful eyes what meekness and holy compassion!
Hark! how those lips still repeat the prayer, 'O Father, forgive
    them!'

Let us repeat that prayer in the hour when the wicked assail us,
Let us repeat it now, and say, 'O Father, forgive them!'"
Few were his words of rebuke, but deep in the hearts of his
    people
Sank they, and sobs of contrition succeeded that passionate
    outbreak;
And they repeated his prayer, and said, "O Father, forgive them!"

Then came the evening service. The tapers gleamed from the altar.
Fervent and deep was the voice of the priest, and the people
    responded,
Not with their lips alone, but their hearts; and the Ave Maria
Sang they, and fell on their knees, and their souls, with devotion
    translated,
Rose on the ardor of prayer, like Elijah ascending to heaven.

Meanwhile had spread in the village the tidings of ill, and on all
    sides
Wandered, wailing, from house to house the women and children.
Long at her father's door Evangeline stood, with her right hand
Shielding her eyes from the level rays of the sun, that, descending,
Lighted the village street with mysterious splendor, and roofed
    each
Peasant's cottage with golden thatch, and emblazoned its win
    dows.
Long within had been spread the snow-white cloth on the table;
There stood the wheaten loaf, and the honey fragrant with wild
    flowers;
There stood the tankard of ale, and the cheese fresh brought from
    the dairy;
And at the head of the board the great armchair of the farmer.
Thus did Evangeline wait at her father's door, as the sunset
Threw the long shadows of trees o'er the broad ambrosial
    meadows.
Ah! on her spirit within a deeper shadow had fallen,
And from the fields of her soul a fragrance celestial ascended –
Charity, meekness, love, and hope, and forgiveness, and patience!
Then, all-forgetful of self, she wandered into the village,
Cheering with looks and words the disconsolate hearts of the
    women,
As o'er the darkening fields with lingering steps they departed,

Urged by their household cares, and the weary feet of their
   children.
Down sank the great red sun, and in golden, glimmering vapors
Veiled the light of his face, like the Prophet descending from
   Sinai.
Sweetly over the village the bell of the Angelus sounded.

Meanwhile, amid the gloom, by the church Evangeline lingered.
All was silent within; and in vain at the door and the windows
Stood she, and listened and looked, until, overcome by emotion,
"Gabriel!" cried she aloud with tremulous voice; but no answer
Came from the graves of the dead, nor the gloomier grave of the
   living
Slowly at length she returned to the tenantless house of her father.
Smouldered the fire on the hearth, on the board stood the supper
   untasted,
Empty and drear was each room, and haunted with phantoms of
   terror.
Sadly echoed her step on the stair and the floor of her chamber.
In the dead of the night she heard the whispering rain fall
Loud on the withered leaves of the sycamore-tree by the window.
Keenly the lightning flashed; and the voice of the echoing
   thunder
Told her that God was in heaven, and governed the world he
   created!
Then she remembered the tale she had heard of the justice of
   heaven;
Soothed was her troubled soul, and she peacefully slumbered till
   morning.

V

Four times the sun had risen and set; and now on the fifth day
Cheerily called the cock to the sleeping maids of the farmhouse.
Soon o'er the yellow fields, in silent and mournful procession,
Came from the neighboring hamlets and farms the Acadian
   women,
Driving in ponderous wains their household goods to the
   seashore,
Pausing and looking back to gaze once more on their dwellings,

Ere they were shut from sight by the winding road and the
    woodland.
Close at their sides their children ran, and urged on the oxen,
While in their little hands they clasped some fragments of
    playthings.

Thus to the Gaspereau's mouth they hurried; and there on the
    sea-beach
Piled in confusion lay the household goods of the peasants.
All day long the wains came laboring down from the village.
Late in the afternoon, when the sun was near to his setting,
Echoing far o'er the fields came the roll of drums from the
    churchyard.
Thither the women and children thronged. On a sudden the
    church-doors
Opened, and forth came the guard, and marching in gloomy
    procession
Followed the long-imprisoned, but patient, Acadian farmers.
Even as pilgrims, who journey afar from their homes and their
    country,
Sing as they go, and in singing forget they are weary and
    wayworn,
So with songs on their lips the Acadian peasants descended
Down from the church to the shore, amid their wives and their
    daughters.
Foremost the young men came; and, raising together their voices,
Sang they with tremulous lips a chant of the Catholic Missions –
"Sacred heart of the Saviour! O inexhaustible fountain!
Fill our hearts this day with strength and submission and
    patience!"
Then the old men, as they marched, and the women that stood by
    the wayside
Joined in the sacred psalm, and the birds in the sunshine above
    them
Mingled their notes therewith, like voices of spirits departed.

Halfway down to the shore Evangeline waited in silence,
Not overcome with grief, but strong in the hour of affliction –
Calmly and sadly waited, until the procession approached her,
And she beheld the face of Gabriel pale with emotion.
Tears then filled her eyes, and, eagerly running to meet him,

Clasped she his hands, and laid her head on his shoulder and
  whispered —
"Gabriel! be of good cheer! for if we love one another,
Nothing, in truth, can harm us, whatever mischances may
  happen!"
Smiling she spake these words; then suddenly paused, for her
  father
Saw she slowly advancing. Alas! how changed was his aspect!
Gone was the glow from his cheek, and the fire from his eye, and
  his footstep
Heavier seemed with the weight of the weary heart in his bosom.
But with a smile and a sigh she clasped his neck and embraced
  him,
Speaking words of endearment where words of comfort availed
  not.
Thus to the Gaspereau's mouth moved on that mournful
  procession.

There disorder prevailed, and the tumult and stir of embarking.
Busily plied the freighted boats; and in the confusion
Wives were torn from their husbands, and mothers, too late, saw
  their children
Left on the land, extending their arms, with wildest entreaties.
So unto separate ships were Basil and Gabriel carried,
While in despair on the shore Evangeline stood with her father.
Half the task was not done when the sun went down, and the
  twilight
Deepened and darkened around; and in haste the refluent ocean
Fled away from the shore, and left the line of the sand-beach
Covered with waifs of the tide, with kelp and the slippery sea
  weed.
Farther back in the midst of the household goods and the wagons,
Like to a gypsy camp, or a leaguer after a battle,
All escape cut off by the sea, and the sentinels near them,
Lay encamped for the night the houseless Acadian farmers.
Back to its nethermost caves retreated the bellowing ocean,
Dragging adown the beach the rattling pebbles, and leaving
Inland and far up the shore the stranded boats of the sailors.
Then, as the night descended, the herds returned from their
  pastures;

Sweet was the moist still air with the odor of milk from their
  udders;
Lowing they waited, and long, at the well-known bars of the
  farmyard –
Waited and looked in vain for the voice and the hand of the
  milkmaid.
Silence reigned in the streets; from the church no Angelus
sounded,
Rose no smoke from the roofs, and gleamed no lights from the
  windows.

But on the shores meanwhile the evening fires had been kindled,
Built of the driftwood thrown on the sands from wrecks in the
  tempest.
Round them shapes of gloom and sorrowful faces were gathered,
Voices of women were heard, and of men, and the crying of
  children.
Onward from fire to fire, as from hearth to hearth in his parish,
Wandered the faithful priest, consoling and blessing and cheering,
Like unto shipwrecked Paul on Melita's desolate sea-shore.
Thus he approached the place where Evangeline sat with her
  father,
And in the flickering light beheld the face of the old man,
Haggard and hollow and wan, and without either thought or
  emotion,
E'en as the face of a clock from which the hands have been taken.
Vainly Evangeline strove with words and caresses to cheer him,
Vainly offered him food; yet he moved not, he looked not, he
  spake not,
But, with a vacant stare, ever gazed at the flickering firelight.
"*Benedicite!*" murmured the priest, in tones of compassion.
More he fain would have said, but his heart was full, and his
  accents
Faltered and paused on his lips, as the feet of a child on a
  threshold,
Hushed by the scene he beholds, and the awful presence of
  sorrow.
Silently, therefore, he laid his hand on the head of the maiden,
Raising his eyes, full of tears, to the silent stars that above them
Moved on their way, unperturbed by the wrongs and sorrows of
  mortals.

Then sat he down at her side, and they wept together in silence.

Suddenly rose from the south a light, as in autumn the blood-red
Moon climbs the crystal walls of heaven, and o'er the horizon
Titan-like stretches its hundred hands upon mountain and
    meadow,
Seizing the rocks and the rivers, and piling huge shadows together.
Broader and ever broader it gleamed on the roofs of the village,
Gleamed on the sky and the sea, and the ships that lay in the
    roadstead.
Columns of shining smoke uprose, and flashes of flame were
Thrust through their folds and withdrawn, like the quivering
    hands of a martyr.
Then as the wind seized the gleeds and the burning thatch, and,
    uplifting,
Whirled them aloft through the air, at once from a hundred
    housetops
Started the sheeted smoke with flashes of flame intermingled.

These things beheld in dismay the crowd on the shore and on
    shipboard.
Speechless at first they stood, then cried aloud in their anguish,
"We shall behold no more our homes in the village of
    Grand-Pre!"
Loud on a sudden the cocks began to crow in the farmyards,
Thinking the day had dawned; and anon the lowing of cattle
Came on the evening breeze, by the barking of dogs interrupted.
Then rose a sound of dread, such as startles the sleeping
    encampments
Far in the western prairies or forests that skirt the Nebraska,
When the wild horses affrighted sweep by with the speed of the
    whirlwind,
Or the loud bellowing herds of buffaloes rush to the river.
Such was the sound that arose on the night, as the herds and the
    horses
Broke through their folds and fences, and madly rushed o'er the
    meadows.

Overwhelmed with the sight, yet speechless, the priest and the
    maiden

Gazed on the scene of terror that reddened and widened before
   them;
And as they turned at length to speak to their silent companion,
Lo! from his seat he had fallen, and stretched abroad on the
   seashore
Motionless lay his form from which the soul had departed.
Slowly the priest uplifted the lifeless head, and the maiden
Knelt at her father's side, and wailed aloud in her terror.
Then in a swoon she sank, and lay with her head on his bosom.
Through the long night she lay in deep, oblivious slumber;
And when she woke from the trance, she beheld a multitude near
   her.
Faces of friends she beheld, that were mournfully gazing upon
   her,
Pallid, with tearful eyes, and looks of saddest compassion.
Still the blaze of the burning village illumined the landscape,
Reddened the sky overhead, and gleamed on the faces around her,
And like the day of doom it seemed to her wavering senses,
Then a familiar voice she heard, as it said to the people —
"Let us bury him here by the sea. When a happier season
Brings us again to our homes from the unknown land of our
   exile,
Then shall his sacred dust be piously laid in the churchyard."
Such were the words of the priest. And there in haste by the
   seaside,
Having the glare of the burning village for funeral torches,
But without bell or book, they buried the farmer of Grand-Pre.
And as the voice of the priest repeated the service of sorrow,
Lo! with a mournful sound, like the voice of a vast congregation,
Solemnly answered the sea, and mingled its roar with the dirges.
'T was the returning tide, that afar from the waste of the ocean,
With the first dawn of the day, came heaving and hurrying
   landward.
Then recommenced once more the stir and noise of embarking;
And with the ebb of that tide the ships sailed out of the harbor,
Leaving behind them the dead on the shore, and the village in
   ruins.

PART THE SECOND

I

Many a weary year had passed since the burning of Grand-Pre,
When on the falling tide the freighted vessels departed,
Bearing a nation, with all its household gods, into exile,
Exile without an end, and without an example in story.
Far asunder, on separate coasts, the Acadians landed;
Scattered were they, like flakes of snow when the wind from the
    northeast
Strikes aslant through the fogs that darken the Banks of
    Newfoundland.
Friendless, homeless, hopeless, they wandered from city to city,
From the cold lakes of the North to sultry Southern savannas –
From the bleak shores of the sea to the lands where the Father of
    Waters
Seizes the hills in his hands, and drags them down to the ocean,
Deep in their sands to bury the scattered bones of the mammoth.
Friends they sought and homes; and many, despairing,
    heartbroken,
Asked of the earth but a grave, and no longer a friend nor a
    fireside.
Written their history stands on tablets of stone in the churchyards.
Long among them was seen a maiden who waited and wandered,
Lowly and meek in spirit, and patiently suffering all things.
Fair was she and young; but, alas! before her extended,
Dreary and vast and silent, the desert of life, with its pathway
Marked by the graves of those who had sorrowed and suffered
    before her,
Passions long extinguished, and hopes long dead and abandoned,
As the emigrant's way o'er the Western desert is marked by
Camp-fires long consumed, and bones that bleach in the sunshine.
Something there was in her life incomplete, imperfect, unfinished;
As if a morning of June, with all its music and sunshine,
Suddenly paused in the sky, and, fading, slowly descended
Into the east again, from whence it late had arisen.
Sometimes she lingered in towns, till, urged by the fever within
    her,
Urged by a restless longing, the hunger and thirst of the spirit,
She would commence again her endless search and endeavor;

Sometimes in churchyards strayed, and gazed on the crosses and
    tombstones,
Sat by some nameless grave, and thought that perhaps in its bosom
He was already at rest, and she longed to slumber beside him.
Sometimes a rumor, a hearsay, an inarticulate whisper,
Came with its airy hand to point and beckon her forward.
Sometimes she spake with those who had seen her beloved and
    known him,
But it was long ago, in some far-off place or forgotten.
"Gabriel Lajeunesse!" said they; "O, yes! we have seen him.
He was with Basil the blacksmith, and both have gone to the
    prairies;
Coureurs-des-Bois are they, and famous hunters and trappers,"
"Gabriel Lajeunesse!" said others; "O, yes! we have seen him.
He is a Voyageur in the lowlands of Louisiana."
Then would they say: "Dear child! why dream and wait for him
    longer?
Are there not other youths as fair as Gabriel? others
Who have hearts as tender and true, and spirits as loyal?
Here is Baptiste Leblanc, the notary's son, who has loved thee
Many a tedious year; come, give him thy hand and be happy!
Thou art too fair to be left to braid St. Catherine's tresses."
Then would Evangeline answer, serenely but sadly — "I cannot!
Whither my heart has gone, there follows my hand, and not
    elsewhere.
For when the heart goes before, like a lamp, and illumines the
    pathway,
Many things are made clear, that else lie hidden in darkness."
Thereupon the priest, her friend and father-confessor,
Said, with a smile — "O daughter! thy God thus speaketh within
    thee!
Talk not of wasted affection, affection never was wasted;
If it enrich not the heart of another, its waters, returning
Back to their springs, like the rain, shall fill them full of
    refreshment;
That which the fountain sends forth returns again to the fountain.
Patience; accomplish thy labor; accomplish thy work of affection!
Sorrow and silence are strong, and patient endurance is godlike,
Therefore accomplish thy labor of love, till the heart is made
    godlike,

Purified, strengthened, perfected, and rendered more worthy of
    heaven!"
Cheered by the good man's words, Evangeline labored and waited.
Still in her heart she heard the funeral dirge of the ocean,
But with its sound there was mingled a voice that whispered,
    "Despair not!"
Thus did that poor soul wander in want and cheerless discomfort,
Bleeding, barefooted, over the shards and thorns of existence.
Let me essay, O Muse! to follow the wanderer's footsteps;
Not through each devious path, each changeful year of existence;
But as a traveler follows a streamlet's course through the valley;
Far from its margin at times, and seeing the gleam of its water
Here and there, in some open space, and at intervals only:
Then drawing nearer its banks, through sylvan glooms that
    conceal it,
Though he behold it not, he can hear its continuous murmur;
Happy, at length, if he find the spot where it reaches an outlet.

II

It was the month of May. Far down the Beautiful River,
Past the Ohio shore and past the mouth of the Wabash,
Into the golden stream of the broad and swift Mississippi,
Floated a cumbrous boat, that was rowed by Acadian boatmen.
It was a band of exiles; a raft, as it were, from the shipwrecked
Nation, scattered along the coast, now floating together,
Bound by the bonds of a common belief and a common
    misfortune;
Men and women and children, who, guided by hope or by
    hearsay,
Sought for their kith and their kin among the few-acred farmers
On the Acadian coast, and the prairies of fair Opelousas.
With them Evangeline went, and her guide, the Father Felician.
Onward, o'er sunken sands, through a wilderness somber with
    forests,
Day after day they glided adown the turbulent river;
Night after night, by their blazing fires, encamped on its borders,
Now through rushing chutes, among green islands, where
    plumelike

Cotton-trees nodded their shadowy crests, they swept with the
    current,
Then emerged into broad lagoons, where silvery sandbars
Lay in the stream, and along the wimpling waves of their margin,
Shining with snow-white plumes, large flocks of pelicans waded.
Level the landscape grew, and along the shores of the river,
Shaded by china-trees, in the midst of luxuriant gardens,
Stood the houses of planters, with negro-cabins and dove-cotes.
They were approaching the region where reigns perpetual
    summer,
Where through the Golden Coast, and groves of orange and
    citron,
Sweeps with majestic curve the river away to the eastward.
They, too, swerved from their course; and, entering the Bayou of
    Plaquemine,
Soon were lost in a maze of sluggish and devious waters,
Which, like a network of steel, extended in every direction.
Over their heads the towering and tenebrous boughs of the
    cypress
Met in a dusky arch, and trailing mosses in mid-air
Waved like banners that hang on the walls of ancient cathedrals.
Deathlike the silence seemed, and unbroken, save by the herons
Home to their roosts in the cedar-trees returning at sunset,
Or by the owl, as he greeted the moon with demoniac laughter.
Lovely the moonlight was as it glanced and gleamed on the water,
Gleamed on the columns of cypress and cedar sustaining the
    arches,
Down through whose broken vaults it fell as through chinks in a
    ruin.
Dreamlike, and indistinct, and strange were all things around
    them;
And o'er their spirits there came a feeling of wonder and sadness
Strange forebodings of ill, unseen and that cannot be compassed.
As, at the tramp of a horse's hoof on the turf of the prairies,
Far in advance are closed the leaves of the shrinking mimosa,
So, at the hoof-beats of fate, with sad forebodings of evil,
Shrinks and closes the heart, ere the stroke of doom has
    attained it.
But Evangeline's heart was sustained by a vision, that faintly
Floated before her eyes, and beckoned her on through the
    moonlight.

It was the thought of her brain that assumed the shape of a
   phantom.
Through those shadowy aisles had Gabriel wandered before her,
And every stroke of the oar now brought him nearer and nearer.

Then in his place, at the prow of the boat, rose one of the
   oarsmen,
And, as a signal sound, if others like them peradventure
Sailed on those gloomy and midnight streams, blew a blast on his
   bugle.
Wild through the dark colonnades and corridors leafy the blast
   rang,
Breaking the seal of silence, and giving tongues to the forest.
Soundless above them the banners of moss just stirred to the
   music.
Multitudinous echoes awoke and died in the distance,
Over the watery floor, and beneath the reverberant branches;
But not a voice replied; no answer came from the darkness;
And when the echoes had ceased, like a sense of pain was the
   silence.
Then Evangeline slept; but the boatmen rowed through the
   midnight,
Silent at times, then singing familiar Canadian boat-songs,
Such as they sang of old on their own Acadian rivers,
And through the night were heard the mysterious sounds of the
   desert,
Far off, indistinct, as of wave or wind in the forest,
Mixed with the whoop of the crane and the roar of the grim
   alligator.

Thus ere another noon they emerged from those shades; and
   before them
Lay, in the golden sun, the lakes of the Atchafalaya.
Water-lilies in myriads rocked on the slight undulations
Made by the passing oars, and, resplendent in beauty, the lotus
Lifted her golden crown above the heads of the boatmen.
Faint was the air with the odorous breath of magnolia blossoms,
And with the heat of noon; and numberless sylvan islands,
Fragrant and thickly embowered with blossoming hedges of roses,
Near to whose shores they glided along, invited to slumber.
Soon by the fairest of these their weary oars were suspended.

Under the boughs of Wachita willows, that grew by the margin,
Safely their boat was moored; and scattered about on the
    greensward,
Tired with their midnight toil, the weary travelers slumbered.
Over them vast and high extended the cope of a cedar.
Swinging from its great arms, the trumpet-flower and the
    grape-vine
Hung their ladder of ropes aloft like the ladder of Jacob,
On whose pendulous stairs the angels ascending, descending,
Were the swift humming-birds, that flitted from blossom to
    blossom.
Such was the vision Evangeline saw as she slumbered beneath it.
Filled was her heart with love, and the dawn of an opening
    heaven
Lighted her soul in sleep with the glory of regions celestial.

Nearer and ever nearer, among the numberless islands,
Darted a light, swift boat, that sped away o'er the water,
Urged on its course by the sinewy arms of hunters and trappers.
Northward its prow was turned, to the land of the bison and
    beaver.
At the helm sat a youth, with countenance thoughtful and
    careworn.
Dark and neglected locks overshadowed his brow, and a sadness
Somewhat beyond his years on his face was legibly written.
Gabriel was it, who, weary with waiting, unhappy and restless,
Sought in the Western wilds oblivion of self and of sorrow.
Swiftly they glided along, close under the lee of the island,
But by the opposite bank, and behind a screen of palmettos,
So that they saw not the boat, where it lay concealed in the
    willows,
And undisturbed by the dash of their oars, and unseen, were the
    sleepers;
Angel of God was there none to awaken the slumbering maiden.
Swiftly they glided away, like the shade of a cloud on the prairie.
After the sound of their oars on the tholes had died in the
    distance,
As from a magic trance the sleepers awoke, and the maiden
Said with a sigh to the friendly priest — "O Father Felician!
Something says in my heart that near me Gabriel wanders.
Is it a foolish dream, an idle vague superstition?

Or has an angel passed, and revealed the truth to my spirit?"
Then, with a blush, she added — "Alas for my credulous fancy!
Unto ears like thine such words as these have no meaning."
But made answer the reverend man, and he smiled as he answered
"Daughter, thy words are not idle; nor are they to me without
    meaning.
Feeling is deep and still; and the word that floats on the surface
Is as the tossing buoy, that betrays where the anchor is hidden.
Therefore trust to thy heart, and to what the world calls illusions.
Gabriel truly is near thee; for not far away to the southward,
On the banks of the Teche are the towns of St. Maur and St.
    Martin.
There the long-wandering bride shall be given again to her
    bridegroom,
There the long-absent pastor regain his flock and his sheepfold.
Beautiful is the land, with its prairies and forests of fruit-trees;
Under the feet a garden of flowers, and the bluest of heavens
Bending above, and resting its dome on the walls of the forest.
They who dwell there have named it the Eden of Louisiana."

With these words of cheer they arose and continued their journey.
Softly the evening came. The sun from the western horizon
Like a magician extended his golden wand o'er the landscape;
Twinkling vapors arose; and sky and water and forest
Seemed all on fire at the touch, and melted and mingled together.
Ranging between two skies, a cloud with edges of silver,
Floated the boat, with its dripping oars, on the motionless water.
Filled was Evangeline's heart with inexpressible sweetness.
Touched by the magic spell, the sacred fountains of feeling
Glowing with the light of love, as the skies and waters around her.
Then from a neighboring thicket the mocking-bird, wildest of
    singers,
Swinging aloft on a willow spray that hung o'er the water,
Shook from his little throat such floods of delirious music,
That the whole air and the woods and the waves seemed silent to
    listen.
Plaintive at first were the tones and sad; then soaring to madness
Seemed they to follow or guide the revel of frenzied Bacchantes.
Single notes were then heard, in sorrowful, low lamentation;
Till, having gathered them all, he flung them abroad in derision,
As when, after a storm, a gust of wind through the tree-tops

Shakes down the rattling rain in a crystal shower on the branches.
With such a prelude as this, and hearts that throbbed with
    emotion,
Slowly they entered the Teche, where it flows through the green
    Opelousas,
And through the amber air, above the crest of the woodland,
Saw the column of smoke that arose from a neighboring dwelling;
Sounds of a horn they heard, and the distant lowing of cattle.

III

Near to the bank of the river, o'ershadowed by oaks, from whose
    branches
Garlands of Spanish moss and of mystic mistletoe flaunted,
Such as the Druids cut down with golden hatchets at Yule-tide,
Stood, secluded and still, the house of the herdsman. A garden
Girded it round about with a belt of luxuriant blossoms,
Filling the air with fragrance. The house itself was of timbers
Hewn from the cypress-tree, and carefully fitted together.
Large and low was the roof; and on slender columns supported,
Rose-wreathed, vine-encircled, a broad and spacious veranda,
Haunt of the humming-bird and the bee, extended around it.
At each end of the house, amid the flowers of the garden,
Stationed the dove-cotes were, as love's perpetual symbol,
Scenes of endless wooing, and endless contentions of rivals.
Silence reigned o'er the place. The line of shadow and sunshine
Ran near the tops of the trees; but the house itself was in shadow,
And from its chimney-top, ascending and slowly expanding
Into the evening air, a thin blue column of smoke rose.
In the rear of the house, from the garden gate, ran a pathway
Through the great groves of oak to the skirts of the limitless
    prairie,
Into whose sea of flowers the sun was slowly descending.
Full in his track of light, like ships with shadowy canvas
Hanging loose from their spars in a motionless calm in the tropics,
Stood a cluster of trees, with tangled cordage of grape-vines.

Just where the woodlands met the flowery surf of the prairie,
Mounted upon his horse, with Spanish saddle and stirrups,
Sat a herdsman, arrayed in gaiters and doublet of deerskin.

Broad and brown was the face that from under the Spanish
    sombrero
Gazed on the peaceful scene, with the lordly look of its master.
Round about him were numberless herds of kine, that were
    grazing
Quietly in the meadows, and breathing the vapory freshness
That uprose from the river, and spread itself over the landscape.
Slowly lifting the horn that hung at his side, and expanding
Fully his broad, deep chest, he blew a blast, that resounded
Wildly and sweet and far, through the still damp air of the
    evening.
Suddenly out of the grass the long white horns of the cattle
Rose like flakes of foam on the adverse currents of ocean.
Silent a moment they gazed, then bellowing rushed o'er the
    prairie,
And the whole mass became a cloud, a shade in the distance.
Then, as the herdsman turned to the house, through the gate of
    the garden
Saw he the forms of the priest and the maiden advancing to meet
    him.
Suddenly down from his horse he sprang in amazement, and
    forward
Rushed with extended arms and exclamations of wonder;
When they beheld his face, they recognized Basil the Blacksmith.
Hearty his welcome was, as he led his guests to the garden.
There in an arbor of roses with endless question and answer
Gave they vent to their hearts, and renewed their friendly em
    braces,
Laughing and weeping by turns, or sitting silent and thoughtful.
Thoughtful, for Gabriel came not; and now dark doubts and
    misgivings
Stole o'er the maiden's heart; and Basil, somewhat embarrassed,
Broke the silence and said – "If you come by the Atchafalaya,
How have you nowhere encountered my Gabriel's boat on the
bayous?"
Over Evangeline's face at the words of Basil a shade passed.
Tears came into her eyes, and she said, with a tremulous accent –
"Gone? is Gabriel gone?" and, concealing her face on his
    shoulder,
All her o'erburdened heart gave way, and she wept and lamented.
Then the good Basil said — and his voice grew blithe as he said it

"Be of good cheer, my child; it is only to-day he departed.
Foolish boy! he has left me alone with my herds and my horses.
Moody and restless grown, and tried and troubled, his spirit
Could no longer endure the calm of this quiet existence.
Thinking ever of thee, uncertain and sorrowful ever,
Ever silent, or speaking only of thee and his troubles,
He at length had become so tedious to men and to maidens,
Tedious even to me, that at length I bethought me and sent him
Unto the town of Adayes to trade for mules with the Spaniards.
Thence he will follow the Indian trails to the Ozark Mountains,
Hunting for furs in the forests, on rivers trapping the beaver.
Therefore be of good cheer; we will follow the fugitive lover;
He is not far on his way, and the Fates and the streams are against
    him.
Up and away to-morrow, and through the red dew of the
    morning
We will follow him fast and bring him back to his prison."

Then glad voices were heard, and up from the banks of the river,
Borne aloft on his comrades' arms, came Michael the fiddler.
Long under Basil's roof had he lived like a god on Olympus,
Having no other care than dispensing music to mortals,
Far renowned was he for his silver locks and his fiddle.
"Long live Michael," they cried, "our brave Acadian minstrel!"
As they bore him aloft in triumphal procession; and straightway
Father Felician advanced with Evangeline, greeting the old man
Kindly and oft, and recalling the past, while Basil, enraptured,
Hailed with hilarious joy his old companions and gossips,
Laughing loud and long, and embracing mothers and daughters.
Much they marvelled to see the wealth of the ci-devant
    blacksmith,
All his domains and his herds, and his patriarchal demeanor;
Much they marveled to hear his tales of the soil and the climate,
And of the prairies, whose numberless herds were his who would
    take them;
Each one thought in his heart that he, too, would go and do
    likewise.
Thus they ascended the steps, and, crossing the airy veranda,
Entered the hall of the house, where already the supper of Basil
Waited his late return; and they rested and feasted together.

Over the joyous feast the sudden darkness descended.
All was silent without, and illuming the landscape with silver,
Fair rose the dewy moon and the myriad stars; but within doors,
Brighter than these, shone the faces of friends in the glimmering
    lamplight.
Then from his station aloft, at the head of the table, the herdsman
Poured forth his heart and his wine together in endless profusion.
Lighting his pipe, that was filled with sweet Natchitoches tobacco,
Thus he spake to his guests, who listened, and smiled as they
    listened:
"Welcome once more, my friends, who so long have been
    friendless and homeless,
Welcome once more to a home, that is better perchance than the
    old one!
Here no hungry winter congeals our blood like the rivers;
Here no stony ground provokes the wrath of the farmer.
Smoothly the plowshare runs through the soil as a keel through
    the water.
All the year round the orange-groves are in blossom; and grass
    grows
More in a single night than a whole Canadian summer.
Here, too, numberless herds run wild and unclaimed in the
    prairies;
Here, too, lands may be had for the asking, and forests of timber
With a few blows of the axe are hewn and framed into houses.
After your houses are built, and your fields are yellow with
    harvests,
No King George of England shall drive you away from your
    homesteads,
Burning your dwellings and barns, and stealing your farms and
    your cattle."
Speaking these words, he blew a wrathful cloud from his nostrils,
And his huge, brawny hand came thundering down on the table,
So that the guests all started; and Father Felician, astounded,
Suddenly paused, with a pinch of snuff half-way to his nostrils.
But the brave Basil resumed, and his words were milder and gayer
"Only beware of the fever, my friends, beware of the fever!
For it is not like that of our cold Acadian climate,
Cured by wearing a spider hung round one's neck in a nutshell!"
Then there were voices heard at the door, and footsteps
    approaching

Sounded upon the stairs and the floor of the breezy veranda.
It was the neighboring Creoles and small Acadian planters,
Who had been summoned all to the house of Basil the Herdsman.
Merry the meeting was of ancient comrades and neighbors;
Friend clasped friend in his arms; and they who before were as
    strangers,
Meeting in exile, became straightway as friends to each other,
Drawn by the gentle bond of a common country together.
But in the neighboring hall a strain of music, proceeding
From the accordant strings of Michael's melodious fiddle,
Broke up all further speech. Away, like children delighted,
All things forgotten beside, they gave themselves to the
    maddening
Whirl of the dizzy dance, as it swept and swayed to the music,
Dreamlike, with beaming eyes and the rush of fluttering garments.

Meanwhile, apart, at the head of the hall, the priest and the
    herdsman
Sat, conversing together of past and present and future;
While Evangeline stood like one entranced, for within her
Olden memories rose, and loud in the midst of the music
Heard she the sound of the sea, and an irrepressible sadness
Came o'er her heart, and unseen she stole forth into the garden.
Beautiful was the night. Behind the black wall of the forest,
Tipping its summit with silver, arose the moon. On the river
Fell here and there through the branches a tremulous gleam of the
    moonlight,
Like the sweet thoughts of love on a darkened and devious spirit.
Nearer and round about her, the manifold flowers of the garden
Poured out their souls in odors, that were their prayers and
    confessions
Unto the night, as it went its way, like a silent Carthusian.
Fuller of fragrance then they, and as heavy with shadows and
    night-dews,
Hung the heart of the maiden. The calm and the magical moon
    light
Seemed to inundate her soul with indefinable longings,
As, through the garden gate, beneath the brown shade of the
    oak-trees,
Passed she along the path to the edge of the measureless prairie.
Silent it lay, with a silvery haze upon it, and the fire-flies

Gleaming and floating away in mingled and infinite numbers.
Over her head the stars, the thoughts of God in the heavens,
Shone on the eyes of man, who had ceased to marvel and
    worship,
Save when a blazing comet was seen on the walls of that temple,
As if a hand had appeared and written upon them, "Upharsin."
And the soul of the maiden, between the stars and the fire-flies,
Wandered alone, and she cried – "O Gabriel! O my beloved!
Art thou so near unto me, and yet I cannot behold thee?
Art thou so near unto me, and yet thy voice does not reach me?
Ah! how often thy feet have trod this path to the prairie!
Ah! how often thine eyes have looked on the woodlands around
    me!
Ah! how often beneath this oak, returning from labor,
Thou hast lain down to rest, and to dream of me in thy slumbers.
When shall these eyes behold, these arms be folded about thee?"
Loud and sudden and near the note of a whippoorwill sounded
Like a flute in the woods; and anon, through the neighboring
    thickets,
Farther and farther away it floated and dropped into silence.
"Patience!" whispered the oaks from oracular caverns of darkness;
And, from the moonlit meadow, a sigh responded, "To-morrow!"

Bright rose the sun next day; and all the flowers of the garden
Bathed his shining feet with their tears, and anointed his tresses
With the delicious balm that they bore in their vases of crystal.
"Farewell!" said the priest, as he stood at the shadowy threshold;
"See that you bring us the Prodigal Son from his fasting and
    famine,
And, too, the Foolish Virgin, who slept when the bridegroom was
    coming."
"Farewell!" answered the maiden, and, smiling, with Basil
    descended
Down to the river's brink, where the boatmen already were
    waiting.
Thus beginning their journey with morning, and sunshine and
    gladness,
Swiftly they followed the flight of him who was speeding before
    them,
Blown by the blast of fate like a dead leaf over the desert.
Not that day, nor the next, nor yet the day that succeeded,

Found they trace of his course, in lake or forest or river,
Nor, after many days, had they found him; but vague and
    uncertain
Rumors alone were their guides through a wild and desolate
    country,
Till, at the little inn of the Spanish town of Adayes,
Weary and worn, they alighted, and learned from the garrulous
    landlord,
That on the day before, with horses and guides and companions,
Gabriel left the village, and took the road of the prairies.

IV

Far in the West there lies a desert land, where the mountains
Lift, through perpetual snows, their lofty and luminous summits.
Down from their jagged, deep ravines, where the gorge, like a
    gateway,
Opens a passage rude to the wheels of the emigrant's wagon,
Westward the Oregon flows and the Walleway and Owyhee.
Eastward, with devious course, among the Windriver Mountains,
Through the Sweetwater Valley precipitate leaps the Nebraska;
And to the south, from Fontaine-qui-bout and the Spanish sierras,
Fretted with sands and rocks, and swept by the wind of the desert,
Numberless torrents, with ceaseless sound, descend to the ocean,
Like the great chords of a harp, in loud and solemn vibrations.
Spreading between these streams are the wondrous, beautiful
    prairies,
Billowy bays of grass ever rolling in shadow and sunshine,
Bright with luxuriant clusters of roses and purple amorphas.
Over them wander the buffalo herds, and the elk and the roebuck;
Over them wander the wolves, and herds of riderless horses;
Fires that blast and blight, and winds that are weary with travel;
Over them wander the scattered tribes of Ishmael's children,
Staining the desert with blood; and above their terrible war-trails
Circles and sails aloft, on pinions majestic, the vulture,
Like the implacable soul of a chieftain slaughtered in battle,
By invisible stairs ascending and scaling the heavens.
Here and there rise smokes from the camps of these savage
    marauders;

Here and there rise groves from the margins of swift-running
    rivers;
And the grim, taciturn bear, the anchorite monk of the desert,
Climbs down their dark ravines to dig for roots by the brookside,
And over all is the sky, the clear and crystalline heaven,
Like the protecting hand of God inverted above them.

Into this wonderful land, at the base of the Ozark Mountains,
Gabriel far had entered, with hunters and trappers behind him.
Day after day, with their Indian guides, the maiden and Basil
followed his flying steps, and thought each day to o'ertake him.
Sometimes they saw, or thought they saw, the smoke of his
    camp-fire
Rise in the morning air from the distant plain; but at nightfall,
When they had reached the place, they found only embers and
    ashes.
And, though their hearts were sad at times and their bodies were
    weary,
Hope still guided them on, as the magic Fata Morgana
Showed them her lakes of light, that retreated and vanished before
    them.
Once, as they sat by their evening fire, there silently entered
Into the little camp an Indian woman, whose features
Wore deep traces of sorrow, and patience as great as her sorrow.
She was a Shawnee woman returning home to her people,
From the far-off hunting-grounds of the cruel Camanches,
Where her Canadian husband, a Coureur-des-Bois, had been
    murdered.
Touched were their hearts at her story, and warmest and
    friendliest welcome
Gave they, with words of cheer, and she sat and feasted among
    them
On the buffalo meat and the venison cooked on the embers.
But when their meal was done, and Basil and all his companions,
Worn with the long day's march and the chase of the deer and the
    bison,
Stretched themselves on the ground, and slept where the
    quivering firelight
Flashed on their swarthy cheeks, and their forms wrapped up in
    their blankets,
Then at the door of Evangeline's tent she sat and repeated

Slowly, with soft, low voice, and the charm of her Indian accent,
All the tale of her love, with its pleasures, and pains, and reverses.
Much Evangeline wept at the tale, and to know that another
Hapless heart like her own had loved and had been disappointed.
Moved to the depths of her soul by pity and woman's compassion,
Yet in her sorrow pleased that one who had suffered was near her,
She in turn related her love and all its disasters.
Mute with wonder the Shawnee sat, and when she had ended
Still was mute; but at length, as if a mysterious horror
Passed through her brain, she spake, and repeated the tale of the
     Mowis;
Mowis, the bridegroom of snow, who won and wedded a maiden,
But, when the morning came, arose and passed from the wigwam,
Fading and melting away and dissolving into the sunshine,
Till she beheld him no more, though she followed far into the
     forest.
Then, in those sweet, low tones, that seem like a weird
     incantation,
Told she the tale of the fair Lilinau, who was wooed by a
     phantom,
That, through the pines o'er her father's lodge, in the hush of the
     twilight,
Breathed like the evening wind, and whispered love to the
     maiden,
Till she followed his green and waving plume through the forest,
And never more returned, nor was seen again by her people.
Silent with wonder and strange surprise Evangeline listened
To the soft flow of her magical words, till the region around her
Seemed like enchanted ground, and her swarthy guest the en
     chantress.
Slowly over the tops of the Ozark Mountains the moon rose,
Lighting the little tent, and with a mysterious splendor
Touching the somber leaves, and embracing and filling the
     woodland.
With a delicious sound the brook rushed by, and the branches
Swayed and sighed overhead in scarcely audible whispers.
Filled with the thoughts of love was Evangeline's heart, but a
     secret,
Subtile sense crept in of pain and indefinite terror,
As the cold, poisonous snake creeps into the nest of the swallow.
It was no earthly fear. A breath from the region of spirits

Seemed to float in the air of night; and she felt for a moment
That, like the Indian maid, she, too, was pursuing a phantom.
And with this thought she slept, and the fear and the phantom
    had vanished.

Early upon the morrow the march was resumed; and the Shawnee
Said, as they journeyed along — "On the western slope of these
    mountains
Dwells in his little village the Black Robe chief of the Mission.
Much he teaches the people, and tells them of Mary and Jesus;
Loud laugh their hearts with joy, and weep with pain, as they hear
    him."
Then, with a sudden and secret emotion, Evangeline answered —
"Let us go to the Mission, for there good tidings await us!"
Thither they turned their steeds; and behind a spur of the
    mountains,
Just as the sun went down, they heard a murmur of voices,
And in a meadow green and broad, by the bank of a river,
Saw the tents of the Christians, the tents of the Jesuit Mission.
Under a towering oak, that stood in the midst of the village,
Knelt the Black Robe chief with his children. A crucifix fastened
High on the trunk of the tree, and overshadowed by grape-vines,
Looked with its agonized face on the multitude kneeling
    beneath it.
This was their rural chapel. Aloft, through the intricate arches
Of its aerial roof, arose the chant of their vespers,
Mingling its notes with the soft susurrus and sighs of the
    branches.
Silent, with heads uncovered, the travelers, nearer approaching,
Knelt on the swarded floor, and joined in the evening devotions.
But when the service was done, and the benediction had fallen
Forth from the hands of the priest, like seed from the hands of the
    sower,
Slowly the reverend man advanced to the strangers, and bade t
    them
Welcome; and when they replied, he smiled with benignant
    expression,
Hearing the homelike sounds of his mother tongue in the forest,
And with words of kindness conducted them into his wigwam.
There upon mats and skins they reposed, and on cakes of the
    maize-ear

Feasted, and slaked their thirst from the water-gourd of the
    teacher.
Soon was their story told; and the priest with solemnity answered:
"Not six suns have risen and set since Gabriel, seated
On this mat by my side, where now the maiden reposes,
Told me this same sad tale; then arose and continued his journey!"
Soft was the voice of the priest, and he spake with an accent of
    kindness;
But on Evangeline's heart fell his words as in winter the
    snowflakes
Fall into some lone nest from which the birds have departed.
"Far to the north he has gone," continued the priest; "but in
    autumn,
When the chase is done, will return again to the Mission."
Then Evangeline said, and her voice was meek and submissive –
"Let me remain with thee, for my soul is sad and afflicted."
So seemed it wise and well unto all; and betimes on the morrow,
Mounting his Mexican steed, with his Indian guides and
    companions,
Homeward Basil returned, and Evangeline stayed at the Mission.

Slowly, slowly, slowly the days succeeded each other –
Days and weeks and months; and the fields of maize that were
    springing
Green from the ground when a stranger she came, now waving
    above her,
Lifted their slender shafts, with leaves interlacing, and forming
Cloisters for mendicant crows and granaries pillaged by squirrels.
Then in the golden weather the maize was busked, and the
    maidens
Blushed at each blood-red ear, for that betokened a lover,
But at the crooked laughed, and called it a thief in the corn-field.
Even the blood-red ear to Evangeline brought not her lover.
"Patience!" the priest would say; "have faith, and thy prayer will
    be answered!
Look at this delicate plant that lifts its head from the meadow,
See how its leaves all point to the north, as true as the magnet;
It is the compass-flower, that the finger of God has suspended
Here in the houseless wild, to direct the traveler's journey
Over the sea-like, pathless, limitless waste of the desert.
Such in the soul of man is faith. The blossoms of passion,

Gay and luxuriant flowers, are brighter and fuller of fragrance,
But they beguile us, and lead us astray, and their odor is deadly.
Only this humble plant can guide us here, and hereafter
Crown us with asphodel flowers, that are wet with the dews of
    nepenthe."

So came the autumn, and passed, and the winter – yet Gabriel
    came not;
Blossomed the opening spring, and the notes of the robin and
    bluebird
Sounded sweet upon wold and in wood, yet Gabriel came not.
But on the breath of the summer winds a rumor was wafted
Sweeter than song of bird, or hue or odor of blossom.
Far to the north and east, it said, in the Michigan forests,
Gabriel had his lodge by the banks of the Saginaw river.
And, with returning guides, that sought the lakes of St. Lawrence,
Saying a sad farewell, Evangeline went from the Mission.
When over weary ways, by long and perilous marches,
She had attained at length the depths of the Michigan forests,
Found she the hunter's lodge deserted and fallen to ruin!

Thus did the long sad years glide on, and in seasons and places
Divers and distant far was seen the wandering maiden;
Now in the tents of grace of the meek Moravian Missions,
Now in the noisy camps and the battle-fields of the army,
Now in secluded hamlets, in towns and populous cities,
Like a phantom she came, and passed away unremembered.
Fair was she and young, when in hope began the long journey;
Faded was she and old, when in disappointment it ended.
Each succeeding year stole something away from her beauty,
Leaving behind it, broader and deeper, the gloom and the shadow.
Then there appeared and spread faint streaks of gray o'er her
    forehead,
Dawn of another life, that broke o'er her earthly horizon,
As in the eastern sky the first faint streaks of the morning.

V

In that delightful land which is washed by the Delaware's waters,
Guarding in sylvan shades the name of Penn the apostle,

Stands on the banks of its beautiful stream the city he founded.
There all the air is balm, and the peach is the emblem of beauty,
And the streets still re-echo the names of the trees of the forest,
As if they fain would appease the Dryads whose haunts they
    molested.
There from the troubled sea had Evangeline landed, an exile,
Finding among the children of Penn a home and a country.
There old Rene Leblanc had died; and when he departed,
Saw at his side only one of all his hundred descendants.
Something at least there was in the friendly streets of the city,
Something that spake to her heart, and made her no longer a
    stranger:
And her ear was pleased with the Thee and Thou of the Quakers,
For it recalled the past, the old Acadian country,
Where all men were equal, and all were brothers and sisters.
So, when the fruitless search, the disappointed endeavor,
Ended, to recommence no more upon earth, uncomplaining,
Thither, as leaves to the light, were turned her thoughts and her
    footsteps.
As from a mountain's top the rainy mists of the morning
Roll away, and afar we behold the landscape below us,
Sun-illumined, with shining rivers and cities and hamlets,
So fell the mists from her mind, and she saw the world far below
    her,
Dark no longer, but all illumined with love; and the pathway
Which she had climbed so far, lying smooth and fair in the
    distance.
Gabriel was not forgotten. Within her heart was his image,
Clothed in the beauty of love and youth, as last she beheld him,
Only more beautiful made by his deathlike silence and absence.
Into her thoughts of him time entered not, for it was not.
Over him years had no power; he was not changed, but
    transfigured;
He had become to her heart as one who is dead, and not absent;
Patience and abnegation of self, and devotion to others,
This was the lesson a life of trial and sorrow had taught her.
So was her love diffused, but, like to some odorous spices,
Suffered no waste nor loss, though filling the air with aroma.
Other hope had she none, nor wish in life, but to follow
Meekly, with reverent steps, the sacred feet of her Saviour.
Thus many years she lived as a Sister of Mercy; frequenting

Lonely and wretched roofs in the crowded lanes of the city,
Where distress and want concealed themselves from the sunlight,
Where disease and sorrow in garrets languished neglected.
Night after night, when the world was asleep, as the watchman
  repeated
Loud, through the gusty streets, that all was well in the city,
High at some lonely window he saw the light of her taper.
Day after day, in the gray of the dawn, as slow through the suburbs
Plodded the German farmer, with flowers and fruits for the
  market,
Met he that meek, pale face, returning home from its watchings.

Then it came to pass that a pestilence fell on the city,
Presaged by wondrous signs, and mostly by flocks of wild pigeons,
Darkening the sun in their flight, with naught in their craws but
  an acorn.
And, as the tides of the sea arise in the month of September,
Flooding some silver stream, till it spreads to a lake in a meadow,
So death flooded life, and o'erflowing its natural margin,
Spread to a brackish lake, the silver stream of existence.
Wealth had no power to bribe, nor beauty to charm, the
  oppressor;
But all perished alike beneath the scourge of his anger —
Only, alas! the poor, who had neither friends nor attendants,
Crept away to die in the almshouse, home of the homeless;
Then in the suburbs it stood, in the midst of meadows and
  woodlands —

Now the city surrounds it; but still with its gateway and wicket
Meek, in the midst of splendor, its humble walls seem to echo
Softly the words of the Lord – "The poor ye always have with
  you."
Thither, by night and by day, came the Sister of Mercy. The dying
Looked up into her face, and thought, indeed, to behold there
Gleams of celestial light encircle her forehead with splendor,
Such as the artist paints o'er the brows of saints and apostles,
Or such as hangs by night o'er a city seen at a distance.
Unto their eyes it seemed the lamps of the city celestial,
Into whose shining gates ere long their spirits would enter.

Thus, on a Sabbath morn, through the streets, deserted and silent,
Wending her quiet way, she entered the door of the almshouse.
Sweet on the summer air was the odor of flowers in the garden;
And she paused on her way to gather the fairest among them,
That the dying once more might rejoice in their fragrance and
    beauty.
Then, as she mounted the stairs to the corridors, cooled by the
    east wind,
Distant and soft on her ear fell the chimes from the belfry of
    Christ Church,
While, intermingled with these, across the meadows were wafted
Sounds of psalms, that were sung by the Swedes in their church at
    Wicaco.
Soft as descending wings fell the calm of the hour on her spirit;
Something within her said — "At length thy trials are ended;"
And, with a light in her looks, she entered the chambers of
    sickness.
Noiselessly moved about the assiduous, careful attendants,
Moistening the feverish lip, and the aching brow, and in silence
Closing the sightless eyes of the dead, and concealing their faces,
Where on their pallets they lay, like drifts of snow by the roadside.
Many a languid head, upraised as Evangeline entered,
Turned on its pillow of pain to gaze while she passed, for her
    presence
Fell on their hearts like a ray of the sun on the walls of a prison.
And, as she looked around, she saw how Death, the consoler,
Laying his hand upon many a heart, had healed it forever.
Many familiar forms had disappeared in the night-time;
Vacant their places were, or filled already by strangers.

Suddenly, as if arrested by fear or a feeling of wonder,
Still she stood with her colorless lips apart, while a shudder
Ran through her frame, and, forgotten, the flowerets dropped
from her fingers,
And from her eyes and cheeks the light and bloom of the
    morning.
Then there escaped from her lips a cry of such terrible anguish,
That the dying heard it, and started up from their pillows.
On the pallet before her was stretched the form of an old man.
Long, and thin, and gray were the locks that shaded his temples;
But, as he lay in the morning light, his face for a moment

Seemed to assume once more the forms of its earlier manhood;
So are wont to be changed the faces of those who are dying.
Hot and red on his lips still burned the flush of the fever,
As if life, like the Hebrew, with blood had besprinkled its portals,
That the Angel of Death might see the sign, and pass over,
Motionless, senseless, dying, he lay, and his spirit exhausted
Seemed to be sinking down to infinite depths in the darkness,
Darkness of slumber and death, forever sinking and sinking.
Then through those realms of shade, in multiplied reverberations,
Heard he that cry of pain, and through the hush that succeeded
Whispered a gentle voice, in accents tender and saint-like,
"Gabriel! O my beloved!" and died away into silence.
Then he beheld, in a dream, once more the home of his
     childhood;
Green Acadian meadows, with sylvan rivers among them,
Village, and mountain, and woodlands; and, walking under their
     shadow,
As in the days of her youth, Evangeline rose in his vision.
Tears came into his eyes; and as slowly he lifted his eyelids,
Vanished the vision away, but Evangeline knelt by his bedside.
Vainly he strove to whisper her name, for the accents unuttered
Died on his lips, and their motion revealed what his tongue
     would have spoken.
Vainly he strove to rise; and Evangeline, kneeling beside him,
Kissed his dying lips, and laid his head on her bosom
Sweet was the light of his eyes; but it suddenly sank into darkness,
As when a lamp is blown out by a gust of wind at a casement.

All was ended now, the hope, and the fear, and the sorrow,
All the aching of heart, the restless, unsatisfied longing,
All the dull, deep pain, and constant anguish of patience!
And, as she pressed once more the lifeless head to her bosom,
Meekly she bowed her own, and murmured, "Father, I thank
     thee!"

Still stands the forest primeval; but far away from its shadow,
Side by side, in their nameless graves, the lovers are sleeping.
Under the humble walls of the little Catholic churchyard,
In the heart of the city, they lie, unknown and unnoticed;
Daily the tides of life go ebbing and flowing beside them,

Thousands of throbbing hearts, where theirs are at rest and
    forever,
Thousands of aching brains, where theirs no longer are busy,
Thousands of toiling hands, where theirs have ceased from their
    labors,
Thousands of weary feet, where theirs have completed their
    journey!

Still stands the forest primeval; but under the shade of its branches
Dwells another race, with other customs and language.
Only along the shore of the mournful and misty Atlantic
Linger a few Acadian peasants, whose fathers from exile
Wandered back to their native land to die in its bosom;
In the fisherman's cot the wheel and the loom are still busy;
Maidens still wear their Norman caps and their kirtles of
    homespun,
And by the evening fire repeat Evangeline's story,
While from its rocky caverns the deep-voiced, neighboring ocean
Speaks, and in accents disconsolate answers the wail of the forest.

The Song of Hiawatha

Introduction

Should you ask me, whence these stories?
Whence these legends and traditions,
With the odors of the forest
With the dew and damp of meadows,
With the curling smoke of wigwams,
With the rushing of great rivers,
With their frequent repetitions,
And their wild reverberations
As of thunder in the mountains?
    I should answer, I should tell you,
"From the forests and the prairies,
From the great lakes of the Northland,
From the land of the Ojibways,
From the land of the Dacotahs,
From the mountains, moors, and fen-lands
Where the heron, the Shuh-shuh-gah,
Feeds among the reeds and rushes.
I repeat them as I heard them
From the lips of Nawadaha,
The musician, the sweet singer."
    Should you ask where Nawadaha
Found these songs so wild and wayward,
Found these legends and traditions,
I should answer, I should tell you,
"In the bird's-nests of the forest,
In the lodges of the beaver,
In the hoofprint of the bison,
In the eyry of the eagle!
    "All the wild-fowl sang them to him,
In the moorlands and the fen-lands,
In the melancholy marshes;
Chetowaik, the plover, sang them,
Mahng, the loon, the wild-goose, Wawa,
The blue heron, the Shuh-shuh-gah,
And the grouse, the Mushkodasa!"
    If still further you should ask me,

Saying, "Who was Nawadaha?
Tell us of this Nawadaha,"
I should answer your inquiries
Straightway in such words as follow.
"In the Vale of Tawasentha,
In the green and silent valley,
By the water-courses,
Dwelt the singer Nawadaha.
Round about the Indian village
Spread the meadows and the corn-fields,
And beyond them stood the forest,
Stood the groves of singing pine-trees,
Green in Summer, white in Winter,
Ever sighing, ever singing.

    "And the pleasant water-courses,
You could trace them through the valley,
By the rushing in the Spring-time,
By the alders in the Summer,
By the white fog in the Autumn,
By the black line in the Winter;
And beside them dwelt the singer,
In the vale of Tawasentha,
In the green and silent valley.

    "There he sang of Hiawatha,
Sang the Song of Hiawatha,
Sang his wondrous birth and ,
How he prayed and how be fasted,
How he lived, and toiled, and suffered,
That the tribes of men might prosper,
That he might advance his people!"

    Ye who love the haunts of Nature,
Love the sunshine of the meadow,
Love the shadow of the forest,
Love the wind among the branches,
And the rain-shower and the snow-storm,
And the rushing of great rivers
Through their palisades of pine-trees,
And the thunder in the mountains,
Whose innumerable echoes
Flap like eagles in their eyries;–

Listen to these wild traditions,
To this Song of Hiawatha!
    Ye who love a nation's legends,
Love the ballads of a people,
That like voices from afar off
Call to us to pause and listen,
Speak in tones so plain and childlike,
Scarcely can the ear distinguish
Whether they are sung or spoken;-
Listen to this Indian Legend,
To this Song of Hiawatha!
    Ye whose hearts are fresh and simple,
Who have faith in God and Nature,
Who believe that in all ages
Every human heart is human,
That in even savage bosoms
There are longings, yearnings, strivings
For the they comprehend not,
That the feeble hands and helpless,
Groping blindly in the darkness,
Touch God's right hand in that darkness
And are lifted up and strengthened;-
Listen to this simple story,
To this Song of Hiawatha!
    Ye, who sometimes, in your rambles
Through the green lanes of the country,
Where the tangled barberry-bushes
Hang their tufts of crimson berries
Over stone walls gray with mosses,
Pause by some neglected graveyard,
For a while to muse, and ponder
On a half-effaced inscription,
Written with little skill of song-craft,
Homely phrases, but each letter
Full of hope and yet of heart-break,
Full of all the tender pathos
Of the Here and the Hereafter; —
Stay and read this rude inscription,
Read this Song of Hiawatha!

I

The Peace-Pipe

On the Mountains of the Prairie,
On the great Red Pipe-stone Quarry,
Gitche Manito, the mighty,
He the Master of Life, descending,
On the red crags of the quarry
Stood erect, and called the nations,
Called the tribes of men together.
From his footprints flowed a river,
Leaped into the light of morning,
O'er the precipice plunging downward
Gleamed like Ishkoodah, the comet.
And the Spirit, stooping earthward,
With his finger on the meadow
Traced a winding pathway for it,
Saying to it, "Run in this way!"
From the red stone of the quarry
With his hand he broke a fragment,
Moulded it into a pipe-head,
Shaped and fashioned it with figures;
From the margin of the river
Took a long reed for a pipe-stem,
With its dark green leaves upon it;
Filled the pipe with bark of willow,
With the bark of the red willow;
Breathed upon the neighboring forest,
Made its great boughs chafe together,
Till in flame they burst and kindled;
And erect upon the mountains,
Gitche Manito, the mighty,
Smoked the calumet, the Peace-Pipe,
As a signal to the nations.
And the smoke rose slowly, slowly,
Through the air of morning,
First a single line of darkness,
Then a denser, bluer vapor,
Then a snow-white cloud unfolding,
Like the tree-tops of the forest,

Ever rising, rising, rising,
Till it the top of heaven,
Till it broke against the heaven,
And rolled outward all around it.
      From the Vale of Tawasentha,
From the Valley of Wyoming,
From the groves of Tuscaloosa,
From the far-off Rocky Mountains,
From the Northern lakes and rivers
All the tribes beheld the signal,
Saw the distant smoke ascending,
The Pukwana of the Peace-Pipe.
And the Prophets of the nations
Said: "Behold it, the Pukwana!
By the signal of the Peace-Pipe,
Bending like a wand of willow,
Waving like a hand that beckons,
Gitche Manito, the mighty,
Calls the tribes of men together,
Calls the warriors to his council!"
      Down the rivers, o'er the prairies,
Came the warriors of the nations,
Came the Delawares and Mohawks,
Came the Choctaws and Camanches,
Came the Shoshonies and Blackfeet,
Came the Pawnees and Omahas,
Came the Mandans and Dacotahs,
Came the Hurons and Ojibways,
All the warriors drawn together
By the signal of the Peace-Pipe,
To the Mountains of the Prairie,
To the great Red Pipe-stone Quarry,
      And they stood there on the meadow,
With their weapons and their war-gear,
Painted like the leaves of Autumn,
Painted like the sky of morning,
Wildly glaring at each other;
In their faces stem defiance,
In their hearts the feuds of ages,
The hereditary hatred,

The ancestral thirst of vengeance.
        Gitche Manito, the mighty,
The creator of the nations,
Looked upon them with compassion ,
With paternal love and pity;
Looked upon their wrath and wrangling
But as quarrels among children,
But as feuds and fights of children!
        Over them he stretched his right hand,
To subdue their stubborn natures,
To allay their thirst and fever,
By the shadow of his right hand;
Spake to them with voice majestic
As the sound of far-off waters,
Falling into deep abysses,
Warning, chiding, spake in this wise: —
        "O my children! my poor children!
Listen to the words of wisdom,
Listen to the words of warning,
From the lips of the Great Spirit ,
From the Master of Life, who made you!
        "I have given you lands to hunt in,
I have given you streams to fish in,
I have given you bear and bison,
I have given you roe and reindeer,
I have given you brant and beaver,
Filled the marshes full of wild-fowl,
Filled the rivers full of fishes:
Why then are you not contented?
Why then will you hunt each other?
        "I am weary of your quarrels,
Weary of your wars and bloodshed,
Weary of your prayers for vengeance,
Of your wranglings and dissensions;
All your strength is in your union,
All your danger is in discord;
Therefore be at peace henceforward,
And as brothers live together.
        "I will send a Prophet to you,
A Deliverer of the nations,

Who shall guide you and shall teach you,
Who shall toil and suffer with you.
If you listen to his counsels,
You will multiply and prosper;
If his warnings pass unheeded,
You will fade away and perish!
  "Bathe now in the stream before you,
Wash the war-paint from your faces,
Wash the blood-stains from your fingers,
Bury your war-clubs and your weapons,
Break the red stone from this quarry,
Mould and make it into Peace-Pipes,
Take the reeds that beside you,
Deck them with your brightest feathers,
Smoke the calumet together,
And as brothers live henceforward!"
  Then upon the ground the warriors
Threw their cloaks and shirts of deerskin,
Threw their weapons and their war-gear,
Leaped into the rushing river,
Washed the war-paint from their faces.
Clear above them flowed the water,
Clear and limpid from the footprints
Of the Master of Life descending;
Dark below them flowed the water,
Soiled and stained with streaks of crimson,
As if blood were mingled with it!
  From the river came the warriors,
Clean and washed from all their war-paint;
On the banks their clubs they buried,
Buried all their warlike weapons.
Gitche Manito, the mighty,
The Great Spirit, the creator,
Smiled upon his helpless children!
  And in silence all the warriors
Broke the red stone of the quarry,
Smoothed and formed it into Peace-Pipes,
Broke the long reeds by the river,
Decked them with their brightest feathers,
And departed each one homeward,

While the Master of Life, ascending,
Through the opening of cloud-curtains,
Through the doorways of the heaven,
Vanished from before their faces,
In the smoke that rolled around him,
The Pukwana of the Peace-Pipe!

II
The Four Winds

"Honor be to Mudjekeewis!"
Cried the warriors, cried the old men,
When he came in triumph homeward
With the sacred Belt of Wampum,
From the regions of the North-Wind,
From the kingdom of Wabasso,
From the land of the White Rabbit.
He had stolen the Belt of Wampum
From the neck of Mishe-Mokwa,
From the Great Bear of the mountains,
From the terror of the nations,
As he lay asleep and cumbrous
On the summit of the mountains,
Like a rock with mosses on it,
Spotted brown and gray with mosses.
Silently he stole upon him
Till the red nails of the monster
Almost touched him, almost scared him,
Till the hot breath of his nostrils
Warmed the hands of Mudjekeewis,
As he drew the Belt of Wampum
Over the round ears, that heard not,
Over the small eyes, that saw not,
Over the long nose and nostrils,
The black muffle of the nostrils,
Out of which the heavy breathing
Warmed the hands of Mudjekeewis.
Then he swung aloft his war-club,
Shouted loud and long his war-cry,

Smote the mighty Mishe-Mokwa
In the middle of the forehead,
Right between the eyes he smote him.
    With the heavy blow bewildered,
Rose the Great Bear of the mountains;
But his knees beneath him trembled,
And he whimpered like a woman,
As he reeled and staggered forward,
As he sat upon his haunches;
And the mighty Mudjekeewis,
Standing fearlessly before him,
Taunted him in loud derision,
Spake disdainfully in this wise: –
    "Hark you, Bear! you are a coward;
And no Brave, as you pretended;
Else you would not cry and whimper
Like a miserable woman!
Bear! you know our tribes are hostile,
Long have been at war together;
Now you find that we are strongest,
You go sneaking in the forest,
You go hiding in the mountains!
Had you conquered me in battle
Not a groan would I have uttered;
But you, Bear! sit here and whimper,
And disgrace your tribe by crying,
Like a wretched Shaugodaya,
Like a cowardly old woman!"
    Then again he raised his war-club,
Smote again the Mishe-Mokwa
In the middle of his forehead,
Broke his skull, as ice is broken
When one goes to fish in Winter.
Thus was slain the Mishe-Mokwa,
He the Great Bear of the mountains,
He the terror of the nations.
    "Honor be to Mudjekeewis!"
With a shout exclaimed the people,
"Honor be to Mudjekeewis!
Henceforth he shall be the West-Wind,

And hereafter and forever
Shall he hold supreme dominion
Over all the winds of heaven.
Call him no more Mudjekeewis,
Call him Kabeyun, the West-Wind!"
    Thus was Mudjekeewis chosen
Father of the Winds of Heaven.
For himself he kept the West-Wind,
Gave the others to his children;
Unto Wabun gave the East-Wind,
Gave the South to Shawondasee,
And the North-Wind, wild and cruel,
To the fierce Kabibonokka.
    Young and beautiful was Wabun;
He it was who brought the morning,
He it was whose silver arrows
Chased the dark o'er hill and valley;
He it was whose cheeks were painted
With the brightest streaks of crimson,
And whose voice the village,
Called the deer, and called the hunter.
Lonely in the sky was Wabun;
Though the birds sang gayly to him,
Though the wild-flowers of the meadow
Filled the air with odors for him;
Though the forests and the rivers
Sang and shouted at his coming,
Still his heart was sad within him,
For he was alone in heaven.
But one morning, gazing earthward,
While the village still was sleeping,
And the fog lay on the river,
Like a ghost, that goes at sunrise,
He beheld a maiden walking
All alone upon a meadow,
Gathering water-flags and rushes
By a river in the meadow.
    Every morning, gazing earthward,
Still the first thing he beheld there
Was her blue eyes looking at him,

Two blue lakes among the rushes.
And he loved the lonely maiden,
Who thus waited for his coming;
For they both were solitary,
She on earth and he in heaven.

And he wooed her with caresses,
Wooed her with his smile of sunshine,
With his flattering words he wooed her,
With his sighing and his singing,
Gentlest whispers in the branches,
Softest music, sweetest odors,
Till he drew her to his bosom,
Folded in his robes of crimson,
Till into a star he changed her,
Trembling still upon his bosom;
And forever in the heavens
They are seen together walking,
Wabun and the Wabun-Annung,
Wabun and the Star of Morning.

But the fierce Kabibonokka
Had his dwelling among icebergs,
In the everlasting snow-drifts,
In the kingdom of Wabasso,
In the land of the White Rabbit.
He it was whose hand in Autumn
Painted all the trees with scarlet,
Stained the leaves with red and yellow;
He it was who sent the snow-flake,
Sifting, hissing through the forest,
Froze the ponds, the lakes, the rivers,
Drove the loon and sea-gull southward,
Drove the cormorant and curlew
To their nests of sedge and sea-tang
In the realms of Shawondasee.

Once the fierce Kabibonokka
Issued from his lodge of snow-drifts
From his home among the icebergs,
And his hair, with snow besprinkled
Streamed behind him like a river,
Like a black and wintry river,

As he howled and hurried southward,
Over frozen lakes and moorlands.
    There among the reeds and rushes
Found he Shingebis, the diver,
Trailing strings of fish behind him,
O'er the frozen fens and moorlands,
Lingering still among the moorlands,
Though his tribe had long departed
To the land of Shawondasee.
    Cried the fierce Kabibonokka,
"Who is this that dares to brave me?
Dares to stay in my dominions,
When the Wawa has departed,
When the wild-goose has gone southward,
And the heron, the Shuh-shuh gah,
Long ago departed southward?
I will go into his wigwam,
I will put his smouldering fire out!"
    And at night Kabibonokka,
To the lodge came wild and wailing,
Heaped the snow in drifts about it,
Shouted down into the smoke-flue,
Shook the lodge-poles in his fury,
Flapped the curtain of the door-way.
Shingebis, the diver, feared not,
Shingebis, the diver, cared not;
Four great logs had he for firewood,
One for each moon of the winter,
And for food the fishes served him.
By his blazing fire he sat there,
Warm and merry, eating, laughing,
Singing, "O Kabibonokka,
You are but my fellow-mortal!"
    Then Kabibonokka entered,
And though Shingebis, the diver,
Felt his presence by the coldness,
Felt his icy breath upon him,
Still he did not his singing,
Still he did not leave his laughing,
Only turned the log a little,

Only made the fire burn brighter,
Made the sparks fly up the smoke-flue.
      From Kabibonokka's forehead,
From his snow-besprinkled tresses,
Drops of sweat fell fast and heavy,
Making dints upon the ashes,
As along the eaves of lodges,
As from drooping boughs of hemlock,
Drips the melting snow in spring-time,
Making hollows in the snow-drifts.
      Till at last he rose defeated.
Could not bear the heat and laughter,
Could not bear the merry singing,
But rushed headlong through the door-way,
Stamped upon the crusted snow-drifts,
Stamped upon the lakes and rivers,
Made the snow upon them harder,
Made the ice upon them thicker,
Challenged Shingebis, the diver,
To come forth and wrestle with him,
To come forth and wrestle naked
On the frozen fens and moorlands.
Forth went Shingebis, the diver,
Wrestled all night with the North-Wind,
Wrestled naked on the moorlands
With the fierce Kabibonokka,
Till his panting breath fainter,
Till his frozen grasp feebler,
Till he reeled and staggered backward,
And retreated, baffled, beaten,
To the kingdom of Wabasso,
To the land of the White Rabbit,
 still the gusty laughter,
 Shingebis, the diver,
Singing, "O Kabibonokka,
You are but my fellow-mortal!"
      Shawondasee, fat and lazy,
Had his dwelling far to southward,
In the drowsy, dreamy sunshine,
In the never-ending Summer.

He it was who sent the wood-birds,
Sent the robin, the Opechee,
Sent the bluebird, the Owaissa,
Sent the Shawshaw, sent the swallow,
Sent the wild-goose, Wawa, northward,
Sent the melons and tobacco,
And the grapes in purple clusters.

From his pipe the smoke ascending
Filled the sky with haze and vapor,
Filled the air with softness,
Gave a twinkle to the water,
Touched the rugged hills with smoothness,
Brought the tender Indian Summer
To the melancholy north-land,
In the dreary Moon of Snow-shoes.

Listless, careless Shawondasee!
In his life he had one shadow,
In his heart one had he.
Once, as he was gazing northward,
Far away upon a prairie
He beheld a maiden standing,
Saw a tall and slender maiden
All upon a prairie;
Brightest green were all her garments,
And her hair was like the sunshine.

Day by day he gazed upon her,
Day by day he sighed with passion,
Day by day his heart within him
Grew more hot with love and longing
For the maid with yellow tresses.
But he was too fat and lazy
To bestir himself and woo her.
Yes, too indolent and easy
To pursue her and persuade her;
So he only gazed upon her,
Only sat and sighed with passion
For the maiden of the prairie.

Till one morning, looking northward,
He beheld her yellow tresses
Changed and covered o'er with whiteness,

Covered as with whitest snow-flakes.
"Ah! my brother from the North-land,
From the kingdom of Wabasso,
From the land of the White Rabbit!
You have stolen the maiden from me,
You have laid your hand upon her,
You have wooed and won my maiden,
With your stories of the North-land!"
  Thus the wretched Shawondasee
Breathed into the air his sorrow;
And the South-Wind o'er the prairie
Wandered warm with sighs of passion,
With the sighs of Shawondasee,
Till the air seemed full of snow-flakes,
Full of thistle-down the prairie,
And the maid with hair like sunshine
Vanished from his forever;
Never more did Shawondasee
See the maid with yellow tresses!
Poor, deluded Shawondasee!
'T was no woman that you gazed at,
'T was no maiden that you sighed for,
'T was the prairie dandelion
That through all the Summer
You had gazed at with such longing,
You had sighed for with such passion,
And had puffed away forever,
Blown into the air with sighing.
Ah! deluded Shawondasee!
  Thus the Four Winds were divided
Thus the sons of Mudjekeewis
Had their stations in the heavens,
At the corners of the heavens;
For the West-Wind only
Kept the mighty Mudjekeewis.

Hiawatha's Childhood

Downward through the evening twilight,
In the days that are forgotten,
In the unremembered ages,
From the full moon fell Nokomis,
Fell the beautiful Nokomis,
She a wife, but not a mother.

    She was sporting with her women,
Swinging in a swing of grape-vines,
When her rival, the rejected,
Full of jealousy and of hatred,
Cut the leafy swing asunder,
Cut in twain the twisted grape-vines,
And Nokomis fell affrighted
Downward through the evening twilight,
On the Muskoday, the meadow,
On the prairie full of blossoms.
"See! a star falls!" said the people;
"From the sky a star is falling!"

    There among the ferns and mosses,
There among the prairie lilies,
On the Muskoday, the meadow,
In the moonlight and the starlight,
Fair Nokomis bore a daughter.
And she called her name Wenonah,
As the first-born of her daughters.
And the daughter of Nokomis
Grew up like the prairie lilies,
Grew a tall and slender maiden,
With the beauty of the moonlight,
With the beauty of the starlight.

    And Nokomis warned her often,
Saying oft, and oft repeating,
"Oh, beware of Mudjekeewis,
Of the West-Wind, Mudjekeewis;
Listen not to what he tells you;
Lie not down upon the meadow,
Stoop not down among the lilies,

Lest the West-Wind come and harm you!"
    But she heeded not the warning,
Heeded not those words of wisdom,
And the West-Wind came at evening,
Walking lightly o'er the prairie,
Whispering to the leaves and blossoms,
Bending low the flowers and grasses,
Found the beautiful Wenonah,
Lying there among the lilies,
Wooed her with his words of sweetness,
Wooed her with his soft caresses,
Till she bore a son in sorrow,
Bore a son of love and sorrow .
    Thus was born my Hiawatha,
Thus was born the child of wonder;
But the daughter of Nokomis,
Hiawatha's gentle mother,
In her anguish died deserted
By the West-Wind, false and faithless,
By the heartless Mudjekeewis.
    For her daughter long and loudly
Wailed and wept the sad Nokomis;
"Oh that I were dead!" she murmured,
"Oh that I were dead, as thou art!
No more work, and no more weeping,
Wahonowin! Wahonowin!"
    By the shores of Gitche Gumee,
By the shining Big-Sea-Water,
Stood the wigwam of Nokomis,
Daughter of the Moon, Nokomis.
Dark behind it rose the forest,
Rose the black and gloomy pine-trees,
Rose the firs with cones upon them;
Bright before it beat the water,
Beat the clear and sunny water,
Beat the shining Big-Sea-Water.
    There the wrinkled old Nokomis
Nursed the little Hiawatha,
Rocked him in his linden cradle,
Bedded soft in moss and rushes,

Safely bound with reindeer sinews;
Stilled his fretful wail by saying,
"Hush! the Naked Bear will get thee!"
Lulled him into Slumber, singing,
"Ewa-yea! my little owlet!
Who is this, that lights the wigwam?
With his great eyes lights the wigwam?
Ewa-yea! my little owlet!"
    Many things Nokomis taught him
Of the stars that shine in heaven;
Showed him Ishkoodah, the comet,
Ishkoodah, with fiery tresses;
Showed the Death-Dance of the spirits ,
Warriors with their plumes and war-clubs,
Flaring far away to northward
In the frosty nights of Winter;
Showed the broad white road in heaven,
Pathway of the ghosts, the shadows,
Running straight across the heavens,
Crowded with the ghosts, the shadows.
    At the door on summer evenings
Sat the little Hiawatha;
Heard the whispering of the pine-trees,
Heared the lapping of the waters,
Sounds of music, words of wonder;
'Minne-wawa!" said the Pine-trees,
Mudway-aushka!" said the water.
    Saw the fire-fly, Wah-wah-taysee,
Flitting through the dusk of evening,
With the twinkle of its candle
Lighting up the brakes and bushes,
And he sang the song of children,
Sang the song Nokomis taught him:
"Wah-wah-taysee, little fire-fly,
Little, flitting, white-fire insect,
Little, dancing, white-fire creature,
Light me with your little candle,
Ere upon my bed I lay me,
Ere in sleep I close my eyelids!"
    Saw the moon rise from the water

Rippling, rounding from the water,
Saw the flecks and shadows on it,
Whispered, "What is that, Nokomis?"
And the Nokomis answered:
"Once a warrior, very angry,
Seized his grandmother, and threw her
Up into the sky at midnight;
Right against the moon he threw her;
'T is her body that you there."

Saw the rainbow in the heaven,
In the eastern sky, the rainbow,
Whispered, "What is that, Nokomis?"
And the good Nokomis answered:
"'T is the heaven of flowers you there;
All the wild-flowers of the forest,
All the lilies of the prairie,
When on earth they fade and perish,
Blossom in that heaven above us."

When he heard the owls at midnight,
Hooting, laughing in the forest,
"What is that?" he cried in terror,
"What is that," he said, "Nokomis?"
And the good Nokomis answered:
"That is but the owl and owlet,
Talking in their native language,
Talking, scolding at each other."

Then the little Hiawatha
Learned of every bird its language,
Learned their names and all their secrets,
How they built their nests in Summer,
Where they hid themselves in Winter,
Talked with them whene'er he met them,
Called them "Hiawatha's Chickens."

Of all beasts he learned the language,
Learned their names and all their secrets,
How the beavers built their lodges,
Where the squirrels hid their acorns,
How the reindeer ran so swiftly,
Why the rabbit was so timid,
Talked with them whene'er he met them,

Called them "Hiawatha's Brothers."
    Then Iagoo, the great boaster,
He the marvellous story-teller,
He the traveller and the talker,
He the friend of old Nokomis,
Made a bow for Hiawatha;
From a branch of ash he made it,
From an oak-bough made the arrows,
Tipped with flint, and winged with feathers,
And the cord he made of deer-skin.
    Then he said to Hiawatha:
"Go, my son, into the forest,
Where the red deer herd together,
Kill for us a famous roebuck,
Kill for us a deer with antlers!"
    Forth into the forest straightway
All alone walked Hiawatha
Proudly, with his bow and arrows;
And the birds sang round him, o'er him,
"Do not shoot us, Hiawatha!"
Sang the robin, the Opechee,
Sang the bluebird, the Owaissa,
"Do not shoot us, Hiawatha!"
    Up the oak-tree, close beside him,
Sprang the squirrel, Adjidaumo,
In and out among the branches,
Coughed and chattered from the oak-tree,
Laughed, and said between his laughing,
"Do not shoot me, Hiawatha!"
    And the rabbit from his pathway
Leaped aside, and at a distance
Sat erect upon his haunches,
Half in fear and half in frolic,
Saying to the little hunter,
"Do not shoot me, Hiawatha!"
    But he heeded not, nor heard them,
For his thoughts were with the red deer;
On their tracks his eyes were fastened,
Leading downward to the river,
To the ford across the river,

And as one in slumber walked he.
    Hidden in the alder-bushes,
There he waited till the deer came,
Till he saw two antlers lifted,
Saw two eyes look from the thicket,
Saw two nostrils point to windward,
And a deer came down the pathway,
Flecked with leafy light and shadow.
And his heart within him fluttered,
Trembled like the leaves above him,
Like the birch-leaf palpitated,
As the deer came down the pathway.
    Then, upon one knee uprising,
Hiawatha aimed an arrow;
Scarce a twig moved with his motion,
Scarce a leaf was stirred or rustled,
But the wary roebuck started,
Stamped with all his hoofs together,
Listened with one foot uplifted,
Leaped as if to meet the arrow;
Ah! the singing, fatal arrow,
Like a wasp it buzzed and stung him!
    Dead he lay there in the forest,
By the ford across the river;
Beat his timid heart no longer,
But the heart of Hiawatha
Throbbed and shouted and exulted,
As he bore the red deer homeward,
And Iagoo and Nokomis
Hailed his coming with applauses.
From the red deer's hide Nokomis
Made a cloak for Hiawatha,
From the red deer's flesh Nokomis
Made a banquet to his honor.
All the village came and feasted,
All the guests praised Hiawatha,
Called him Strong-Heart, Soan-ge-taha!
Called him Loon-Heart, Mahn-go-taysee!

IV

Hiawatha and Mudjekeewis

Out of childhood into manhood
Now had my Hiawatha,
Skilled in all the craft of hunters,
Learned in all the lore of old men,
In all youthful sports and pastimes,
In all manly arts and labors.

    Swift of foot was Hiawatha;
He could shoot an arrow from him,
And run forward with such fleetness,
That the arrow fell behind him!
Strong of arm was Hiawatha;
He could shoot ten arrows upward,
Shoot them with such strength and swiftness,
That the tenth had left the bow-string
Ere the first to earth had fallen!

    He had mittens, Minjekahwun,
Magic mittens made of deer-skin;
When upon his hands he wore them,
He could smite the rocks asunder,
He could grind them into powder.
He had moccasins enchanted,
Magic moccasins of deer-skin;
When he bound them round his ankles,
When upon his feet he tied them,
At each stride a mile he measured!

    Much he questioned old Nokomis
Of his father Mudjekeewis;
Learned from her the fatal secret
Of the beauty of his mother,
Of the falsehood of his father;
And his heart was hot within him,
Like a living coal his heart was.

    Then he said to old Nokomis,
"I will go to Mudjekeewis,
 how fares it with my father,
At the doorways of the West-Wind,
At the portals of the Sunset!"

From his lodge went Hiawatha,
Dressed for travel, armed for hunting;
Dressed in deer-skin shirt and leggings,
Richly wrought with quills and wampum;
On his head his eagle-feathers,
Round his waist his belt of wampum,
In his hand his bow of ash-wood,
Strung with sinews of the reindeer;
In his quiver oaken arrows,
Tipped with jasper, winged with feathers;
With his mittens, Minjekahwun,
With his moccasins enchanted.

Warning said the old Nokomis,
"Go not forth, O Hiawatha!
To the kingdom of the West-Wind,
To the realms of Mudjekeewis,
Lest he harm you with his magic,
Lest he kill you with his cunning!"

But the fearless Hiawatha
Heeded not her woman's warning;
Forth he strode into the forest,
At each stride a mile he measured;
Lurid seemed the sky above him,
Lurid seemed the earth beneath him,
Hot and close the air around him,
Filled with smoke and fiery vapors,
As of burning woods and prairies,
For his heart was hot within him,
Like a living coal his heart was.

So he journeyed westward, westward,
Left the fleetest deer behind him,
Left the antelope and bison;
Crossed the rushing Esconaba,
Crossed the mighty Mississippi,
Passed the Mountains of the Prairie,
Passed the land of Crows and Foxes,
Passed the dwellings of the Blackfeet,
Came unto the Rocky Mountains,
To the kingdom of the West-Wind,
Where upon the gusty summits

Sat the ancient Mudjekeewis,
Ruler of the winds of heaven.
    Filled with awe was Hiawatha
At the aspect of his father.
On the air about him wildly
Tossed and streamed his cloudy tresses,
Gleamed like drifting snow his tresses,
Glared like Ishkoodah, the comet,
Like the star with fiery tresses.
    Filled with was Mudjekeewis
When he looked on Hiawatha,
Saw his youth rise up before him
In the face of Hiawatha,
Saw the beauty of Wenonah
From the grave rise up before him.
    "Welcome!" said he, "Hiawatha,
To the kingdom of the West-Wind!
Long have I been waiting for you
Youth is lovely, age is lonely,
Youth is fiery, age is frosty;
You bring back the days departed,
You bring back my youth of passion,
And the beautiful Wenonah!"
    Many days they talked together,
Questioned, listened, waited, answered;
Much the mighty Mudjekeewis
Boasted of his ancient prowess,
Of his perilous adventures,
His indomitable courage,
His invulnerable body.
    Patiently sat Hiawatha,
Listening to his father's boasting;
With a smile he sat and listened,
Uttered neither threat nor menace,
Neither word nor look betrayed him,
But his heart was hot within him,
Like a living coal his heart was.
    Then he said, "O Mudjekeewis,
Is there nothing that can harm you?
Nothing that you are afraid of?"

And the mighty Mudjekeewis,
Grand and gracious in his boasting,
Answered, saying, "There is nothing,
Nothing but the black rock yonder,
Nothing but the fatal Wawbeek!"

And he looked at Hiawatha
With a wise look and benignant,
With a countenance paternal,
Looked with pride upon the beauty
Of his tall and graceful figure,
Saying, "O my Hiawatha!
Is there anything can harm you?
Anything you are afraid of?"

But the wary Hiawatha
Paused awhile, as if uncertain,
Held his peace, as if resolving,
And then answered, "There is nothing,
Nothing but the bulrush yonder,
Nothing but the great Apukwa!"

And as Mudjekeewis, rising,
Stretched his hand to pluck the bulrush,
Hiawatha cried in terror,
Cried in well-dissembled terror,
"Kago! kago! do not touch it!"
"Ah, kaween!" said Mudjekeewis,
"No indeed, I will not touch it!"

Then they talked of other matters;
First of Hiawatha's brothers,
First of Wabun, of the East-Wind,
Of the South-Wind, Shawondasee,
Of the North, Kabibonokka;
Then of Hiawatha's mother,
Of the beautiful Wenonah,
Of her birth upon the meadow,
Of her death, as old Nokomis
Had remembered and related.

And he cried, "O Mudjekeewis,
It was you who killed Wenonah,
Took her young life and her beauty,
Broke the Lily of the Prairie,

Trampled it beneath your footsteps;
You confess it! you confess it!"
And the mighty Mudjekeewis
Tossed upon the wind his tresses,
Bowed his hoary head in anguish,
With a silent nod assented.

Then up started Hiawatha,
And with threatening look and gesture
Laid his hand upon the black rock,
On the fatal Wawbeek laid it,
With his mittens, Minjekahwun,
Rent the jutting crag asunder,
Smote and crushed it into fragments,
Hurled them madly at his father,
The remorseful Mudjekeewis,
For his heart was hot within him,
Like a living coal his heart was.

But the ruler of the West-Wind
Blew the fragments backward from him,
With the breathing of his nostrils,
With the tempest of his anger,
Blew them back at his assailant;
Seized the bulrush, the Apukwa,
Dragged it with its roots and fibres
From the margin of the meadow,
From its ooze the giant bulrush;
Long and loud laughed Hiawatha!

Then began the deadly conflict,
Hand to hand among the mountains;
From his eyry screamed the eagle,
The Keneu, the great war-eagle,
Sat upon the crags around them,
Wheeling flapped his wings above them.

Like a tall tree in the tempest
Bent and lashed the giant bulrush;
And in masses huge and heavy
Crashing fell the fatal Wawbeek;
Till the earth shook with the tumult
And comfusion of the battle,
And the air was full of shoutings,

And the thunder of the mountains,
Starting, answered, "Baim-wawa!"

Back retreated Mudjekeewis,
Rushing westward o'er the mountains,
Stumbling westward down the mountains,
Three whole days retreated fighting,
Still pursued by Hiawatha
To the doorways of the West-Wind,
To the portals of the Sunset,
To the earth's remotest border,
Where into the empty spaces
Sinks the sun, as a flamingo
Drops into her nest at nightfall
In the melancholy marshes.

"Hold!" at length cried Mudjekeewis,
"Hold, my son, my Hiawatha!
'T is impossible to kill me,
For you cannot kill the immortal
I have put you to this trial,
But to know and prove your courage;
Now receive the prize of valor!

"Go back to your home and people,
Live among them, toil among them,
Cleanse the earth from all that harms it,
Clear the fishing-grounds and rivers,
Slay all monsters and magicians,
All the Wendigoes, the giants,
All the serpents, the Kenabeeks,
As I slew the Mishe-Mokwa,
Slew the Great Bear of the mountains.

"And at last when Death draws near you,
When the awful eyes of Pauguk
Glare upon you in the darkness,
I will share my kingdom with you,
Ruler shall you be thenceforward
Of the Northwest-Wind, Keewaydin,
Of the home-wind, the Keewaydin."

Thus was fought that famous battle
In the dreadful days of Shah-shah,
In the days long since departed,

In the kingdom of the West-Wind.
Still the hunter sees its traces
Scattered far o'er hill and valley;
Sees the giant bulrush growing
By the ponds and water-courses,
Sees the masses of the Wawbeek
Lying still in every valley.

　　Homeward now went Hiawatha;
Pleasant was the landscape round him,
Pleasant was the air above him,
For the bitterness of anger
Had departed wholly from him,
From his brain the thought of vengeance,
From his heart the burning fever.

　　Only once his pace he slackened,
Only once he paused or halted,
Paused to purchase heads of arrows
Of the ancient Arrow-maker,
In the land of the Dacotahs,
Where the Falls of Minnehaha
Flash and gleam among the oak-trees,
Laugh and leap into the valley.

　　There the ancient Arrow-maker
Made his arrow-heads of sandstone,
Arrow-heads of chalcedony,
Arrow-heads of flint and jasper,
Smoothed and sharpened at the edges,
Hard and polished, keen and costly.

　　With him dwelt his dark-eyed daughter,
Wayward as the Minnehaha,
With her moods of shade and sunshine,
Eyes that smiled and frowned alternate,
Feet as rapid as the river,
Tresses flowing like the water,
And as musical a laughter:
And he named her from the river,
From the water-fall he named her,
Minnehaha, Laughing Water.

　　Was it then for heads of arrows,
Arrow-heads of chalcedony,

Arrow-heads of flint and jasper,
That my Hiawatha halted
In the land of the Dacotahs?
　　Was it not to see the maiden,
See the face of Laughing Water
Peeping from behind the curtain,
Hear the rustling of her garments
From behind the waving curtain,
As one hears the Minnehaha
Gleaming, glancing through the branches,
As one hears the Laughing Water
From behind its screen of branches?
　　Who shall say what thoughts and visions
Fill the fiery brains of young men?
Who shall say what dreams of beauty
Filled the heart of Hiawatha?
All he told to old Nokomis,
When he reached the lodge at sunset,
Was the meeting with his father,
Was his fight with Mudjekeewis;
Not a word he said of arrows,
Not a word of Laughing Water.

V

Hiawatha's Fasting

You shall hear how Hiawatha
Prayed and fasted in the forest,
Not for greater skill in hunting,
Not for greater craft in fishing,
Not for triumphs in the battle,
And renown among the warriors,
But for profit of the people,
For advantage of the nations.
　　First he built a lodge for fasting,
Built a wigwam in the forest,
By the shining Big-Sea-Water,
In the blithe and Spring-time,
In the Moon of Leaves he built it,

And, with and visions many,
Seven whole days and nights he fasted.
     On the first day of his fasting
Through the leafy woods he wandered;
Saw the deer start from the thicket,
Saw the rabbit in his burrow,
Heard the pheasant, Bena, drumming,
Heard the squirrel, Adjidaumo,
     Rattling in his hoard of acorns,
Saw the pigeon, the Omeme,
Building nests among the pinetrees,
And in flocks the wild-goose, Wawa,
Flying to the fen-lands northward,
Whirring, wailing far above him.
"Master of Life!" he cried, desponding,
"Must our lives depend on these things?"
     On the next day of his fasting
By the river's brink he wandered,
Through the Muskoday, the meadow,
Saw the wild rice, Mahnomonee,
Saw the blueberry, Meenahga,
And the strawberry, Odahmin,
And the gooseberry, Shahbomin,
And the grape.vine, the Bemahgut,
Trailing o'er the alder-branches,
Filling all the air with fragrance!
"Master of Life!" he cried, desponding,
"Must our lives depend on these things?"
     On the third day of his fasting
By the lake he sat and pondered,
By the still, transparent water;
Saw the sturgeon, Nahma, leaping,
Scattering drops like beads of wampum,
Saw the yellow perch, the Sahwa,
Like a sunbeam in the water,
Saw the pike, the Maskenozha,
And the herring, Okahahwis,
And the Shawgashee, the crawfish!
"Master of Life!" he cried, desponding,
"Must our lives depend on these things?"

On the fourth day of his fasting
In his lodge he lay exhausted;
From his couch of leaves and branches
Gazing with half-open eyelids,
Full of shadowy dreams and visions,
On the dizzy, swimming landscape,
On the gleaming of the water,
On the splendor of the sunset.

And he saw a youth approaching,
Dressed in garments green and yellow,
Coming through the purple twilight,
Through the splendor of the sunset;
Plumes of green bent o'er his forehead,
And his hair was soft and golden.

Standing at the open doorway,
Long he looked at Hiawatha,
Looked with pity and compassion
On his wasted and features,
And, in accents like the sighing
Of the South-Wind in the tree-tops,
Said he, "O my Hiawatha!
All your prayers are in heaven,
For you pray not like the others;
Not for greater skill in hunting,
Not for greater craft in fishing,
Not for triumph in the battle,
Nor renown among the warriors,
But for profit of the people,
For advantage of the nations.

"From the Master of Life descending,
I, the friend of man, Mondamin,
Come to warn you and instruct you,
How by struggle and by labor
You shall gain what you have prayed for.
Rise up from your bed of branches,
Rise, O youth, and wrestle with me!"

Faint with famine, Hiawatha
Started from his bed of branches,
From the twilight of his wigwam
Forth into the flush of sunset

Came, and wrestled with Mondamin;
At his touch he felt new courage
Throbbing in his brain and bosom,
Felt new life and hope and vigor
Run through every nerve and fibre.

So they wrestled there together
In the glory of the sunset,
And the more they strove and struggled,
Stronger still grew Hiawatha;
Till the darkness fell around them,
And the heron, the Shuh-shuh-gah,
From her nest among the pine-trees,
Gave a cry of lamentation,
Gave a scream of pain and famine.

"'T is enough!" then said Mondamin,
Smiling upon Hiawatha,
"But tomorrow, when the sun sets,
I will come again to try you."
And he vanished, and was seen not;
Whether sinking as the rain sinks,
Whether rising as the mists rise,
Hiawatha saw not, knew not,
Only that he had vanished,
Leaving him alone and fainting,
With the misty lake below him,
And the reeling stars above him.

On the morrow and the next day,
When the sun through heaven descending,
Like a red and burning cinder
From the hearth of the Great Spirit,
Fell into the western waters,
Came Mondamin for the trial,
For the strife with Hiawatha;
Came as silent as the dew comes,
From the empty air appearing,
Into empty air returning,
Taking shape when earth it touches,
But invisible to all men
In its coming and its going.

Thrice they wrestled there together

In the glory of the sunset,
Till the darkness fell around them,
Till the heron, the Shuh-shuh-gah,
From her nest among the pine-trees,
Uttered her loud cry of famine,
And Mondamin paused to listen.

Tall and beautiful he stood there,
In his garments green and yellow;
To and fro his plumes above him,
Waved and nodded with his breathing,
And the sweat of the encounter
Stood like drops of dew upon him.

And he cried, "O Hiawatha!
Bravely have you wrestled with me,
Thrice have wrestled stoutly with me,
And the Master of Life, who us,
He will give to you the triumph!"

Then he smiled, and said: "To-morrow
Is the last day of your conflict,
Is the last day of your fasting.
You will conquer and o'ercome me;
Make a bed for me to lie in,
Where the rain may fall upon me,
Where the sun may come and warm me;
Strip these garments, green and yellow,
Strip this nodding plumage from me,
Lay me in the earth, and make it
Soft and loose and light above me.

"Let no hand disturb my slumber,
Let no weed nor worm molest me,
Let not Kahgahgee, the raven,
Come to haunt me and molest me,
Only come yourself to watch me,
Till I wake, and start, and quicken,
Till I leap into the sunshine"

And thus saying, he departed;
Peacefully slept Hiawatha,
But he heard the Wawonaissa,
Heard the whippoorwill complaining,
Perched upon his lonely wigwam;

Heard the rushing Sebowisha,
Heard the rivulet rippling near him,
Talking to the darksome forest;
Heard the sighing of the branches,
As they lifted and subsided
At the passing of the night-wind,
Heard them, as one hears in slumber
Far-off murmurs, dreamy whispers:
Peacefully slept Hiawatha.

On the morrow came Nokomis,
On the seventh day of his fasting,
Came with food for Hiawatha,
Came imploring and bewailing,
Lest his hunger should o'ercome him,
Lest his fasting should be fatal.

But he tasted not, and touched not,
Only said to her, "Nokomis,
Wait until the sun is setting,
Till the darkness falls around us,
Till the heron, the Shuh-shuh-gah,
Crying from the desolate marshes,
Tells us that the day is ended."

Homeward weeping went Nokomis,
Sorriwing for her Hiawatha,
Fearing lest his strength should fail him,
Lest his fasting should be fatal.
He meanwhile sat weary waiting
For the coming of Mondamin,
Till the shadows, pointing eastward,
Lengthened over field and forest,
Till the sun dropped from the heaven,
Floating on the waters westward,
As a red leaf in the Autumn
Falls and floats upon the water,
Falls and sinks into its bosom.

And behold! the young Mondamin,
With his soft and shining tresses,
With his garments green and yellow,
With his long and glossy plumage,
Stood and beckoned at the doorway.

And as one in slumber walking,
Pale and haggard, but undaunted,
From the wigwam Hiawatha
Came and wrestled with Mondamin.

Round about him spun the landscape,
Sky and forest reeled together,
And his strong heart leaped within him,
As the sturgeon leaps and struggles
In a net to break its meshes.
Like a ring of fire around him
Blazed and flared the red horizon,
And a hundred suns seemed looking
At the combat of the wrestlers.

Suddenly upon the greensward
All alone stood Hiawatha,
Panting with his wild exertion,
Palpitating with the struggle;
And before him breathless, lifeless,
Lay the youth, with hair dishevelled,
Plumage torn, and garments tattered,
Dead he lay there in the sunset.

And victorious Hiawatha
Made the grave as he commanded,
Stripped the garments from Mondamin,
Stripped his tattered plumage from him,
Laid him in the earth, and made it
Soft and loose and light above him;
And the heron, the Shuh-shuh-gah,
From the melancholy moorlands,
Gave a cry of lamentation,
Gave a cry of pain and anguish!

Homeward then went Hiawatha
To the lodge of old Nokomis,
And the seven days of his fasting
Were accomplished and completed.
But the place was not forgotten
Where he wrestled with Mondamin;
Nor forgotten nor neglected
Was the grave where lay Mondamin,
Sleeping in the rain and sunshine,

Where his scattered plumes and garments
Faded in the rain and sunshine.
　　Day by day did Hiawatha
Go to wait and watch beside it;
Kept the dark mould soft above it,
Kept it clean from weeds and insects,
Drove away, with scoffs and shoutings,
Kahgahgee, the king of ravens.
　　Till at length a small green feather
From the earth shot slowly upward,
Then another and another,
And before the Summer ended
Stood the maize in all its beauty,
With its shining robes about it,
And its long, soft, yellow tresses;
And in rapture Hiawatha
Cried aloud, "It is Mondamin!
Yes, the friend of man, Mondamin!"
　　Then he called to old Nokomis
And Iagoo, the great boaster,
Showed them where the maize was growing,
Told them of his wondrous vision,
Of his wrestling and his triumph,
Of this new gift to the nations,
Which should be their food forever.
　　And still later, when the Autumn
Changed the long, green leaves to yellow,
And the soft and juicy kernels
Grew like wampum hard and yellow,
Then the ripened ears he gathered,
Stripped the withered husks from off them,
As he once had stripped the wrestler,
Gave the first Feast of Mondamin,
And made known unto the people
This new gift of the Great Spirit.

VI
Hiawatha's Friends

Two good friends had Hiawatha,
Singled out from all the others,
Bound to him in closest union,
And to whom he gave the right hand
Of his heart, in joy and sorrow:
Chibiabos, the musician,
And the very strong man, Kwasind.

    Straight between them ran the pathway,
Never grew the grass upon it;
Singing birds, that utter falsehoods,
Story-tellers, mischief-makers,
Found no eager ear to listen,
Could not breed ill-will between them,
For they kept each other's counsel,
Spake with naked hearts together,
Pondering much and much contriving
How the tribes of men might prosper.

    Most beloved by Hiawatha
Was the gentle Chibiabos,
He the best of all musicians,
He the sweetest of all singers.
Beautiful and childlike was he,
Brave as man is, soft as woman,
Pliant as a wand of willow,
Stately as a deer with antlers.

    When he sang, the village listened;
All the warriors gathered round him,
All the women came to him;
Now he stirred their souls to passion,
Now he melted them to pity.

    From the hollow reeds he fashioned
Flutes so musical and mellow,
That the brook, the Sebowisha,
Ceased to murmur in the woodland,
That the wood-birds from singing,
And the squirrel, Adjidaumo,
Ceased his chatter in the oak-tree,

And the rabbit, the Wabasso,
Sat upright to look and listen.
    Yes, the brook, the Sebowisha,
Pausing, said, "O Chibiabos,
Teach my waves to flow in music,
Softly as your words in singing!"
    Yes, the bluebird, the Owaissa,
Envious, said, "O Chibiabos,
Teach me tones as wild and wayward,
Teach me songs as full of frenzy!"
    Yes, the robin, the Opechee,
Joyous, said, "O Chibiabos,
Teach me tones as sweet and tender,
Teach me songs as full of gladness!"
    And the whippoorwill, Wawonaissa,
Sobbing, said, "O Chibiabos,
Teach me tones as melancholy,
Teach me songs as full of sadness!"
    All the many sounds of nature
Borrowed sweetness from his singing;
All the hearts of men were softened
By the pathos of his music;
For he sang of peace and freedom,
Sang of beauty, love, and longing;
Sang of death, and life undying
In the Islands of the Blessed,
In the kingdom of Ponemah,
In the land of the Hereafter.
    Very dear to Hiawatha
Was the gentle Chibiabos,
He the best of all musicians,
He the sweetest of all singers;
For his gentleness he loved him,
And the magic of his singing.
    Dear, too, unto Hiawatha
Was the very strong man, Kwasind,
He the strongest of all mortals,
He the mightiest among many;
For his very strength he loved him,
For his strength allied to goodness.

Idle in his youth was Kwasind,
Very listless, dull, and dreamy,
Never played with other children,
Never fished and never hunted,
Not like other children was he;
But they that much he fasted,
Much his Manito entreated,
Much besought his Guardian Spirit.

"Lazy Kwasind!" said his mother,
"In my work you never help me!
In the Summer you are roaming
Idly in the fields and forests;
In the Winter you are cowering
O'er the firebrands in the wigwam!
In the coldest days of Winter
I must break the ice for fishing;
With my nets you never help me!
At the door my nets are hanging,
Dripping, freezing with the water;
Go and wring them, Yenadizze!
Go and dry them in the sunshine!"

Slowly, from the ashes, Kwasind
Rose, but made no angry answer;
From the lodge went forth in silence,
Took the nets, that hung together,
Dripping, freezing at the doorway;
Like a wisp of straw he wrung them,
Like a wisp of straw he broke them,
Could not wring them without breaking,
Such the strength was in his fingers.

"Lazy Kwasind!" said his father,
"In the hunt you never help me;
Every bow you touch is broken,
Snapped asunder every arrow;
Yet come with me to the forest,
You shall bring the hunting homeward."

Down a narrow pass they wandered,
Where a brooklet led them onward,
Where the trail of deer and bison
Marked the soft mud on the margin,

Till they found all further passage
Shut against them, barred securely
By the trunks of trees uprooted,
Lying lengthwise, lying crosswise,
And forbidding further passage.
    "We must go back," said the old man,
"O'er these logs we cannot clamber;
Not a woodchuck could get through them,
Not a squirrel clamber o'er them!"
And straightway his pipe he lighted,
And sat down to smoke and ponder.
But before his pipe was finished,
Lo! the path was cleared before him;
All the trunks had Kwasind lifted,
To the right hand, to the left hand,
Shot the pine-trees swift as arrows,
Hurled the cedars light as lances.
    "Lazy Kwasind!" said the young men,
As they sported in the meadow:
"Why stand idly looking at us,
Leaning on the rock behind you?
Come and wrestle with the others,
Let us pitch the quoit together!"
Lazy Kwasind made no answer,
To their challenge made no answer,
Only rose, and slowly turning,
Seized the huge rock in his fingers,
Tore it from its deep foundation,
Poised it in the air a moment,
Pitched it sheer into the river,
Sheer into the swift Pauwating,
Where it still is seen in Summer.
    Once as down that foaming river,
Down the rapids of Pauwating,
Kwasind sailed with his companions,
In the stream he saw a beaver,
Saw Ahmeek, the King of Beavers,
Struggling with the rushing currents,
Rising, sinking in the water.
Without speaking, without pausing,

Kwasind leaped into the river,
Plunged beneath the bubbling surface,
Through the whirlpools chased the beaver,
Followed him among the islands,
Stayed so long beneath the water,
That his terrified companions
Cried, "Alas! good-by to Kwasind!
We shall never more see Kwasind!"
But he reappeared triumphant,
And upon his shining shoulders
Brought the beaver, dead and dripping,
Brought the King of all the Beavers.
    And these two, as I have told you,
Were the friends of Hiawatha,
Chibiabos, the musician,
And the very strong man, Kwasind.
Long they lived in peace together,
Spake with naked hearts together,
Pondering much and much contriving
How the tribes of men might prosper.

VII
Hiawatha's Sailing

"Give me of your bark, O Birch-tree!
Of your yellow bark, O Birch-tree!
Growing by the rushing river,
Tall and stately in the valley!
I a light canoe will build me,
Build a swift Cheemaun for sailing,
That shall float on the river,
Like a yellow leaf in Autumn,
Like a yellow water-lily!
    "Lay aside your cloak, O Birch-tree!
Lay aside your white-skin wrapper,
For the Summer-time is coming,
And the sun is warm in heaven,
And you need no white-skin wrapper!"
    Thus aloud cried Hiawatha

In the solitary forest,
By the rushing Taquamenaw,
When the birds were singing gayly,
In the Moon of Leaves were singing,
And the sun, from sleep awaking,
Started up and said, "Behold me!
Gheezis, the great Sun, behold me!"
    And the tree with all its branches
Rustled in the breeze of morning,
Saying, with a sigh of patience,
"Take my cloak, O Hiawatha!"
    With his knife the tree he girdled;
Just beneath its lowest branches,
Just above the roots, he cut it,
Till the sap came oozing outward;
Down the trunk, from top to bottom,
Sheer he cleft the bark asunder,
With a wooden wedge he raised it,
Stripped it from the trunk unbroken.
    "Give me of your boughs, O Cedar!
Of your strong and pliant branches,
My canoe to make more steady,
Make more strong and firm beneath me!"
    Through the summit of the Cedar
Went a sound, a cry of horror,
Went a murmur of resistance;
But it whispered, bending downward,
'Take my boughs, O Hiawatha!"
    Down he hewed the boughs of cedar,
Shaped them straightway to a frame-work,
Like two bows he formed and shaped them,
Like two bended bows together.
    "Give me of your roots, O Tamarack!
Of your fibrous roots, O Larch-tree!
My canoe to bind together,
So to bind the ends together
That the water may not enter,
That the river may not wet me!"
    And the Larch, with all its fibres,
Shivered in the air of morning,

his forehead with its tassels,
Slid, with one long sigh of sorrow.
"Take them all, O Hiawatha!"
　　From the earth he tore the fibres,
Tore the tough roots of the Larch-tree,
Closely sewed the bark together,
Bound it closely to the frame-work.
　　"Give me of your balm, O Fir-tree!
Of your balsam and your resin,
So to close the seams together
That the water may not enter,
That the river may not wet me!"
　　And the Fir-tree, tall and sombre,
Sobbed through all its robes of darkness,
Rattled like a shore with pebbles,
Answered wailing, answered weeping,
"Take my balm, O Hiawatha!"
　　And he took the tears of balsam,
Took the resin of the Fir-tree,
Smeared therewith each seam and fissure,
Made each crevice safe from water.
　　"Give me of your quills, O Hedgehog!
All your quills, O Kagh, the Hedgehog!
I will make a necklace of them,
Make a girdle for my beauty,
And two stars to deck her bosom!"
　　From a hollow tree the Hedgehog
With his sleepy eyes looked at him,
Shot his shining quills, like arrows,
Saying with a drowsy murmur,
Through the tangle of his whiskers,
"Take my quills, O Hiawatha!"
　　From the ground the quills he gathered,
All the little shining arrows,
Stained them red and blue and yellow,
With the juice of roots and berries;
Into his canoe he wrought them,
Round its waist a shining girdle,
Round its bows a gleaming necklace,
On its breast two stars resplendent.

Thus the Birch Canoe was builded
In the valley, by the river,
In the bosom of the forest;
And the forest's life was in it,
All its mystery and its magic,
All the lightness of the birch-tree,
All the toughness of the cedar,
All the larch's supple sinews;
And it floated on the river
Like a yellow leaf in Autumn,
Like a yellow water-lily.

Paddles none had Hiawatha,
Paddles none he had or needed,
For his as paddles served him,
And his wishes served to guide him;
Swift or slow at will he glided,
Veered to right or left at pleasure.

Then he called aloud to Kwasind,
To his friend, the strong man, Kwasind,
Saying, "Help me clear this river
Of its sunken logs and sand-bars."

Straight into the river Kwasind
Plunged as if he were an otter,
Dived as if he were a beaver,
Stood up to his waist in water,
To his arm-pits in the river,
Swam and scouted in the river,
Tugged at sunken logs and branches,
With his hands he scooped the sand-bars,
With his feet the ooze and tangle.

And thus sailed my Hiawatha
Down the rushing Taquamenaw,
Sailed through all its bends and windings,
Sailed through all its deeps and shallows,
While his friend, the strong man, Kwasind,
Swam the deeps, the shallows waded.

Up and down the river went they,
In and out among its islands,
Cleared its bed of root and sand-bar,
Dragged the dead trees from its channel,

Made its passage safe and certain,
Made a pathway for the people,
From its springs among the mountains,
To the waters of Pauwating,
To the bay of Taquamenaw.

VIII
Hiawatha's Fishing

Forth upon the Gitche Gumee,
On the shining Big-Sea-Water,
With his fishing-line of cedar,
Of the twisted bark of cedar,
Forth to catch the sturgeon Nahma,
Mishe-Nahma, King of Fishes,
In his birch canoe exulting
All alone went Hiawatha.
    Through the clear, transparent water
He could the fishes swimming
Far down in the depths below him;
See the yellow perch, the Sahwa,
Like a sunbeam in the water,
See the Shawgashee, the craw-fish,
Like a spider on the bottom,
On the white and sandy bottom.
    At the stern sat Hiawatha,
With his fishing-line of cedar;
In his plumes the breeze of morning
Played as in the hemlock branches;
On the bows, with tail erected,
Sat the squirrel, Adjidaumo;
In his fur the breeze of morning
Played as in the prairie grasses.
    On the white sand of the bottom
Lay the monster Mishe-Nahma,
Lay the sturgeon, King of Fishes;
Through his gills he breathed the water,
With his fins he fanned and winnowed,
With his tail he swept the sand-floor.

There he lay in all his armor;
On each side a shield to guard him,
Plates of bone upon his forehead,
Down his sides and back and shoulders
Plates of bone with spines projecting
Painted was he with his war-paints,
Stripes of yellow, red, and azure,
Spots of brown and spots of sable;
And he lay there on the bottom,
Fanning with his fins of purple,
As above him Hiawatha
In his birch canoe came sailing,
With his fishing-line of cedar.

    "Take my bait," cried Hiawatha,
Dawn into the depths beneath him,
"Take my bait, O Sturgeon, Nahma!
Come up from below the water,
Let us see which is the stronger!"
And he dropped his line of cedar
Through the clear, transparent water,
Waited vainly for an answer,
Long sat waiting for an answer,
And repeating loud and louder,
"Take my bait, O King of Fishes!"

    Quietlay the sturgeon, Nahma,
Fanning slowly in the water,
Looking up at Hiawatha,
Listening to his call and clamor,
His unnecessary tumult,
Till he wearied of the shouting;
And he said to the Kenozha,
To the pike, the Maskenozha,
"Take the bait of this rude fellow,
Break the line of Hiawatha!"

    In his fingers Hiawatha
Felt the loose line jerk and tighten,
As he drew it in, it tugged so
That the birch canoe stood endwise,
Like a birch log in the water,
With the squirrel, Adjidaumo,

Perched and frisking on the summit.
    Full of scorn was Hiawatha
When he saw the fish rise upward,
Saw the pike, the Maskenozha,
Coming nearer, nearer to him,
And he shouted through the water,
"Esa! esa! shame upon you!
You are but the pike, Kenozha,
You are not the fish I wanted,
You are not the King of Fishes!"
    Reeling downward to the bottom
Sank the pike in great confusion,
And the mighty sturgeon, Nahma,
Said to Ugudwash, the sun-fish,
To the bream, with scales of crimson,
"Take the bait of this great boaster,
Break the line of Hiawatha!"
    Slowly upward, wavering, gleaming,
Rose the Ugudwash, the sun-fish,
Seized the line of Hiawatha,
Swung with all his weight upon it,
Made a whirlpool in the water,
Whirled the birch canoe in circles,
Round and round in gurgling eddies,
Till the circles in the water
Reached the far-off sandy beaches,
Till the water-flags and rushes
Nodded on the distant margins.
    But when Hiawatha saw him
Slowly rising through the water,
Lifting up his disk refulgent,
Loud he shouted in derision,
"Esa! esa! shame upon you!
You are Ugudwash, the sun-fish,
You are not the fish I wanted,
You are not the King of Fishes!"
Slowly downward, wavering, gleaming,
Sank the Ugudwash, the sun-fish,
And again the sturgeon, Nahma,
Heard the shout of Hiawatha,

Heard his challenge of defiance,
The unnecessary tumult,
Ringing far across the water.

From the white sand of the bottom
Up he rose with angry gesture,
Quivering in each nerve and fibre,
Clashing all his plates of armor,
Gleaming bright with all his war-paint;
In his wrath he darted upward,
Flashing leaped into the sunshine,
Opened his great jaws, and swallowed
Both canoe and Hiawatha.

Down into that darksome cavern
Plunged the headlong Hiawatha,
As a log on some black river
Shoots and plunges down the rapids,
Found in utter darkness,
Groped about in helpless wonder,
Till he a great heart beating,
Throbbing in that utter darkness.

And he smote it in his anger,
With his fist, the heart of Nahma,
Felt the mighty King of Fishes
Shudder through each nerve and fibre,
Heard the water gurgle round him
As he leaped and staggered through it,
Sick at heart, and faint and weary.

Crosswise then did Hiawatha
Drag his birch-canoe for safety,
Lest from out the jaws of Nahma,
In the turmoil and confusion,
Forth he might be hurled and perish.
And the squirrel, Adjidaumo,
Frisked and chatted very gayly,
Toiled and tugged with Hiawatha
Till the labor was completed.

Then said Hiawatha to him,
"O my little friend, the squirrel,
Bravely have you toiled to me;
Take the thanks of Hiawatha,

And the name which now he gives you;
For hereafter and forever
Boys shall call you Adjidaumo,
Tail-in-air the boys shall call you!"

And again the sturgeon, Nahma,
Gasped and quivered in the water,
Then was still, and drifted landward
Till he grated on the pebbles,
Till the listening Hiawatha
Heard him grate upon the margin,
Felt him strand upon the pebbles,
Knew that Nahma, King of Fishes,
Lay there dead upon the margin.

Then he heard a clang and flapping,
As of many wings assembling,
Heard a screaming and confusion,
As of birds of prey contending,
Saw a gleam of light above him,
Shining through the ribs of Nahma,
Saw the glittering eyes of sea-gulls,
Of Kayoshk, the sea-gulls, peering,
Gazing at him through the opening,
Heard them saying to each other,
"'T is our brother, Hiawatha!"

And he shouted from below them,
Cried exulting from the caverns:
"O ye sea-gulls! O my brothers!
I have slain the sturgeon, Nahma;
Make the rifts a little larger,
With your claws the openings widen,
Set me free from this dark prison,
And henceforward and forever
Men shall speak of your achievements,
Calling you Kayoshk, the sea-gulls,
Yes, Kayoshk, the Noble Scratchers!"

And the wild and clamorous sea-gulls
Toiled with beak and claws together,
Made the rifts and openings wider
In the mighty ribs of Nahma,
And from peril and from prison,

From the body of the sturgeon,
From the peril of the water,
They released my Hiawatha.

He was standing near his wigwam,
On the margin of the water,
And he called to old Nokomis,
Called and beckoned to Nokomis,
Pointed to the sturgeon, Nahma,
Lying lifeless on the pebbles,
With the sea-gulls feeding on him.

"I have slain the Mishe-Nahma,
Slain the King of Fishes!" said he'
"Look! the sea-gulls feed upon him,
Yes, my friends Kayoshk, the sea-gulls;
Drive them not away, Nokomis,
They have saved me from great peril
In the body of the sturgeon;
Wait until their meal is ended,
Till their craws are full with feasting,
Till they homeward fly, at sunset,
To their nests among the marshes;
Then bring all your pots and kettles,
And make oil for us in Winter."

And she waited till the sun set,
Till the pallid moon, the Night-sun,
Rose above the tranquil water,
Till Kayoshk, the sated sea-gulls,
From their banquet rose with clamor,
And across the fiery sunset
Winged their way to far-off islands,
To their nests among the rushes.

To his sleep went Hiawatha,
And Nokomis to her labor,
Toiling patient in the moonlight,
Till the sun and moon changed places,
Till the sky was red with sunrise,
And Kayoshk, the hungry sea-gulls,
Came back from the reedy islands,
Clamorous for their morning banquet.

Three whole days and nights alternate

Old Nokomis and the sea-gulls
Stripped the oily flesh of Nahma,
Till the waves washed through the rib-bones,
Till the sea-gulls came no longer,
And upon the sands lay nothing
But the skeleton of Nahma.

IX

Hiawatha and the Pearl-Feather

On the shores of Gitche Gumee,
Of the shining Big-Sea-Water,
Stood Nokomis, the old woman,
Pointing with her finger westward,
O'er the water pointing westward,
To the purple clouds of sunset.
    Fiercely the red sun descending
Burned his way along the heavens,
Set the sky on fire behind him,
As war-parties, when retreating,
Burn the prairies on their war-trail;
And the moon, the Night-Sun, eastward,
Suddenly starting from his ambush,
Followed fast those bloody footprints,
Followed in that fiery war-trail,
With its glare upon his features.
    And Nokomis, the old woman,
Pointing with her finger westward,
Spake these words to Hiawatha:
"Yonder dwells the great Pearl-Feather,
Megissogwon, the Magician,
Manito of Wealth and Wampum,
Guarded by his fiery serpents,
Guarded by the black pitch-water.
You can see his fiery serpents,
The Kenabeek, the great serpents,
Coiling, playing in the water;
You can see the black pitch-water
Stretching far away beyond them,

To the purple clouds of sunset!
    "He it was who slew my father,
By his wicked wiles and cunning,
When he from the moon descended,
When he came on earth to seek me.
He, the mightiest of Magicians,
Sends the fever from the marshes,
Sends the pestilential vapors,
Sends the poisonous exhalations,
Sends the white fog from the fen-lands,
Sends disease and death among us!
    "Take your bow, O Hiawatha,
Take your arrows, jasper-headed,
Take your war-club, Puggawaugua,
And your mittens, Minjekahwun,
And your birch-canoe for sailing,
And the oil of Mishe-Nahma,
So to smear its sides, that swiftly
You may pass the black pitch-water;
Slay this merciless magician,
Save the people from the fever
That he breathes across the fen-lands,
And avenge my father's murder!"
    Straightway then my Hiawatha
Armed himself with all his war-gear,
Launched his birch-canoe for sailing;
With his palm its sides he patted,
Said with glee, "Cheemaun, my darling,
O my Birch-Canoe! leap forward,
Where you the fiery serpents,
Where you the black pitch-water!"
    Forward leaped Cheemaun exulting,
And the noble Hiawatha
Sang his war-song wild and woful,
And above him the war-eagle,
The Keneu, the great war-eagle,
Master of all fowls with feathers,
Screamed and hurtled through the heavens.
    Soon he reached the fiery serpents,
The Kenabeek, the great serpents,

Lying huge upon the water,
Sparkling, rippling in the water,
Lying coiled across the passage,
With their blazing crests uplifted,
Breathing fiery fogs and vapors,
So that none could pass beyond them.
   But the fearless Hiawatha
Cried aloud, and spake in this wise:
"Let me pass my way, Kenabeek,
Let me go upon my journey!"
And they answered, hissing fiercely,
With their fiery breath made answer:
"Back, go back! O Shaugodaya!
Back to old Nokomis, Faint-heart!"
   Then the angry Hiawatha
Raised his mighty bow of ash-tree,
Seized his arrows, jasper-headed,
Shot them fast among the serpents;
Every twanging of the bow-string
Was a war-cry and a death-cry,
Every whizzing of an arrow
Was a death-song of Kenabeek.
   Weltering in the bloody water,
Dead lay all the fiery serpents,
And among them Hiawatha
Harmless sailed, and cried exulting:
"Onward, O Cheemaun, my darling!
Onward to the black pitch-water!"
   Then he took the oil of Nahma,
And the bows and sides anointed,
Smeared them well with oil, that swiftly
He might pass the black pitch-water.
   All night long he sailed upon it,
Sailed upon that sluggish water,
Covered with its mould of ages,
Black with rotting water-rushes,
Rank with flags and leaves of lilies,
Stagnant, lifeless, dreary, dismal,
Lighted by the shimmering moonlight,
And by will-o'-the-wisps illumined,

Fires by ghosts of dead men kindled,
In their weary night-encampments.

All the air was white with moonlight,
All the water black with shadow,
And around him the Suggema,
The mosquito, sang his war-song,
And the fire-flies, Wah-wah-taysee,
Waved their torches to mislead him;
And the bull-frog, the Dahinda,
Thrust his head into the moonlight,
Fixed his yellow eyes upon him,
Sobbed and sank beneath the surface;
And anon a thousand whistles,
Answered over all the fen-lands,
And the heron, the Shuh-shuh-gah,
Far off on the reedy margin,
Heralded the hero's coming.

Westward thus fared Hiawatha,
Toward the realm of Megissogwon,
Toward the land of the Pearl-Feather,
Till the level moon stared at him
In his face stared pale and haggard,
Till the sun was hot behind him,
Till it burned upon his shoulders,
And before him on the upland
He could the Shining Wigwam
Of the Manito of Wampum,
Of the mightiest of Magicians.

Then once more Cheemaun he patted,
To his birch-canoe said, "Onward!"
And it stirred in all its fibres,
And with one great bound of triumph
Leaped across the water-lilies,
Leaped through tangled flags and rushes,
And upon the beach beyond them
Dry-shod landed Hiawatha.

Straight he took his bow of ash-tree,
On the sand one end he rested,
With his knee he pressed the middle,
Stretched the bow-string tighter,

Took an arrow, jasper-headed,
Shot it at the Shining Wigwam,
Sent it singing as a herald,
As a bearer of his message,
Of his challenge loud and lofty:
"Come forth from your lodge, Pearl-Feather!
Hiawatha waits your coming!"
    Straightway from the Shining Wigwam
Came the mighty Megissogwon,
Tall of stature, broad of shoulder,
Dark and terrible in aspect,
Clad from head to foot in wampum,
Armed with all his warlike weapons,
Painted like the sky of morning,
Streaked with crimson, blue, and yellow,
Crested with great eagle-feathers,
Streaming upward, streaming outward.
    "Well I know you, Hiawatha!"
Cried he in a voice of thunder,
In a tone of loud derision.
"Hasten back, O Shaugodaya!
Hasten back among the women,
Back to old Nokomis, Faint-heart!
I will slay you as you stand there,
As of old I slew her father!"
    But my Hiawatha answered,
Nothing daunted, fearing nothing:
"Big words do not smite like war-clubs,
Boastful breath is not a bow-string,
Taunts are not so sharp as arrows,
Deeds are better things than words are,
Actions mightier than boastings!"
    Then began the greatest battle
That the sun had ever looked on,
That the war-birds ever witnessed.
All a Summer's day it lasted,
From the sunrise to the sunset;
For the shafts of Hiawatha
Harmless hit the shirt of wampum,
Harmless fell the blows he dealt it

With his mittens, Minjekahwun,
Harmless fell the heavy war-club;
It could dash the rocks asunder,
But it could not break the meshes
Of that magic shirt of wampum.

   Till at sunset Hiawatha,
Leaning on his bow of ash-tree,
Wounded, weary, and desponding,
With his mighty war-club broken,
With his mittens torn and tattered,
And three useless arrows only,
Paused to rest beneath a pine-tree,
From whose branches trailed the mosses,
And whose trunk was coated over
With the Dead-man's Moccasin-leather,
With the fungus white and yellow.

   Suddenly from the boughs above him
Sang the Mama, the woodpecker:
"Aim your arrows, Hiawatha,
At the head of Megissogwon,
Strike the tuft of hair upon it,
At their roots the long black tresses;
There alone can he be wounded!"

   Winged with feathers, tipped with jasper,
Swift flew Hiawatha's arrow,
Just as Megissogwon, stooping,
Raised a heavy stone to throw it.
Full upon the crown it struck him,
At the roots of his long tresses,
And he reeled and staggered forward,
Plunging like a wounded bison,
Yes, like Pezhekee, the bison,
When the snow is on the prairie.

   Swifter flew the second arrow,
In the pathway of the other,
Piercing deeper than the other,
Wounding sorer than the other;
And the knees of Megissogwon
Shook like windy reeds beneath him,
Bent and trembled like the rushes.

But the third and latest arrow
Swiftest flew, and wounded sorest,
And the mighty Megissogwon
Saw the fiery eyes of Pauguk,
Saw the eyes of Death glare at him,
Heard his voice call in the darkness;
At the feet of Hiawatha
Lifeless lay the great Pearl-Feather,
Lay the mightiest of Magicians.
    Then the grateful Hiawatha
Called the Mama, the woodpecker,
From his perch among the branches
Of the melancholy pine-tree,
And, in honor of his service,
Stained with blood the tuft of feathers
On the little head of Mama;
Even to this day he wears it,
Wears the tuft of crimson feathers,
As a symbol of his service.
    Then he stripped the shirt of wampum
From the back of Megissogwon,
As a trophy of the battle,
As a signal of his conquest.
On the shore he left the body,
Half on land and half in water,
In the sand his feet were buried,
And his face was in the water.
And above him, wheeled and clamored
The Keneu, the great war-eagle,
Sailing round in narrower circles,
Hovering nearer, nearer, nearer.
    From the wigwam Hiawatha
Bore the wealth of Megissogwon,
All his wealth of skins and wampum,
Furs of bison and of beaver,
Furs of sable and of ermine,
Wampum belts and strings and pouches,
Quivers wrought with beads of wampum,
Filled with arrows, silver-headed.
    Homeward then he sailed exulting,

Homeward through the black pitch-water,
Homeward through the weltering serpents,
With the trophies of the battle,
With a shout and song of triumph.
　　On the shore stood old Nokomis,
On the shore stood Chibiabos,
And the very strong man, Kwasind,
Waiting for the hero's coming,
Listening to his songs of triumph.
And the people of the village
Welcomed him with songs and dances,
Made a feast, and shouted:
'Honor be to Hiawatha!
He has slain the great Pearl-Feather,
Slain the mightiest of Magicians,
Him, who sent the fiery fever,
Sent the white fog from the fen-lands,
Sent disease and death among us!"
　　Ever dear to Hiawatha
Was the memory of Mama!
And in token of his friendship,
As a mark of his remembrance,
He adorned and decked his pipe-stem
With the crimson tuft of feathers,
With the blood-red crest of Mama.
But the wealth of Megissogwon,
All the trophies of the battle,
He divided with his people,
Shared it equally among them.

X
Hiawatha's Wooing

"As unto the bow the cord is,
So unto the man is woman;
Though she bends him, she obeys him,
Though she draws him, yet she follows;
Useless each without the other!"
　　Thus the youthful Hiawatha

Said within himself and pondered,
Much perplexed by various feelings,
Listless, longing, hoping, fearing,
Dreaming still of Minnehaha,
Of the lovely Laughing Water,
In the land of the Dacotahs.

    "Wed a maiden of your people,"
Warning said the old Nokomis;
"Go not eastward, go not westward,
For a stranger, whom we know not!
Like a fire upon the hearth-stone
Is a neighbor's homely daughter,
Like the starlight or the moonlight
Is the handsomest of strangers!"

    Thus dissuading spake Nokomis,
And my Hiawatha answered
Only this: "Dear old Nokomis,
Very pleasant is the firelight,
But I like the starlight better,
Better do I like the moonlight!"

    Gravely then said old Nokomis:
"Bring not here an idle maiden,
Bring not here a useless woman,
Hands unskilful, feet unwilling;
Bring a wife with nimble fingers,
Heart and hand that move together,
Feet that run on willing errands!"

    Smiling answered Hiawatha:
'In the land of the Dacotahs
Lives the Arrow-maker's daughter,
Minnehaha, Laughing Water,
Handsomest of all the women.
I will bring her to your wigwam,
She shall run upon your errands,
Be your starlight, moonlight, firelight,
Be the sunlight of my people!"

    Still dissuading said Nokomis:
"Bring not to my lodge a stranger
From the land of the Dacotahs!
Very fierce are the Dacotahs,

Often is there war between us,
There are feuds yet unforgotten,
Wounds that ache and still may open!"
    Laughing answered Hiawatha:
"For that reason, if no other,
Would I wed the fair Dacotah,
That our tribes might be united,
That old feuds might be forgotten,
And old wounds be healed forever!"
    Thus departed Hiawatha
To the land of the Dacotahs,
To the land of handsome women;
Striding over moor and meadow,
Through interminable forests,
Through uninterrupted silence.
    With his moccasins of magic,
At each stride a mile he measured;
Yet the way seemed long before him,
And his heart outran his footsteps;
And he journeyed without resting,
Till he heard the cataract's laughter,
Heard the Falls of Minnehaha
Calling to him through the silence.
"Pleasant is the sound!" he murmured,
"Pleasant is the voice that calls me!"
    On the outskirts of the forests,
'Twixt the shadow and the sunshine,
Herds of fallow deer were feeding,
But they saw not Hiawatha;
To his bow he whispered, "Fail not!"
To his arrow whispered, "Swerve not!"
Sent it singing on its errand,
To the red heart of the roebuck;
Threw the deer across his shoulder,
And sped forward without pausing.
    At the doorway of his wigwam
Sat the ancient Arrow-maker,
In the land of the Dacotahs,
Making arrow-heads of jasper,
Arrow-heads of chalcedony.

At his side, in all her beauty,
Sat the lovely Minnehaha,
Sat his daughter, Laughing Water,
Plaiting mats of flags and rushes
Of the past the old man's thoughts were,
And the maiden's of the future.

He was thinking, as he sat there,
Of the days when with such arrows
He had struck the deer and bison,
On the Muskoday, the meadow;
Shot the wild goose, flying southward
On the wing, the clamorous Wawa;
Thinking of the great war-parties,
How they came to buy his arrows,
Could not fight without his arrows.
Ah, no more such noble warriors
Could be found on earth as they were!
Now the men were all like women,
Only used their tongues for weapons!

She was thinking of a hunter,
From another tribe and country,
Young and tall and very handsome,
Who one morning, in the Spring-time,
Came to buy her father's arrows,
Sat and rested in the wigwam,
Lingered long about the doorway,
Looking back as he departed.
She had her father praise him,
Praise his courage and his wisdom;
Would he come again for arrows
To the Falls of Minnehaha?
On the mat her hands lay idle,
And her eyes were very dreamy.

Through their thoughts they heard a footstep,
Heard a rustling in the branches,
And with glowing cheek and forehead,
With the deer upon his shoulders,
Suddenly from out the woodlands
Hiawatha stood before them.

Straight the ancient Arrow-maker

Looked up gravely from his labor,
Laid aside the unfinished arrow,
Bade him enter at the doorway,
Saying, as he rose to meet him,
"Hiawatha, you are welcome!"
    At the feet of Laughing Water
Hiawatha laid his burden,
Threw the red deer from his shoulders;
And the maiden looked up at him,
Looked up from her mat of rushes,
Said with gentle look and accent,
"You are welcome, Hiawatha!"
    Very spacious was the wigwam,
Made of deer-skins dressed and whitened,
With the Gods of the Dacotahs
Drawn and painted on its curtains,
And so tall the doorway, hardly
Hiawatha stooped to enter,
Hardly touched his eagle-feathers
As he entered at the doorway.
    Then uprose the Laughing Water,
From the ground fair Minnehaha,
Laid aside her mat unfinished,
Brought forth food and set before them,
Water brought them from the brooklet,
Gave them food in earthen vessels,
Gave them drink in bowls of bass-wood,
Listened while the guest was speaking,
Listened while her father answered,
But not once her lips she opened,
Not a single word she uttered.
    Yes, as in a dream she listened
To the words of Hiawatha,
As he talked of old Nokomis,
Who had nursed him in his childhood,
As he told of his companions,
Chibiabos, the musician,
And the very strong man, Kwasind,
And of happiness and plenty
In the land of the Ojibways,

In the pleasant land and peaceful.
    "After many years of warfare,
Many years of strife and bloodshed,
There is peace between the Ojibways
And the tribe of the Dacotahs."
Thus continued Hiawatha,
And then added, speaking slowly,
"That this peace may last forever,
And our hands be clasped more closely,
And our hearts be more united,
Give me as my wife this maiden,
Minnehaha, Laughing Water,
Loveliest of Dacotah women!"
    And the ancient Arrow-maker
Paused a moment ere he answered,
Smoked a little while in silence,
Looked at Hiawatha proudly,
Fondly looked at Laughing Water,
And made answer very gravely:
"Yes, if Minnehaha wishes;
Let your heart speak, Minnehaha!"
    And the lovely Laughing Water
Seemed more lovely as she stood there,
Neither willing nor reluctant,
As she went to Hiawatha,
Softly took the seat beside him,
While she said, and blushed to say it,
"I will follow you, my husband!"
    This was Hiawatha's wooing!
Thus it was he won the daughter
Of the ancient Arrow-maker,
In the land of the Dacotahs!
    From the wigwam he departed,
Leading with him Laughing Water;
Hand in hand they went together,
Through the woodland and the meadow,
Left the old man standing
At the doorway of his wigwam,
Heard the Falls of Minnehaha
Calling to them from the distance,

Crying to them from afar off,
"Fare thee well, O Minnehaha!"
    And the ancient Arrow-maker
Turned again unto his labor,
Sat down by his sunny doorway,
Murmuring to himself, and saying:
"Thus it is our daughters leave us,
Those we love, and those who love us!
Just when they have learned to help us,
When we are old and lean upon them,
Comes a youth with flaunting feathers,
With his flute of reeds, a stranger
Wanders piping through the village,
Beckons to the fairest maiden,
And she follows where he leads her,
Leaving all things for the stranger!"
    Pleasant was the journey homeward,
Through interminable forests,
Over meadow, over mountain,
Over river, hill, and hollow.
Short it seemed to Hiawatha,
Though they journeyed very slowly,
Though his pace he checked and slackened
To the steps of Laughing Water.
    Over wide and rushing rivers
In his arms he bore the maiden;
Light he thought her as a feather,
As the plume upon his head-gear;
Cleared the tangled pathway for her,
Bent aside the swaying branches,
Made at night a lodge of branches,
And a bed with boughs of hemlock,
And a fire before the doorway
With the dry cones of the pine-tree.
    All the travelling winds went with them,
O'er the meadows, through the forest;
All the stars of night looked at them,
Watched with sleepless eyes their slumber;
From his ambush in the oak-tree
Peeped the squirrel, Adjidaumo,

Watched with eager eyes the lovers;
And the rabbit, the Wabasso,
Scampered from the path before them,
Peering, peeping from his burrow,
Sat erect upon his haunches,
Watched with curious eyes the lovers.
    Pleasant was the journey homeward!
All the birds sang loud and sweetly
Songs of happiness and heart's-ease;
Sang the bluebird, the Owaissa,
"Happy are you, Hiawatha,
Having such a wife to love you!"
Sang the robin, the Opechee,
"Happy are you, Laughing Water,
Having such a noble husband!"
    From the sky the sun benignant
Looked upon them through the branches,
Saying to them, "O my children,
Love is sunshine, hate is shadow,
Life is checkered shade and sunshine,
Rule by love, O Hiawatha!"
    From the sky the moon looked at them,
Filled the lodge with mystic splendors,
Whispered to them, "O my children,
Day is restless, night is quiet,
Man imperious, woman feeble;
Half is mine, although I follow;
Rule by patience, Laughing Water!"
    Thus it was they journeyed homeward;
Thus it was that Hiawatha
To the lodge of old Nokomis
Brought the moonlight, starlight, firelight,
Brought the sunshine of his people,
Minnehaha, Laughing Water,
Handsomest of all the women
In the land of the Dacotahs,
In the land of handsome women.

XI
Hiawatha's Wedding-Feast

You shall hear how Pau-Puk-Keewis,
How the handsome Yenadizze
Danced at Hiawatha's wedding;
How the gentle Chibiabos,
He the sweetest of musicians,
Sang his songs of love and longing;
How Iagoo, the great boaster,
He the marvellous story-teller,
Told his tales of strange adventure,
That the feast might be more joyous,
That the time might pass more gayly,
And the guests be more contented.

    Sumptuous was the feast Nokomis
Made at Hiawatha's wedding;
All the bowls were made of bass-wood,
White and polished very smoothly,
All the spoons of horn of bison,
Black and polished very smoothly.

    She had sent through all the village
Messengers with wands of willow,
As a sign of invitation,
As a token of the feasting;
And the wedding guests assembled,
Clad in all their richest raiment,
Robes of fur and belts of wampum,
Splendid with their paint and plumage,
Beautiful with beads and tassels.

    First they ate the sturgeon, Nahma,
And the pike, the Maskenozha,
Caught and cooked by old Nokomis;
Then on pemican they feasted,
Pemican and buffalo marrow,
Haunch of deer and hump of bison,
Yellow cakes of the Mondamin,
And the wild rice of the river.

    But the gracious Hiawatha,
And the lovely Laughing Water,

And the careful old Nokomis,
Tasted not the food before them,
Only waited on the others
Only served their guests in silence.

And when all the guests had finished,
Old Nokomis, brisk and busy,
From an ample pouch of otter,
Filled the red-stone pipes for smoking
With tobacco from the South-land,
Mixed with bark of the red willow,
And with herbs and leaves of fragrance.

Then she said, "O Pau-Puk-Keewis,
Dance for us your merry dances,
Dance the Beggar's Dance to please us,
That the feast may be more joyous,
That the time may pass more gayly,
And our guests be more contented!"

Then the handsome Pau-Puk-Keewis,
He the idle Yenadizze,
He the merry mischief-maker,
Whom the people called the Storm-Fool,
Rose among the guests assembled.

Skilled was he in sports and pastimes,
In the merry dance of snow-shoes,
In the play of quoits and ball-play;
Skilled was he in games of hazard,
In all games of skill and hazard,
Pugasaing, the Bowl and Counters,
Kuntassoo, the Game of Plum-stones.

Though the warriors called him Faint-Heart,
Called him coward, Shaugodaya,
Idler, gambler, Yenadizze,
Little heeded he their jesting,
Little cared he for their insults,
For the women and the maidens
Loved the handsome Pau-Puk-Keewis.

He was dressed in shirt of doe-skin,
White and soft, and fringed with ermine,
All inwrought with beads of wampum;
He was dressed in deer-skin leggings,

Fringed with hedgehog quills and ermine,
And in moccasins of buck-skin,
Thick with quills and beads embroidered.
On his head were plumes of swan's down,
On his heels were tails of foxes,
In one hand a fan of feathers,
And a pipe was in the other.

    Barred with streaks of red and yellow,
Streaks of blue and bright vermilion,
Shone the face of Pau-Puk-Keewis.
From his forehead fell his tresses,
Smooth, and parted like a woman's,
Shining bright with oil, and plaited,
Hung with braids of scented grasses,
As among the guests assembled,
To the sound of flutes and singing,
To the sound of drums and voices,
Rose the handsome Pau-Puk-Keewis,
And began his mystic dances.

    First he danced a solemn measure,
Very slow in step and gesture,
In and out among the pine-trees,
Through the shadows and the sunshine,
Treading softly like a panther.
Then more swiftly and still swifter,
Whirling, spinning round in circles,
Leaping o'er the guests assembled,
Eddying round and round the wigwam,
Till the leaves went whirling with him,
Till the dust and wind together
Swept in eddies round about him.

    Then along the sandy margin
Of the lake, the Big-Sea-Water,
On he sped with frenzied gestures,
Stamped upon the sand, and tossed it
Wildly in the air around him;
Till the wind became a whirlwind,
Till the sand was blown and sifted
Like great snowdrifts o'er the landscape,
Heaping all the shores with Sand Dunes,

Sand Hills of the Nagow Wudjoo!
    Thus the merry Pau-Puk-Keewis
Danced his Beggar's Dance to please them,
And, returning, sat down laughing
There among the guests assembled,
Sat and fanned serenely
With his fan of turkey-feathers
    Then they said to Chibiabos,
To the friend of Hiawatha,
To the sweetest of all singers,
To the best of all musicians,
"Sing to us, O Chibiabos!
Songs of love and songs of longing,
That the feast may be more joyous,
That the time may pass more gayly,
And our guests be more contented!"
    And the gentle Chibiabos
Sang in accents sweet and tender,
Sang in tones of deep emotion,
Songs of love and songs of longing;
Looking still at Hiawatha,
Looking at fair Laughing Water,
Sang he softly, sang in this wise:
    "Onaway! Awake, beloved!
Thou the wild-flower of the forest!
Thou the wild-bird of the prairie!
Thou with eyes so soft and fawn-like!
    "If thou only lookest at me,
I am happy, I am happy,
As the lilies of the prairie,
When they feel the dew upon them!
    "Sweet thy breath is as the fragrance
Of the wild-flowers in the morning,
As their fragrance is at evening,
In the Moon when leaves are falling.
    "Does not all the blood within me
Leap to meet thee, leap to meet thee,
As the springs to meet the sunshine,
In the Moon when nights are brightest?
    "Onaway! my heart sings to thee,

Sings with joy when thou art near me,
As the sighing, singing branches
In the pleasant Moon of Strawberries!

"When thou art not pleased, beloved,
Then my heart is sad and darkened,
As the shining river darkens
When the clouds drop shadows on it!

"When thou smilest, my beloved,
Then my troubled heart is brightened,
As in sunshine gleam the ripples
That the cold wind makes in rivers.

"Smiles the earth, and smile the waters,
Smile the cloudless skies above us,
But I lose the way of smiling
When thou art no longer near me!

"I myself, myself! behold me!
Blood of my beating heart, behold me!
O awake, awake, beloved!
Onaway! awake, beloved!"

Thus the gentle Chibiabos
Sang his song of love and longing;
And Iagoo, the great boaster,
He the marvellous story-teller,
He the friend of old Nokomis,
Jealous of the sweet musician,
Jealous of the applause they gave him,
Saw in all the eyes around him,
Saw in all their looks and gestures,
That the wedding guests assembled
Longed to hear his pleasant stories,
His immeasurable falsehoods.

Very boastful was Iagoo;
Never heard he an adventure
But himself had met a greater;
Never any deed of daring
But himself had done a bolder;
Never any marvellous story
But himself could tell a stranger.

Would you listen to his boasting,
Would you only give him credence,

No one ever shot an arrow
Half so far and high as he had;
Ever caught so many fishes,
Ever killed so many reindeer,
Ever trapped so many beaver!
    None could run so fast as he could,
None could dive so deep as he could,
None could swim so far as he could;
None had made so many journeys,
None had seen so many wonders,
As this wonderful Iagoo,
As this marvellous story-teller!
    Thus his name became a by-word
And a jest among the people;
And whene'er a boastful hunter
Praised his own address too highly,
Or a warrior, home returning,
Talked too much of his achievements,
All his hearers cried, "Iagoo!
Here's Iagoo come among us!"
    He it was who carved the cradle
Of the little Hiawatha,
Carved its framework out of linden,
Bound it strong with reindeer sinews;
He it was who taught him later
How to make his bows and arrows,
How to make the bows of ash-tree,
And the arrows of the oak-tree.
So among the guests assembled
At my Hiawatha's wedding
Sat Iagoo, old and ugly,
Sat the marvellous story-teller.
    And they said, "O good Iagoo,
Tell us now a tale of wonder,
Tell us of some strange adventure,
That the feast may be more joyous,
That the time may pass more gayly,
And our guests be more contented!"
    And Iagoo answered straightway,
"You shall hear a tale of wonder,

You shall hear the strange adventures
Of Osseo, the Magician,
From the Evening Star descending."

XII

The Son of the Evening Star

Can it be the sun descending
O'er the level plain of water?
Or the Red Swan floating, flying,
Wounded by the magic arrow,
Staining all the waves with crimson,
With the crimson of its life-blood,
Filling all the air with splendor,
With the splendor of its plumage?
   Yes; it is the sun descending,
Sinking down into the water;
All the sky is stained with purple,
All the water flushed with crimson!
No; it is the Red Swan floating,
Diving down beneath the water;
To the sky its wings are lifted,
With its blood the waves are reddened!
   Over it the Star of Evening
Melts and trembles through the purple,
Hangs suspended in the twilight.
No; it is a bead of wampum
On the robes of the Great Spirit
As he passes through the twilight,
Walks in silence through the heavens.
   This with joy beheld Iagoo
And he said in haste: "Behold it!
See the sacred Star of Evening!
You shall hear a tale of wonder,
Hear the story of Osseo,
Son of the Evening Star, Osseo!
   "Once, in days no more remembered,
Ages nearer the beginning,
When the heavens were closer to us,

And the Gods were more familiar,
In the North-land lived a hunter,
With ten young and comely daughters,
Tall and lithe as wands of willow;
Only Oweenee, the youngest,
She the wilful and the wayward,
She the silent, dreamy maiden,
Was the fairest of the sisters.

  "All these women married warriors,
Married brave and haughty husbands;
Only Oweenee, the youngest,
Laughed and flouted all her lovers,
All her young and handsome suitors,
And then married old Osseo,
Old Osseo, poor and ugly,
Broken with age and weak with coughing,
Always coughing like a squirrel.

  "Ah, but beautiful within him
Was the spirit of Osseo,
From the Evening Star descended,
Star of Evening, Star of Woman,
Star of tenderness and passion!
All its fire was in his bosom,
All its beauty in his spirit,
All its mystery in his being,
All its splendor in his language!

  "And her lovers, the rejected,
Handsome men with belts of wampum,
Handsome men with paint and feathers.
Pointed at her in derision,
Followed her with jest and laughter.
But she said:'I care not for you,
Care not for your belts of wampum,
Care not for your paint and feathers,
Care not for your jests and laughter;
I am happy with Osseo!'

  "Once to some great feast invited,
Through the damp and dusk of evening,
Walked together the ten sisters,
Walked together with their husbands;

Slowly followed old Osseo,
With fair Oweenee beside him;
All the others chatted gayly,
These two only walked in silence.
     "At the western sky Osseo
Gazed intent, as if imploring,
Often stopped and gazed imploring
At the trembling Star of Evening,
At the tender Star of Woman;
And they heard him murmur softly,
'Ah, *showain nemeshin, Nosa!*
Pity me, pity me, my father!'
"'Listen!' said the eldest sister,
'He is praying to his father!
What a pity that the old man
Does not stumble in the pathway,
Does not break his neck by falling!'
And they laughed till all the forest
Rang with their unseemly laughter.
     "On their pathway through the woodlands
Lay an oak, by storms uprooted,
Lay the great trunk of an oak-tree,
Buried half in leaves and mosses,
Mouldering, crumbling, huge and hollow.
And Osseo, when he saw it,
Gave a shout, a cry of anguish,
Leaped into its yawning cavern,
At one end went in an old man,
Wasted, wrinkled, old, and ugly;
From the other came a young man,
Tall and straight and strong and handsome.
     "Thus Osseo was transfigured,
Thus restored to youth and beauty;
But, alas for good Osseo,
And for Oweenee, the faithful!
Strangely, too, was she transfigured.
Changed into a weak old woman,
With a staff she tottered onward,
Wasted, wrinkled, old, and ugly!
And the sisters and their husbands

Laughed until the echoing forest
Rang with their unseemly laughter.
    "But Osseo turned not from her,
Walked with slower step beside her,
Took her hand, as brown and withered
As an oak-leaf is in Winter,
Called her sweetheart, Nenemoosha,
Soothed her with soft words of kindness,
Till they reached the lodge of feasting,
Till they sat down in the wigwam,
Sacred to the Star of Evening,
To the tender Star of Woman.
    "Wrapt in visions, lost in dreaming,
At the banquet sat Osseo;
All were merry, all were happy,
All were joyous but Osseo.
Neither food nor drink he tasted,
Neither did he speak nor listen;
But as one bewildered sat he,
Looking dreamily and sadly,
First at Oweenee, then upward
At the gleaming sky above them.
    "Then a voice was heard, a whisper,
Coming from the starry distance,
Coming from the empty vastness,
Low, and musical, and tender;
And the voice said: 'O Osseo!
O my son, my best beloved!
Broken are the spells that bound you,
All the charms of the magicians,
All the magic powers of evil;
Come to me; ascend, Osseo!
    " 'Taste the food that stands before you:
It is blessed and enchanted,
It has magic virtues in it,
It will change you to a spirit.
All your bowls and all your kettles
Shall be wood and clay no longer;
But the bowls be changed to wampum,
And the kettles shall be silver;

They shall shine like shells of scarlet,
Like the fire shall gleam and glimmer.
   "'And the women shall no longer
Bear the dreary doom of labor,
But be changed to birds, and glisten
With the beauty of the starlight,
Painted with the dusky splendors
Of the skies and clouds of evening!'

   "What Osseo heard as whispers,
What as words he comprehended,
Was but music to the others,
Music as of birds afar off,
Of the whippoorwill afar off,
Of the lonely Wawonaissa
Singing in the darksome forest.

   "Then the lodge began to tremble,
Straight began to shake and tremble,
And they felt it rising, rising,
Slowly through the air ascending,
From the darkness of the tree-tops
Forth into the dewy starlight,
Till it passed the topmost branches;
And behold! the wooden dishes
All were changed to shells of scarlet!
And behold! the earthen kettles
All were changed to bowls of silver!
And the roof-poles of the wigwam
Were as glittering rods of silver,
And the roof of bark upon them
As the shining shards of beetles.

   "Then Osseo gazed around him,
And he saw the nine fair sisters,
All the sisters and their husbands,
Changed to birds of various plumage.
Some were jays and some were magpies,
Others thrushes, others blackbirds;
And they hopped, and sang, and twittered,
Perked and fluttered all their feathers,
Strutted in their shining plumage,
And their tails like fans unfolded.

"Only Oweenee, the youngest,
Was not changed, but sat in silence,
Wasted, wrinkled, old, and ugly,
Looking sadly at the others;
Till Osseo, gazing upward,
Gave another cry of anguish,
Such a cry as he had uttered
By the oak-tree in the forest.

     "Then returned her youth and beauty,
And her soiled and tattered garments
Were to robes of ermine,
And her staff became a feather,
Yes, a shining silver feather!

     "And again the wigwam trembled,
Swayed and rushed through airy currents,
Through transparent cloud and vapor,
And amid celestial splendors
On the Evening Star alighted,
As a snow-flake falls on snow-flake,
As a leaf drops on a river,
As the thistledown on water.

     "Forth with cheerful words of welcome
Came the father of Osseo,
He with radiant locks of silver,
He with eyes serene and tender.
And he said: `My son, Osseo,
Hang the cage of birds you bring there,
Hang the cage with rods of silver,
And the birds with glistening feathers,
At the doorway of my wigwam.'

     "At the door he hung the bird-cage,
And they entered in and gladly
Listened to Osseo's father,
Ruler of the Star of Evening,
As he said: `O my Osseo!
I have had on you,
Given you back your youth and beauty,
Into birds of various plumage
Changed your sisters and their husbands;
Changed them thus because they mocked you

In the figure of the old man,
In that aspect sad and wrinkled,
Could not see your heart of passion,
Could not see your youth immortal;
Only Oweenee, the faithful,
Saw your naked heart and loved you.
  "In the lodge that glimmers yonder,
In the little star that twinkles
Through the vapors, on the left hand,
Lives the envious Evil Spirit,
The Wabeno, the magician,
Who transformed you to an old man.
Take heed lest his beams fall on you,
For the rays he darts around him
Are the power of his enchantment,
Are the arrows that he uses.'
  "Many years, in peace and quiet,
On the peaceful Star of Evening
Dwelt Osseo with his father;
Many years, in song and flutter,
At the doorway of the wigwam,
Hung the cage with rods of silver,
And fair Oweenee, the faithful,
Bore a son unto Osseo,
With the beauty of his mother,
With the courage of his father.
  "And the boy grew up and prospered,
And Osseo, to delight him,
Made him little bows and arrows,
Opened the great cage of silver,
And let loose his aunts and uncles,
All those birds with glossy feathers,
For his little son to shoot at.
  "Round and round they wheeled and darted,
Filled the Evening Star with music,
With their songs of joy and freedom
Filled the Evening Star with splendor,
With the fluttering of their plumage;
Till the boy, the little hunter,
Bent his bow and shot an arrow,

Shot a swift and fatal arrow,
And a bird, with shining feathers,
At his feet fell wounded sorely.

"But, O wondrous transformation!
'T was no bird he saw before him,
'T was a beautiful young woman,
With the arrow in her bosom!

"When her blood fell on the planet,
On the sacred Star of Evening,
Broken was the spell of magic,
Powerless was the strange enchantment,
And the youth, the fearless bowman,
Suddenly felt himself descending,
Held by unseen hands, but sinking
Downward through the empty spaces,
Downward through the clouds and vapors,
Till he rested on an island,
On an island, green and grassy,
Yonder in the Big-Sea-Water.

"After him he saw descending
All the birds with shining feathers,
Fluttering, falling, wafted downward,
Like the painted leaves of Autumn;
And the lodge with poles of silver,
With its roof like wings of beetles,
Like the shining shards of beetles,
By the winds of heaven uplifted,
Slowly sank upon the island,
Bringing back the good Osseo,
Bringing Oweenee, the faithful.

"Then the birds, again transfigured,
Reassumed the shape of mortals,
Took their shape, but not their stature;
They remained as Little People,
Like the pygmies, the Puk-Wudjies,
And on pleasant nights of Summer,
When the Evening Star was shining,
Hand in hand they danced together
On the island's craggy headlands,
On the sand-beach low and level.

"Still their glittering lodge is seen there,
On the tranquil Summer evenings,
And upon the shore the fisher
Sometimes hears their happy voices,
Sees them dancing in the starlight !"

When the story was completed,
When the wondrous tale was ended,
Looking round upon his listeners,
Solemnly Iagoo added:
"There are great men, I have known such,
Whom their people understand not,
Whom they even make a jest of,
Scoff and jeer at in derision.
From the story of Osseo
Let us learn the fate of jesters!"

All the wedding guests delighted
Listened to the marvellous story,
Listened laughing and applauding,
And they whispered to each other:
"Does he mean himself, I wonder?
And are we the aunts and uncles?"

Then again sang Chibiabos,
Sang a song of love and longing,
In those accents sweet and tender,
In those tones of pensive sadness,
Sang a maiden's lamentation
For her lover, her Algonquin.

"When I think of my beloved,
Ah me! think of my beloved,
When my heart is thinking of him,
O my sweetheart, my Algonquin!
"Ah me! when I parted from him,
Round my neck he hung the wampum,
As a pledge, the snow-white wampum,
O my sweetheart, my Algonquin!
"I will go with you, he whispered,
Ah me! to your native country;
Let me go with you, he whispered,
O my sweetheart, my Algonquin!
"Far away, away, I answered,

Very far away, I answered,
Ah me! is my native country,
O my sweetheart, my Algonquin!
    "When I looked back to behold him,
Where we parted, to behold him,
After me he still was gazing,
O my sweetheart, my Algonquin!
    "By the tree he still was standing,
By the fallen tree was standing,
That had dropped into the water,
O my sweetheart, my Algonquin!
    "When I think of my beloved,
Ah me! think of my beloved,
When my heart is thinking of him,
O my sweetheart, my Algonquin!"
    Such was Hiawatha's Wedding,
Such the dance of Pau-Puk-Keewis,
Such the story of Iagoo,
Such the songs of Chibiabos;
Thus the wedding banquet ended,
And the wedding guests departed,
Leaving Hiawatha happy
With the night and Minnehaha.

XIII
Blessing the Cornfields

Sing, O Song of Hiawatha,
Of the happy days that followed,
In the land of the Ojibways,
In the pleasant land and peaceful!
Sing the mysteries of Mondamin,
Sing the Blessing of the Cornfields!
    Buried was the bloody hatchet,
Buried was the dreadful war-club,
Buried were all warlike weapons,
And the war-cry was forgotten.
There was peace among the nations;
Unmolested roved the hunters,

Built the birch-canoe for sailing,
Caught the fish in lake and river,
Shot the deer and trapped the beaver;
Unmolested worked the women,
Made their sugar from the maple,
Gathered wild rice in the meadows,
Dressed the skins of deer and beaver.
    All around the happy village
Stood the maize-fields, green and shining,
Waved the green plumes of Mondamin,
Waved his soft and sunny tresses,
Filling all the land with plenty.
'T was the women who in Spring-time
Planted the broad fields and fruitful,
Buried in the earth Mondamin;
'T was the women who in Autumn
Stripped the yellow husks of harvest,
Stripped the garments from Mondamin,
Even as Hiawatha taught them.
    Once, when all the maize was planted,
Hiawatha, wise and thoughtful,
Spake and said to Minnehaha,
To his wife, the Laughing Water:
"You shall bless to-night the cornfields,
Draw a magic circle round them,
To protect them from destruction,
Blast of mildew, blight of insect,
Wagemin, the thief of cornfields,
Paimosaid, who steals the maize-ear!
    "In the night, when all Is silence,'
In the night, when all is darkness,
When the Spirit of Sleep, Nepahwin,
Shuts the doors of all the wigwams,
So that not an ear can hear you,
So that not an eye can see you,
Rise up from your bed in silence,
Lay aside your garments wholly,
Walk around the fields you planted,
Round the borders of the cornfields,
Covered by your tresses only,

Robed with darkness as a garment.
    "Thus the fields shall be more fruitful,
And the passing of your footsteps
Draw a magic circle round them,
So that neither blight nor mildew,
Neither burrowing worm nor insect,
Shall pass o'er the magic circle;
Not the dragon-fly, Kwo-ne-she,
Nor the spider, Subbekashe,
Nor the grasshopper, Pah-puk-keena;
Nor the mighty caterpillar,
Way-muk-kwana, with the bear-skin,
King of all the caterpillars!"
    On the tree-tops near the cornfields
Sat the hungry crows and ravens,
Kahgahgee, the King of Ravens,
With his band of black marauders.
And they laughed at Hiawatha,
Till the tree-tops shook with laughter,
With their melancholy laughter,
At the words of Hiawatha.
"Hear him!" said they; "hear the Wise Man,
Hear the plots of Hiawatha!"
    When the noiseless night descended
Broad and dark o'er field and forest,
When the mournful Wawonaissa
Sorrowing sang among the hemlocks,
And the Spirit of Sleep, Nepahwin,
Shut the doors of all the wigwams,
From her bed rose Laughing Water,
Laid aside her garments wholly,
And with darkness clothed and guarded,
Unashamed and unaffrighted,
Walked securely round the cornfields,
Drew the sacred, magic circle
Of her footprints round the cornfields.
    No one but the Midnight only
Saw her beauty in the darkness,
No one but the Wawonaissa
Heard the panting of her bosom

Guskewau, the darkness, wrapped her
Closely in his sacred mantle,
So that none might see her beauty,
So that none might boast, "I saw her!"
   On the morrow, as the day dawned,
Kahgahgee, the King of Ravens,
Gathered all his black marauders,
Crows and blackbirds, jays and ravens,
Clamorous on the dusky tree-tops,
And descended, fast and fearless,
On the fields of Hiawatha,
On the grave of the Mondamin.
   "We will drag Mondamin," said they,
"From the grave where he is buried,
Spite of all the magic circles
Laughing Water draws around it,
Spite of all the sacred footprints
Minnehaha stamps upon it!"
   But the wary Hiawatha,
Ever thoughtful, careful, watchful,
Had o'erheard the scornful laughter
When they mocked him from the tree-tops.
"Kaw!" he said, "my friends the ravens!
Kahgahgee, my King of Ravens!
I will teach you all a lesson
That shall not be soon forgotten!"
   He had risen before the daybreak,
He had spread o'er all the cornfields
Snares to catch the black marauders,
And was lying now in ambush
In the neighboring grove of pine-trees,
Waiting for the crows and blackbirds,
Waiting for the jays and ravens.
   Soon they came with caw and clamor,
Rush of wings and cry of voices,
To their work of devastation,
Settling down upon the cornfields,
Delving deep with beak and talon,
For the body of Mondamin.
And with all their craft and cunning,

All their skill in wiles of warfare,
They perceived no danger near them,
Till their claws became entangled,
Till they found themselves imprisoned
In the snares of Hiawatha.

From his place of ambush came he,
Striding terrible among them,
And so awful was his aspect
That the bravest quailed with terror.
Without mercy he destroyed them
Right and left, by tens and twenties,
And their wretched, lifeless bodies
Hung aloft on poles for scarecrows
Round the consecrated cornfields,
As a signal of his vengeance,
As a warning to marauders.

Only Kahgahgee, the leader,
Kahgahgee, the King of Ravens,
He alone was spared among them
As a hostage for his people.
With his prisoner-string he bound him,
Led him captive to his wigwam,
Tied him fast with cords of elm-bark
To the ridge-pole of his wigwam.

"Kahgahgee, my raven!" said he,
"You the leader of the robbers,
You the plotter of this mischief,
The contriver of this outrage,
I will keep you, I will hold you,
As a hostage for your people,
As a pledge of good behavior !"

And he left him, grim and sulky,
Sitting in the morning sunshine
On the summit of the wigwam,
Croaking fiercely his displeasure,
Flapping his great sable pinions,
Vainly struggling for his freedom,
Vainly calling on his people!

Summer passed, and Shawondasee
Breathed his sighs o'er all the landscape,

From the South-land sent his ardor,
Wafted kisses warm and tender;
And the maize-field grew and ripened,
Till it stood in all the splendor
Of its garments green and yellow,
Of its tassels and its plumage,
And the maize-ears full and shining
Gleamed from bursting sheaths of verdure.
    Then Nokomis, the old woman,
Spake, and said to Minnehaha:
" 'T is the Moon when, leaves are falling;
All the wild rice has been gathered,
And the maize is ripe and ready;
Let us gather in the harvest,
Let us wrestle with Mondamin,
Strip him of his plumes and tassels,
Of his garments green and yellow!"
    And the merry Laughing Water
Went rejoicing from the wigwam,
With Nokomis, old and wrinkled,
And they called the women round them,
Called the young men and the maidens,
To the harvest of the cornfields,
To the husking of the maize-ear.
    On the border of the forest,
Underneath the fragrant pine-trees,
Sat the old men and the warriors
Smoking in the pleasant shadow.
In uninterrupted silence
Looked they at the gamesome labor
Of the young men and the women;
Listened to their noisy talking,
To their laughter and their singing,
Heard them chattering like the magpies,
Heard them laughing like the blue-jays,
Heard them singing like the robins.
    And whene'er some lucky maiden
Found a red ear in the husking,
Found a maize-ear red as blood is,
"Nushka!" cried they all together,

"Nushka! you shall have a sweetheart,
You shall have a handsome husband!"
"Ugh!" the old men all responded
From their seats beneath the pine-trees.
    And whene'er a youth or maiden
Found a crooked ear in husking,
Found a maize-ear in the husking
Blighted, mildewed, or misshapen,
Then they laughed and sang together,
Crept and limped about the cornfields,
Mimicked in their gait and gestures
Some old man, bent almost double,
Singing singly or together:
"Wagemin, the thief of cornfields!
Paimosaid, who steals the maize-ear!"
    Till the cornfields rang with laughter,
Till from Hiawatha's wigwam
Kahgahgee, the King of Ravens,
Screamed and quivered in his anger,
And from all the neighboring tree-tops
Cawed and croaked the black marauders.
"Ugh!" the old men all responded,
From their seats beneath the pine-trees!

XIV
Picture-Writing

In those days said Hiawatha,
"Lo! how all things fade and perish!
From the memory of the old men
Pass away the great traditions,
The achievements of the warriors,
The adventures of the hunters,
All the wisdom of the Medas,
All the craft of the Wabenos,
All the marvellous dreams and visions
Of the Jossakeeds, the Prophets!
    "Great men die and are forgotten,
Wise men speak; their words of wisdom

Perish in the ears that hear them,
Do not reach the generations
That, as yet unborn, are waiting
In the great, mysterious darkness
Of the speechless days that shall be!
    "On the grave-posts of our fathers
Are no signs, no figures painted;
Who are in those graves we know not,
Only know they are our fathers.
Of what kith they are and kindred,
From what old, ancestral Totem,
Be it Eagle, Bear, or Beaver,
They descended, this we know not,
Only they are our fathers.
    "Face to face we speak together,
But we cannot speak when absent,
Cannot send our voices from us
To the friends that dwell afar off;
Cannot send a secret message,
But the bearer learns our secret,
May pervert it, may betray it,
May reveal it unto others."
    Thus said Hiawatha, walking
In the solitary forest,
Pondering, musing in the forest,
On the welfare of his people.
    From his pouch he took his colors,
Took his paints of different colors,
On the smooth bark of a birch-tree
Painted many shapes and figures,
Wonderful and mystic figures,
And each figure had a meaning,
Each some word or thought suggested.
    Gitche Manito the Mighty,
He, the Master of Life, was painted
As an egg, with points projecting
To the four winds of the heavens.
Everywhere is the Great Spirit,
Was the meaning of this symbol.
    Gitche Manito the Mighty,

He the dreadful Spirit of Evil,
As a serpent was depicted,
As Kenabeek, the great serpent.
Very crafty, very cunning,
Is the creeping Spirit of Evil,
Was the meaning of this symbol.

Life and Death he drew as circles,
Life was white, but Death was darkened;
Sun and moon and stars he painted,
Man and beast, and fish and reptile,
Forests, mountains, lakes, and rivers.

For the earth he drew a straight line,
For the sky a bow above it;
White the space between for day-time,
Filled with little stars for night-time;
On the left a point for sunrise,
On the right a point for sunset,
On the top a point for noontide,
And for rain and cloudy weather
Waving lines descending from it.

Footprints pointing towards a wigwam
Were a sign of invitation,
Were a sign of guests assembling;
Bloody hands with palms uplifted
Were a symbol of destruction,
Were a hostile sign and symbol.

All these things did Hiawatha
Show unto his wondering people,
And interpreted their meaning,
And he said: "Behold, your grave-posts
Have no mark, no sign, nor symbol,
Go and paint them all with figures;
Each one with its household symbol,
With its own ancestral Totem;
So that those who follow after
May distinguish them and know them."

And they painted on the grave-posts
On the graves yet unforgotten,
Each his own ancestral Totem,
Each the symbol of his household;

Figures of the Bear and Reindeer,
Of the Turtle, Crane, and Beaver,
Each inverted as a token
That the owner was departed,
That the chief who bore the symbol
Lay beneath in dust and ashes.
    And the Jossakeeds, the Prophets,
The Wabenos, the Magicians,
And the Medicine-men, the Medas,
Painted upon bark and deer-skin
Figures for the songs they chanted,
For each song a separate symbol,
Figures mystical and awful,
Figures strange and brightly colored;
And each figure had its meaning,
Each some magic song suggested.
    The Great Spirit, the Creator,
Flashing light through all the heaven;
The Great Serpent, the Kenabeek,
With his bloody crest erected,
Creeping, looking into heaven;
In the sky the sun, that listens,
And the moon eclipsed and dying;
Owl and eagle, crane and hen-hawk,
And the cormorant, bird of magic;
Headless men, that walk the heavens,
Bodies lying pierced with arrows,
Bloody hands of death uplifted,
Flags on graves, and great war-captains
Grasping both the earth and heaven!
    Such as these the shapes they painted
On the birch-bark and the deer-skin;
Songs of war and songs of hunting,
Songs of medicine and of magic,
All were written in these figures,
For each figure had its meaning,
Each its separate song recorded.
    Nor forgotten was the Love-Song,
The most subtle of all medicines,
The most potent spell of magic,

Dangerous more than war or hunting!
Thus the Love-Song was recorded,
Symbol and interpretation.

First a human figure standing,
Painted in the brightest scarlet;
'T is the lover, the musician,
And the meaning is, "My painting
Makes me powerful over others."

Then the figure seated, singing,
Playing on a drum of magic,
And the interpretation, "Listen!
'T is my voice you hear, my singing!"

Then the same red figure seated
In the shelter of a wigwam,
And the meaning of the symbol,
"I will come and sit beside you
In the mystery of my passion!"

Then two figures, man and woman,
Standing hand in hand together
With their hands so clasped together
That they seemed in one united,
And the words thus represented
Are, "I see your heart within you,
And your cheeks are red with blushes!"

Next the maiden on an island,
In the centre of an Island;
And the song this shape suggested
Was, "Though you were at a distance,
Were upon some far-off island,
Such the spell I cast upon you,
Such the magic power of passion,
I could straightway draw you to me!"

Then the figure of the maiden
Sleeping, and the lover near her,
Whispering to her in her slumbers,
Saying, "Though you were far from me
In the land of Sleep and Silence,
Still the voice of love would reach you!"

And the last of all the figures
Was a heart within a circle,

Drawn within a magic circle;
And the image had this meaning:
"Naked lies your heart before me,
To your naked heart I whisper!"
  Thus it was that Hiawatha,
In his wisdom, taught the people
All the mysteries of painting,
All the art of Picture-Writing,
On the smooth bark of the birch-tree,
On the white skin of the reindeer,
On the grave-posts of the village.

XV
Hiawatha's Lamentation

In those days the Evil Spirits,
All the Manitos of mischief,
  Fearing Hiawatha's wisdom,
And his love for Chibiabos,
Jealous of their faithful friendship,
And their noble words and actions,
Made at length a league against them,
To molest them and destroy them.
Hiawatha, wise and wary,
Often said to Chibiabos,
"O my brother! do not leave me,
Lest the Evil Spirits harm you!"
Chibiabos, young and heedless,
Laughing shook his coal-black tresses,
Answered ever sweet and childlike,
"Do not fear for me, O brother!
Harm and evil come not near me!"
  Once when Peboan, the Winter,
Roofed with ice the Big-Sea-Water,
When the snow-flakes, whirling downward,
Hissed among the withered oak-leaves,
Changed the pine-trees into wigwams,
Covered all the earth with silence,
Armed with arrows, shod with snow-shoes,

Heeding not his brother's warning,
Fearing not the Evil Spirits,
Forth to hunt the deer with antlers
All alone went Chibiabos.

Right across the Big-Sea-Water
Sprang with speed the deer before him.
With the wind and snow he followed,
O'er the treacherous ice he followed,
Wild with all the fierce commotion
And the rapture of the hunting.

But beneath, the Evil Spirits
Lay in ambush, waiting for him,
Broke the treacherous ice beneath him,
Dragged him downward to the bottom,
Buried in the sand his body.
Unktahee, the god of water,
He the god of the Dacotahs,
Drowned him in the deep abysses
Of the lake of Gitche Gumee.

From the headlands Hiawatha
Sent forth such a wail of anguish,
Such a fearful lamentation,
That the bison paused to listen,
And the wolves howled from the prairies,
And the thunder in the distance
Starting answered "Baim-wawa!"

Then his face with black he painted,
With his robe his head he covered,
In his wigwam sat lamenting,
Seven long weeks he sat lamenting,
Uttering still this moan of sorrow: –

"He is dead, the sweet musician!
He the sweetest of all singers!
He has gone from us forever,
He has moved a little nearer
To the Master of all music,
To the Master of all singing!
O my brother, Chibiabos!"

And the melancholy fir-trees
Waved their dark green fans above him,

Waved their purple cones above him,
Sighing with him to console him,
Mingling with his lamentation
Their complaining, their lamenting.
　　Came the Spring, and all the forest
Looked in vain for Chibiabos;
Sighed the rivulet, Sebowisha,
Sighed the rushes in the meadow.
　　From the tree-tops sang the bluebird,
Sang the bluebird, the Owaissa,
"Chibiabos! Chibiabos!
He is dead, the sweet musician!"
　　From the wigwam sang the robin,
Sang the robin, the Opechee,
"Chibiabos! Chibiabos!
He is dead, the sweetest singer!"
And at night through all the forest
Went the whippoorwill complaining,
Wailing went the Wawonaissa,
"Chibiabos! Chibiabos!
He is dead, the sweet musician!
He the sweetest of all singers!"
　　Then the Medicine-men, the Medas,
The Magicians, the Wabenos,
And the Jossakeeds, the Prophets,
Came to visit Hiawatha;
Built a Sacred Lodge beside him,
To appease him, to console him,
Walked in silent, grave procession,
Bearing each a pouch of healing,
Skin of beaver, lynx, or otter,
Filled with magic roots and simples,
Filled with very potent medicines.
　　When he heard their steps approaching
Hiawatha ceased lamenting,
Called no more on Chibiabos;
Naught he questioned, naught he answered,
But his mournful head uncovered,
From his face the mourning colors
Washed he slowly and in silence,

Slowly and in silence followed
Onward to the Sacred Wigwam.
    There a magic drink they gave him,
Made of Nahma-wusk, the spearmint,
And Wabeno-wusk, the yarrow,
Roots of power, and herbs of healing;
Beat their drums, and shook their rattles;
Chanted singly and in chorus,
Mystic songs like these, they chanted.
    "I myself, myself! behold me!
'T is the great Gray Eagle talking;
Come, ye white crows, come and hear him!
The loud-speaking thunder helps me;
All the unseen spirits help me;
I can hear their voices calling,
All around the sky I hear them!
I can blow you strong, my brother,
I can heal you, Hiawatha!"
    "Hi-au-ha!" replied the chorus,
"Wayha-way!" the mystic chorus.
    Friends of mine are all the serpents!
Hear me shake my skin of hen-hawk!
Mahng, the white loon, I can kill him;
I can shoot your heart and kill it!
I can blow you strong, my brother,
I can heal you, Hiawatha !"
    "Hi-au-ha!" replied the chorus,
"Wayhaway!" the mystic chorus.
    "I myself, myself! the prophet!
When I speak the wigwam trembles,
Shakes the Sacred Lodge with terror,
Hands unseen begin to shake it!
When I walk, the sky I tread on
Bends and makes a noise beneath me!
I can blow you strong, my brother!
Rise and speak, O Hiawatha!"
    "Hi-au-ha!" replied the chorus,
"Way-ha-way!" the mystic chorus.
    Then they shook their medicine-pouches
O'er the head of Hiawatha,

Danced their medicine-dance around him;
And upstarting wild and haggard,
Like a man from dreams awakened,
He was healed of all his madness.
As the clouds are swept from heaven,
Straightway from his brain departed
All his moody melancholy;
As the ice is swept from rivers,
Straightway from his heart departed
All his sorrow and affliction.

Then they summoned Chibiabos
From his grave beneath the waters,
From the sands of Gitche Gumee
Summoned Hiawatha's brother.
And so mighty was the magic
Of that cry and invocation,
That he heard it as he lay there
Underneath the Big-Sea-Water;
From the sand he rose and listened,
Heard the music and the singing,
Came, obedient to the summons,
To the doorway of the wigwam,
But to enter they forbade him.

Through a chink a coal they gave him,
Through the door a burning fire-brand;
Ruler in the Land of Spirits,
Ruler o'er the dead, they made him,
Telling him a fire to kindle
For all those that died thereafter,
Camp-fires for their night encampments
On their solitary journey
To the kingdom of Ponemah,
To the land of the Hereafter.

From the village of his childhood,
From the homes of those who knew him,
Passing silent through the forest,
Like a smoke-wreath wafted sideways,
Slowly vanished Chibiabos!
Where he passed, the branches moved not,
Where he trod, the grasses bent not,

And the fallen leaves of last year
Made no sound beneath his footstep.
    Four whole days he journeyed onward
Down the pathway of the dead men;
On the dead-man's strawberry feasted,
Crossed the melancholy river,
On the swinging log he crossed it,
Came unto the Lake of Silver,
In the Stone Canoe was carried
To the Islands of the Blessed,
To the land of ghosts and shadows.
    On that journey, moving slowly,
Many weary spirits saw he,
Panting under heavy burdens,
Laden with war-clubs, bows and arrows,
Robes of fur, and pots and kettles,
And with food that friends had given
For that solitary journey.
    "Ah! why do the living," said they,
"Lay such heavy burdens on us!
Better were it to go naked,
Better were it to go fasting,
Than to bear such heavy burdens
On our long and weary journey!"
    Forth then issued Hiawatha,
Wandered eastward, wandered westward,
Teaching men the use of simples
And the antidotes for poisons,
And the cure of all diseases.
Thus was first made known to mortals
All the mystery of Medamin,
All the sacred art of healing.

XVI
Pau-Puk-Keewis

You shall hear how Pau-Puk-Keewis,
He, the handsome Yenadizze,
Whom the people called the Storm-Fool,

Vexed the village with disturbance;
You shall hear of all his mischief,
And his flight from Hiawatha,
And his wondrous transmigrations,
And the end of his adventures.

On the shores of Gitche Gumee,
On the dunes of Nagow Wudjoo,
By the shining Big-Sea-Water
Stood the lodge of Pau-Puk-Keewis.
It was he who in his frenzy
Whirled these drifting sands together,
On the dunes of Nagow Wudjoo,
When, among the guests assembled,
He so merrily and madly
Danced at Hiawatha's wedding,
Danced the Beggar's Dance to please them.

Now, in search of new adventures,
From his lodge went Pau-Puk-Keewis,
Came with speed into the village,
Found the young men all assembled
In the lodge of old Iagoo,
Listening to his monstrous stories,
To his wonderful adventures.

He was telling them the story
Of Ojeeg, the Summer-Maker,
How he made a hole in heaven,
How he climbed up into heaven,
And let out the Summer-weather,
The perpetual, pleasant Summer;
How the Otter first essayed it;
How the Beaver, Lynx, and Badger
Tried in turn the great achievement,
From the summit of the mountain
Smote their fists against the heavens,
Smote against the sky their foreheads,
Cracked the sky, but could not break it;
How the Wolverine, uprising,
Made him ready for the encounter,
Bent his knees down, like a squirrel,
Drew his arms back, like a cricket.

"Once he leaped," said old Iagoo,
"Once he leaped, and lo! above him
Bent the sky, as ice in rivers
When the waters rise beneath it;
Twice he leaped, and lo! above him
Cracked the sky, as ice in rivers
When the freshet is at highest!
Thrice he leaped, and lo! above him
Broke the shattered sky asunder,
And he disappeared within it,
And Ojeeg, the Fisher Weasel,
With a bound went in behind him!"

"Hark you!" shouted Pau-Puk-Keewis
As he entered at the doorway;
"I am tired of all this talking,
Tired of old Iagoo's stories,
Tired of Hiawatha's wisdom.
Here is something to amuse you,
Better than this endless talking."

Then from out his pouch of wolf-skin
Forth he drew, with solemn manner,
All the game of Bowl and Counters,
Pugasaing, with thirteen pieces.
White on one side were they painted,
And vermilion on the other;
Two Kenabeeks or great serpents,
Two Ininewug or wedge-men,
One great war-club, Pugamaugun,
And one slender fish, the Keego,
Four round pieces, Ozawabeeks,
And three Sheshebwug or ducklings.
All were made of bone and painted,
All except the Ozawabeeks;
These were brass, on one side burnished,
And were black upon the other.

In a wooden bowl he placed them,
Shook and jostled them together,
Threw them on the ground before him,
Thus exclaiming and explaining:
"Red side up are all the pieces,

And one great Kenabeek standing
On the bright side of a brass piece,
On a burnished Ozawabeek;
Thirteen tens and eight are counted."
    Then again he shook the pieces,
Shook and jostled them together,
Threw them on the ground before him,
Still exclaiming and explaining:
"White are both the great Kenabeeks,
White the Ininewug, the wedge-men,
Red are all the other pieces;
Five tens and an eight are counted."
    Thus he taught the game of hazard,
Thus displayed it and explained it,
Running through its various chances,
Various changes, various meanings:
Twenty curious eyes stared at him,
Full of eagerness stared at him.
"Many games," said old Iagoo,
"Many games of skill and hazard
Have I seen in different nations,
Have I played in different countries.
He who plays with old Iagoo
Must have very nimble fingers;
Though you think yourself so skilful,
I can beat you, Pau-Puk-Keewis,
I can even give you lessons
In your game of Bowl and Counters!"
    So they sat and played together,
All the old men and the young men,
Played for dresses, weapons, wampum,
Played till midnight, played till morning,
Played until the Yenadizze,
Till the cunning Pau-Puk-Keewis,
Of their treasures had despoiled them,
Of the best of all their dresses,
Shirts of deer-skin, robes of ermine,
Belts of wampum, crests of feathers,
Warlike weapons, pipes and pouches.
Twenty eyes glared wildly at him,

Like the eyes of wolves glared at him.
    Said the lucky Pau-Puk-Keewis:
"In my wigwam I am lonely,
In my wanderings and adventures
I have need of a companion,
Fain would have a Meshinauwa,
An attendant and pipe-bearer.
I will venture all these winnings,
All these garments heaped about me,
All this wampum, all these feathers,
On a single throw will venture
All against the young man yonder!"
'T was a youth of sixteen summers,
'T was a nephew of Iagoo;
Face-in-a-Mist, the people called him.
    As the fire burns in a pipe-head
Dusky red beneath the ashes,
So beneath his shaggy eyebrows
Glowed the eyes of old Iagoo.
"Ugh!" he answered very fiercely;
"Ugh!" they answered all and each one.
    Seized the wooden bowl the old man,
Closely in his bony fingers
Clutched the fatal bowl, Onagon,
Shook it fiercely and with fury,
Made the pieces ring together
As he threw them down before him.
    Red were both the great Kenabeeks,
Red the Ininewug, the wedge-men,
Red the Sheshebwug, the ducklings,
Black the four brass Ozawabeeks,
White the fish, the Keego;
Only five the pieces counted!
    Then the smiling Pau-Puk-Keewis
Shook the bowl and threw the pieces;
Lightly in the air he tossed them,
And they fell about him scattered;
Dark and bright the Ozawabeeks,
Red and white the other pieces,
And upright among the others

One Ininewug was standing,
Even as crafty Pau-Puk-Keewis
Stood alone among the players,
Saying, "Five tens! mine the game is,"

Twenty eyes glared at him fiercely,
Like the eyes of wolves glared at him,
As he turned and left the wigwam,
Followed by his Meshinauwa,
By the nephew of Iagoo,
By the tall and graceful stripling,
Bearing in his arms the winnings,
Shirts of deer-skin, robes of ermine,
Belts of wampum, pipes and weapons.

"Carry them," said Pau-Puk-Keewis,
Pointing with his fan of feathers,
"To my wigwam far to eastward,
On the dunes of Nagow Wudjoo!"

Hot and red with smoke and gambling
Were the eyes of Pau-Puk-Keewis
As he came forth to the freshness
Of the pleasant Summer morning.
All the birds were singing gayly,
All the streamlets flowing swiftly,
And the heart of Pau-Puk-Keewis
Sang with pleasure as the birds sing,
Beat with triumph like the streamlets,
As he wandered through the village,
In the early gray of morning,
With his fan of turkey-feathers,
With his plumes and tufts of swan's down,
Till he reached the farthest wigwam,
Reached the lodge of Hiawatha.

Silent was it and deserted;
No one met him at the doorway,
No one came to bid him welcome;
But the birds were singing round it,
In and out and round the doorway,
Hopping, singing, fluttering, feeding,
And aloft upon the ridge-pole
Kahgahgee, the King of Ravens,

Sat with fiery eyes, and, screaming,
Flapped his wings at Pau–Puk–Keewis.
    "All are gone! the lodge Is empty!"
Thus it was spake Pau–Puk–Keewis,
In his heart resolving mischief
"Gone is wary Hiawatha,
Gone the silly Laughing Water,
Gone Nokomis, the old woman,
And the lodge is left unguarded!"
    By the neck he seized the raven,
Whirled it round him like a rattle,
Like a medicine-pouch he shook it,
Strangled Kahgahgee, the raven,
From the ridge-pole of the wigwam
Left its lifeless body hanging,
As an insult to its master,
As a taunt to Hiawatha.
    With a stealthy step he entered,
Round the lodge in wild disorder
Threw the household things about him,
Piled together in confusion
Bowls of wood and earthen kettles,
Robes of buffalo and beaver,
Skins of otter, lynx, and ermine,
As an insult to Nokomis,
As a taunt to Minnehaha.
    Then departed Pau–Puk–Keewis,
Whistling, singing through the forest,
Whistling gayly to the squirrels,
Who from hollow boughs above him
Dropped their acorn-shells upon him,
Singing gayly to the wood birds,
Who from out the leafy darkness
Answered with a song as merry.
    Then he climbed the rocky headlands,
Looking o'er the Gitche Gumee,
Perched upon their summit,
Waiting full of mirth and mischief
The return of Hiawatha.
    Stretched upon his back he lay there;

Far below him splashed the waters,
Plashed and washed the waters;
Far above him swam the heavens,
Swam the dizzy, dreamy heavens;
Round him hovered, fluttered, rustled
Hiawatha's mountain chickens,
Flock-wise swept and wheeled about him,
Almost brushed him with their pinions.
    And he killed them as he lay there,
Slaughtered them by tens and twenties,
Threw their bodies down the headland,
Threw them on the beach below him,
Till at length Kayoshk, the sea-gull,
Perched upon a crag above them,
Shouted: "It is Pau-Puk-Keewis!
He is slaying us by hundreds!
Send a message to our brother,
Tidings send to Hiawatha!"

XVII
The Hunting of Pau-Puk-Keewis

Full of wrath was Hiawatha
When he came into the village,
Found the people in confusion,
Heard of all the misdemeanors,
All the malice and the mischief,
Of the cunning Pau-Puk-Keewis.
    Hard his breath came through his nostrils,
Through his teeth he buzzed and muttered
Words of anger and resentment,
Hot and humming, like a hornet.
"I will slay this Pau-Puk-Keewis,
Slay this mischief-maker!" said he.
"Not so long and wide the world is,
Not so rude and rough the way is, `
That my wrath shall not attain him,
That my vengeance shall not reach him!"
    Then in swift pursuit departed

Hiawatha and the hunters
On the trail of Pau-Puk-Keewis,
Through the forest, where he passed it,
To the headlands where he rested;
But they found not Pau-Puk-Keewis,
Only in the trampled grasses,
In the whortleberry-bushes,
Found the couch where he had rested,
Found the impress of his body.

From the lowlands far beneath them,
From the Muskoday, the meadow,
Pau-Puk-Keewis, turning backward,
Made a gesture of defiance,
Made a gesture of derision;
And aloud cried Hiawatha,
From the summit of the mountains:
"Not so long and wide the world is,
Not so rude and rough the way is,
But my wrath shall overtake you,
And my vengeance shall overtake you!"

Over rock and over river,
Through bush, and brake, and forest,
Ran the cunning Pau-Puk-Keewis;
Like an antelope he bounded,
Till he came unto a streamlet
In the middle of the forest,
To a streamlet still and tranquil,
That had overflowed its margin,
To a dam made by the beavers,
To a pond of quiet water,
Where knee-deep the trees were standing,
Where the water lilies floated,
Where the rushes waved and whispered.

On the dam stood Pau-Puk-Keewis,
On the dam of trunks and branches,
Through whose chinks the water spouted,
O'er whose summit flowed the streamlet.
From the bottom rose the beaver,
Looked with two great eyes of wonder,
Eyes that seemed to ask a question,

At the stranger, Pau-Puk-Keewis.
   On the dam stood Pau-Puk-Keewis,
O'er his ankles flowed the streamlet,
Flowed the bright and silvery water,
And he spake unto the beaver,
With a smile he spake in this wise:
   "O my friend Ahmeek, the beaver,
Cool and pleasant is the water;
Let me dive into the water,
Let me rest there in your lodges;
Change me, too, into a beaver!"
   Cautiously replied the beaver,
With reserve he thus made answer:
"Let me first consult the others,
Let me ask the other beavers."
Down he sank into the water,
Heavily sank he, as a stone sinks,
Down among the leaves and branches,
Brown and matted at the bottom.
   On the dam stood Pau-Puk-Keewis,
O'er his ankles flowed the streamlet,
Spouted through the chinks below him,
Dashed upon the stones beneath him,
Spread serene and calm before him,
And the sunshine and the shadows
Fell in flecks and gleams upon him,
Fell in little shining patches,
Through the waving, rustling branches.
   From the bottom rose the beavers,
Silently above the surface
Rose one head and then another,
Till the pond seemed full of beavers,
Full of black and shining faces.
   To the beavers Pau-Puk-Keewis
Spake entreating, said in this wise:
"Very pleasant is your dwelling,
O my friends! and safe from danger;
Can you not with all your cunning,
All your wisdom and contrivance,
Change me, too, into a beaver?"

"Yes!" replied Ahmeek, the beaver,
He the King of all the beavers,
"Let yourself slide down among us,
Down into the tranquil water."

Down into the pond among them
Silently sank Pau-Puk-Keewis;
Black became his shirt of deer-skin,
Black his moccasins and leggings,
In a broad black tail behind him
Spread his fox-tails and his fringes;
He was changed into a beaver.

"Make me large," said Pau-Puk-Keewis,
"Make me large and make me larger,
Larger than the other beavers."
"Yes," the beaver chief responded,
"When our lodge below you enter,
In our wigwam we will make you
Ten times larger than the others."

Thus into the clear, brown water
Silently sank Pau-Puk-Keewis:
Found the bottom covered over
With the trunks of trees and branches,
Hoards of food against the winter,
Piles and heaps against the famine;
Found the lodge with arching doorway,
Leading into spacious chambers.

Here they made him large and larger,
Made him largest of the beavers,
Ten times larger than the others.
"You shall be our ruler," said they;
"Chief and King of all the beavers."

But not long had Pau-Puk-Keewis
Sat in state among the beavers,
When there came a voice, of warning
From the watchman at his station
In the water-flags and lilies,
Saying, "Here Is Hiawatha!
Hiawatha with his hunters!"

Then they heard a cry above them,
Heard a shouting and a tramping,

Heard a crashing and a rushing,
And the water round and o'er them
Sank and sucked away in eddies,
And they knew their dam was broken.
    On the lodge's roof the hunters
Leaped, and broke it all asunder;
Streamed the sunshine through the crevice,
Sprang the beavers through the doorway,
Hid themselves in deeper water,
In the channel of the streamlet;
But the mighty Pau-Puk-Keewis
Could not pass beneath the doorway;
He was puffed with pride and feeding,
He was swollen like a bladder.
    Through the roof looked Hiawatha,
Cried aloud, "O Pau-Puk-Keewis
Vain are all your craft and cunning,
Vain your manifold disguises!
Well I know you, Pau-Puk-Keewis!"
    With their clubs they beat and bruised him,
Beat to death poor Pau-Puk-Keewis,
Pounded him as maize is pounded,
Till his skull was crushed to pieces.
    Six tall hunters, lithe and limber,
Bore him home on poles and branches,
Bore the body of the beaver;
But the ghost, the Jeebi in him,
Thought and felt as Pau-Puk-Keewis,
Still lived on as Pau-Puk-Keewis.
    And it fluttered, strove, and struggled,
Waving hither, waving thither,
As the curtains of a wigwam
Struggle with their thongs of deer-skin,
When the wintry wind is blowing;
Till it drew itself together,
Till it rose up from the body,
Till it took the form and features
Of the cunning Pau-Puk-Keewis
Vanishing into the forest.
    But the wary Hiawatha

Saw the figure ere it vanished,
Saw the form of Pau-Puk-Keewis
Glide into the soft blue shadow
Of the pine-trees of the forest;
Toward the squares of white beyond it,
Toward an opening in the forest.
Like a wind it rushed and panted,
Bending all the boughs before it,
And behind it, as the rain comes,
Came the steps of Hiawatha.

    To a lake with many islands
Came the breathless Pau-Puk-Keewis,
Where among the water-lilies
Pishnekuh, the brant, were sailing;
Through the tufts of rushes floating,
Steering through the reedy Islands.
Now their broad black beaks they lifted,
Now they plunged beneath the water,
Now they darkened in the shadow,
Now they brightened in the sunshine.

    "Pishnekuh!" cried Pau-Puk-Keewis,
"Pishnekuh! my brothers!" said he,
"Change me to a brant with plumage,
With a shining neck and feathers,
Make me large, and make me larger,
Ten times larger than the others."

    Straightway to a brant they changed him,
With two huge and dusky pinions,
With a bosom smooth and rounded,
With a bill like two great paddles,
Made him larger than the others,
Ten times larger than the largest,
Just as, shouting from the forest,
On the shore stood Hiawatha.

    Up they rose with cry and clamor,
With a whir and beat of pinions,
Rose up from the reedy Islands,
From the water-flags and lilies.
And they said to Pau-Puk-Keewis:
"In your flying, look not downward,

Take good heed and look not downward,
Lest some strange mischance should happen,
Lest some great mishap befall you!"
 Fast and far they fled to northward,
Fast and far through mist and sunshine,
Fed among the moors and fen-lands,
Slept among the reeds and rushes.
 On the morrow as they journeyed,
Buoyed and lifted by the South-wind,
Wafted onward by the South-wind,
Blowing fresh and strong behind them,
Rose a sound of human voices,
Rose a clamor from beneath them,
From the lodges of a village,
From the people miles beneath them.
 For the people of the village
Saw the flock of brant with wonder,
Saw the wings of Pau-Puk-Keewis
Flapping far up in the ether,
Broader than two doorway curtains.
 Pau-Puk-Keewis heard the shouting,
Knew the voice of Hiawatha,
Knew the outcry of Iagoo,
And, forgetful of the warning,
Drew his neck in, and looked downward,
And the wind that blew behind him
Caught his mighty fan of feathers,
Sent him wheeling, whirling downward!
 All in vain did Pau-Puk-Keewis
Struggle to regain his balance!
Whirling round and round and downward,
He beheld in turn the village
And in turn the flock above him,
Saw the village coming nearer,
And the flock receding farther,
Heard the voices growing louder,
Heard the shouting and the laughter;
Saw no more the flocks above him,
Only saw the earth beneath him;
Dead out of the empty heaven,

Dead among the shouting people,
With a heavy sound and sullen,
Fell the brant with broken pinions.

But his soul, his ghost, his shadow,
Still survived as Pau-Puk-Keewis,
Took again the form and features
Of the handsome Yenadizze,
And again went rushing onward,
Followed fast by Hiawatha,
Crying: "Not so wide the world is,
Not so long and rough the way is,
But my wrath shall overtake you,
But my vengeance shall attain you!"

And so near he came, so near him,
That his hand was stretched to seize him,
His right hand to seize and hold him,
When the cunning Pau-Puk-Keewis
Whirled and spun about in circles,
Fanned the air into a whirlwind,
Danced the dust and leaves about him,
And amid the whirling eddies
Sprang into a hollow oak-tree,
Changed himself into a serpent,
Gliding out through root and rubbish.

With his right hand Hiawatha
Smote amain the hollow oak-tree,
Rent it into shreds and splinters,
Left it lying there in fragments.
But in vain; for Pau-Puk-Keewis,
Once again in human figure,
Full in sight ran on before him,
Sped away in gust and whirlwind,
On the shores of Gitche Gumee,
Westward by the Big-Sea-Water,
Came unto the rocky headlands,
To the Pictured Rocks of sandstone,
Looking over lake and landscape.

And the Old Man of the Mountain,
He the Manito of Mountains,
Opened wide his rocky doorways,

Opened wide his deep abysses,
Giving Pau-Puk-Keewis shelter
In his caverns dark and dreary,
Bidding Pau-Puk-Keewis welcome
To his gloomy lodge of sandstone

    There without stood Hiawatha,
Found the doorways closed against him,
With his mittens, Minjekahwun,
Smote great caverns in the sandstone,
Cried aloud in tones of thunder,
"Open! I am Hiawatha!"
But the Old Man of the Mountain
Opened not, and made no answer
From the silent crags of sandstone,
From the gloomy rock abysses.

    Then he raised his hands to heaven,
Called imploring on the tempest,
Called Waywassimo, the lightning,
And the thunder, Annemeekee;
And they came with night and darkness,
Sweeping down the Big-Sea-Water
From the distant Thunder Mountains;
And the trembling Pau-Puk-Keewis
Heard the footsteps of the thunder,
Saw the red eyes of the lightning,
Was afraid, and crouched and trembled.

    Then Waywassimo, the lightning,
Smote the doorways of the caverns,
With his war-club smote the doorways,
Smote the jutting crags of sandstone,
And the thunder, Annemeekee,
Shouted down into the caverns,
Saying, "Where is Pau-Puk-Keewis!"
And the crags fell, and beneath them
Dead among the rocky ruins
Lay the cunning Pau-Puk-Keewis,
Lay the handsome Yenadizze,
Slain in his own human figure.

    Ended were his wild adventures,
Ended were his tricks and gambols,

Ended all his craft and cunning,
Ended all his mischief-making,
All his gambling and his dancing,
All his wooing of the maidens.
    Then the noble Hiawatha
Took his soul, his ghost, his shadow,
Spake and said: "O Pau-Puk-Keewis,
Never more in human figure
Shall you search for new adventures;
Never more with jest and laughter
Dance the dust and leaves in whirlwinds;
But above there in the heavens
You shall soar and sail in circles;
I will change you to an eagle,
To Keneu, the great war-eagle,
Chief of all the fowls with feathers,
Chief of Hiawatha's chickens."
    And the name of Pau-Puk-Keewis
Lingers still among the people,
Lingers still among the singers,
And among the story-tellers;
And in Winter, when the snow-flakes
Whirl in eddies round the lodges,
When the wind in gusty tumult
O'er the smoke-flue pipes and whistles,
"There," they cry, "comes Pau-Puk-Keewis,
He is dancing through the village,
He is gathering in his harvest!"

XVIII
The Death of Kwasind

Far and wide among the nations
Spread the name and fame of Kwasind;
No man dared to strive with Kwasind,
No man could compete with Kwasind.
But the mischievous Puk-Wudjies,
They the envious Little People,
They the fairies and the pygmies,

Plotted and conspired against him.
        "If this hateful Kwasind," said they,
"If this great, outrageous fellow
Goes on thus a little longer,
Tearing everything he touches,
Rending everything to pieces,
Filling all the world with wonder,
What becomes of the Puk-Wudjies?
Who will care for the Puk-Wudjies?
He will tread us down like mushrooms,
Drive us all into the water,
Give our bodies to be eaten
By the wicked Nee-ba-naw-baigs,
By the Spirits of the water!
        So the angry Little People
All conspired against the Strong Man,
All conspired to murder Kwasind,
Yes, to rid the world of Kwasind,
The audacious, overbearing,
Heartless, haughty, dangerous Kwasind!
        Now this wondrous strength of Kwasind
In his crown alone was seated;
In his crown too was his weakness;
There alone could he be wounded,
Nowhere else could weapon pierce him,
Nowhere else could weapon harm him.
        Even there the only weapon
That could wound him, that could slay him,
Was the seed-cone of the pine-tree,
Was the blue cone of the fir-tree.
This was Kwasind's fatal secret,
Known to no man among mortals;
But the cunning Little People,
The Puk-Wudjies, the secret,
Knew the only way to kill him.
        So they gathered cones together,
Gathered seed-cones of the pine-tree,
Gathered blue cones of the fir-tree,
In the woods by Taquamenaw,
Brought them to the river's margin,

Heaped them in great piles together,
Where the red rocks from the margin
Jutting overhang the river.
There they lay in wait for Kwasind,
The malicious Little People.
　　'T was an afternoon in Summer;
Very hot and still the air was,
Very smooth the gliding river,
Motionless the sleeping shadows:
Insects glistened in the sunshine,
Insects skated on the water,
Filled the drowsy air with buzzing,
With a far resounding war-cry.
　　Down the river came the Strong Man,
In his birch canoe came Kwasind,
Floating slowly down the current
Of the sluggish Taquamenaw,
Very languid with the weather,
Very sleepy with the silence.
　　From the overhanging branches,
From the tassels of the birch-trees,
Soft the Spirit of Sleep descended;
By his airy hosts surrounded,
His invisible attendants,
Came the Spirit of Sleep, Nepahwin;
Like a burnished Dush-kwo-ne-she,
Like a dragon-fly, he hovered
O'er the drowsy head of Kwasind.
　　To his ear there came a murmur
As of waves upon a sea-shore,
As of far-off tumbling waters,
As of winds among the pine-trees;
And he felt upon his forehead
Blows of little airy war-clubs,
Wielded by the slumbrous legions
Of the Spirit of Sleep, Nepahwin,
As of some one breathing on him.
　　At the first blow of their war-clubs,
Fell a drowsiness on Kwasind;
At the second blow they smote him,

Motionless his paddle rested;
At the third, before his vision
Reeled the landscape into darkness,
Very sound asleep was Kwasind.

So he floated down the river,
Like a blind man seated upright,
Floated down the Taquamenaw,
Underneath the trembling birch-trees,
Underneath the wooded headlands,
Underneath the war encampment
Of the pygmies, the Puk-Wudjies.

There they stood, all armed and waiting,
Hurled the pine-cones down upon him,
Struck him on his brawny shoulders,
On his crown defenceless struck him.
"Death to Kwasind!" was the sudden
War-cry of the Little People.

And he sideways swayed and tumbled,
Sideways fell into the river,
Plunged beneath the sluggish water
Headlong, as an otter plunges;
And the birch canoe, abandoned,
Drifted empty down the river,
Bottom upward swerved and drifted
Nothing more was seen of Kwasind.

But the memory of the Strong Man
Lingered long among the people,
And whenever through the forest
Raged and roared the wintry tempest,
And the branches, tossed and troubled,
Creaked and groaned and split asunder,
"Kwasind!" cried they; "that is Kwasind!
He is gathering in his fire-wood!"

XIX
The Ghosts

Never stoops the soaring vulture
On his quarry in the desert,
On the sick or wounded bison,
But another vulture, watching
From his high aerial look-out,
Sees the downward plunge, and follows;
And a third pursues the second,
Coming from the invisible ether,
First a speck, and then a vulture,
Till the air is dark with pinions.

    So disasters come not singly;
But as if they watched and waited,
Scanning one another's motions,
When the first descends, the others
Follow, follow, gathering flock-wise
Round their victim, sick and wounded,
First a shadow, then a sorrow,
Till the air is dark with anguish.

    Now, o'er all the dreary Northland,
Mighty Peboan, the Winter,
Breathing on the lakes and rivers,
Into stone had changed their waters.
From his hair he shook the snowflakes,
Till the plains were strewn with whiteness,
One uninterrupted level,
As if, stooping, the Creator
With his hand had smoothed them over.

    Through the forest, wide and wailing,
Roamed the hunter on his snow-shoes;
In the village worked the women,
Pounded maize, or dressed the deer-skin;
And the young men played together
On the ice the noisy ball-play,
On the plain the dance of snow-shoes.

    One dark evening, after sundown,
In her wigwam Laughing Water
Sat with old Nokomis, waiting

For the steps of Hiawatha
Homeward from the hunt returning.
    On their faces gleamed the firelight,
Painting them with streaks of crimson,
In the eyes of old Nokomis
Glimmered like the watery moonlight,
In the eyes of Laughing Water
Glistened like the sun in water;
And behind them crouched their shadows
In the corners of the wigwam,
And the smoke In wreaths above them
Climbed and crowded through the smoke-flue.
    Then the curtain of the doorway
From without was slowly lifted;
Brighter glowed the fire a moment,
And a moment swerved the smoke-wreath,
As two women entered softly,
Passed the doorway uninvited,
Without word of salutation,
Without sign of recognition,
Sat down in the farthest corner,
Crouching low among the shadows.
    From their aspect and their garments,
Strangers seemed they in the village;
Very pale and haggard were they,
As they sat there sad and silent,
Trembling, cowering with the shadows.
    Was it the wind above the smoke-flue,
Muttering down into the wigwam?
Was it the owl, the Koko-koho,
Hooting from the dismal forest?
Sure a voice said in the silence:
"These are corpses clad in garments,
These are ghosts that come to haunt you,
From the kingdom of Ponemah,
From the land of the Hereafter!"
    Homeward now came Hiawatha
From his hunting in the forest,
With the snow upon his tresses,
And the red deer on his shoulders.

At the feet of Laughing Water
Down he threw his lifeless burden;
Nobler, handsomer she thought him,
Than when first he came to woo her,
First threw down the deer before her,
As a token of his wishes,
As a promise of the future.

Then he turned and saw the strangers,
Cowering, crouching with the shadows;
Said within, "Who are they?
What strange guests has Minnehaha?"
But he questioned not the strangers,
Only spake to bid them welcome
To his lodge, his food, his fireside.

When the evening meal was ready,
And the deer had been divided,
Both the pallid guests, the strangers,
Springing from among the shadows,
Seized upon the choicest portions,
Seized the white fat of the roebuck,
Set apart for Laughing Water,
For the wife of Hiawatha;
Without asking, without thanking,
Eagerly devoured the morsels,
Flitted back among the shadows
In the corner of the wigwam.

Not a word spake Hiawatha,
Not a motion made Nokomis,
Not a gesture Laughing Water;
Not a change came o'er their features;
Only Minnehaha softly
Whispered, saying, "They are famished;
Let them do what best delights them;
Let them eat, for they are famished."

Many a daylight dawned and darkened,
Many a night shook off the daylight
As the pine shakes off the snow-flakes
From the midnight of its branches;
Day by day the guests unmoving
Sat there silent in the wigwam;

But by night, in storm or starlight,
Forth they went into the forest,
Bringing fire-wood to the wigwam,
Bringing pine-cones for the burning,
Always sad and always silent.

And whenever Hiawatha
Came from fishing or from hunting,
When the evening meal was ready,
And the food had been divided,
Gliding from their darksome corner,
Came the pallid guests, the strangers,
Seized upon the choicest portions
Set aside for Laughing Water,
And without rebuke or question
Flitted back among the shadows.

Never once had Hiawatha
By a word or look reproved them;
Never once had old Nokomis
Made a gesture of impatience;
Never once had Laughing Water
Shown resentment at the outrage.
All had they endured in silence,
That the rights of guest and stranger,
That the virtue of free-giving,
By a look might not be lessened,
By a word might not be broken.

Once at midnight Hiawatha,
Ever wakeful, ever watchful,
In the wigwam, dimly lighted
By the brands that still were burning,
By the glimmering, flickering firelight
Heard a sighing, oft repeated,
Heard a sobbing, as of sorrow.

From his couch rose Hiawatha,
From his shaggy hides of bison,
Pushed aside the deer-skin curtain,
Saw the pallid guests, the shadows,
Sitting upright on their couches,
Weeping in the silent midnight.

And he said: "O guests! why is it

That your hearts are so afflicted,
That you sob so in the midnight?
Has perchance the old Nokomis,
Has my wife, my Minnehaha,
Wronged or grieved you by unkindness,
Failed in hospitable duties?"
    Then the shadows ceased from weeping,
Ceased from sobbing and lamenting,
And they said, with gentle voices:
"We are ghosts of the departed,
Souls of those who once were with you.
From the realms of Chibiabos
Hither have we come to try you,
Hither have we come to warn you.
    "Cries of grief and lamentation
Reach us in the Blessed Islands;
Cries of anguish from the living,
Calling back their friends departed,
Sadden us with useless sorrow.
Therefore have we come to try you;
No one knows us, no one heeds us.
We are but a burden to you,
And we see that the departed
Have no place among the living.
    "Think of this, O Hiawatha!
Speak of it to all the people,
That henceforward and forever
They no more with lamentations
Sadden the souls of the departed
In the Islands of the Blessed.
    "Do not lay such heavy burdens
In the graves of those you bury,
Not such weight of furs and wampum,
Not such weight of pots and kettles,
For the spirits faint beneath them.
Only give them food to carry,
Only give them fire to light them.
    "Four days is the spirit's journey
To the land of ghosts and shadows,
Four its lonely night encampments;

Four times must their fires be lighted.
Therefore, when the dead are buried,
Let a fire, as night approaches,
Four times on the grave be kindled,
That the soul upon its journey
May not lack the cheerful firelight,
May not grope about in darkness.
    "Farewell, noble Hiawatha!
We have put you to the trial,
To the proof have put your patience,
By the insult of our presence,
By the outrage of our actions.
We have found you great and noble.
Fail not in the greater trial,
Faint not in the harder struggle."
    When they ceased, a sudden darkness
Fell and filled the silent wigwam.
Hiawatha heard a rustle
As of garments trailing by him,
Heard the curtain of the doorway
Lifted by a hand he saw not,
Felt the cold breath of the night air,
For a moment saw the starlight;
But he saw the ghosts no longer,
Saw no more the wandering
From the kingdom of Ponemah,
From the land of the Hereafter.

XX
The Famine

Oh the long and dreary Winter!
Oh the cold and cruel Winter!
Ever thicker, thicker, thicker
Froze the ice on lake and river,
Ever deeper, deeper, deeper
Fell the snow o'er all the landscape,
Fell the covering snow, and drifted
Through the forest, round the village.

Hardly from his buried wigwam
Could the hunter force a passage;
With his mittens and his snow-shoes
Vainly walked he through the forest,
Sought for bird or beast and found none,
Saw no track of deer or rabbit,
In the snow beheld no footprints,
In the ghastly, gleaming forest
Fell, and could not rise from weakness,
Perished there from cold and hunger.
 O the famine and the fever!
O the wasting of the famine!
O the blasting of the fever!
O the wailing of the children!
O the anguish of the women!
 All the earth was sick and famished;
Hungry was the air around them,
Hungry was the sky above them,
And the hungry stars in heaven
Like the eyes of wolves glared at them!
 Into Hiawatha's wigwam
Came two other guests, as silent
As the ghosts were, and as gloomy,
Waited not to be invited,
Did not parley at the doorway
Sat there without word of welcome
In the seat of Laughing Water;
Looked with haggard eyes and hollow
At the face of Laughing Water.
 And the foremost said: "Behold me!
I am Famine, Bukadawin!"
And the other said: "Behold me!
I am Fever, Ahkosewin!"
 And the lovely Minnehaha
Shuddered as they looked upon her,
Shuddered at the words they uttered,
Lay down on her bed in silence,
Hid her face, but made no answer;
Lay there trembling, freezing, burning
At the looks they cast upon her,

At the fearful words they uttered.
   Forth into the empty forest
Rushed the maddened Hiawatha;
In his heart was deadly sorrow,
In his face a stony firmness;
On his brow the sweat of anguish
Started, but it froze and fell not.
   Wrapped in furs and armed for hunting,
With his mighty bow of ash-tree,
With his quiver full of arrows,
With his mittens, Minjekahwun,
Into the vast and vacant forest
On his snow-shoes strode he forward.
   "Gitche Manito, the Mighty!"
Cried he with his face uplifted
In that bitter hour of anguish,
"Give your children food, O father!
Give us food, or we must perish!
Give me food for Minnehaha,
For my dying Minnehaha!"
   Through the far-resounding forest,
Through the forest vast and vacant
Rang that cry of desolation,
But there came no other answer
Than the echo of his crying,
Than the echo of the woodlands,
"Minnehaha! Minnehaha!"
   All day long roved Hiawatha
In that melancholy forest,
Through the shadow of whose thickets,
In the pleasant days of Summer,
Of that ne'er forgotten Summer,
He had brought his young wife homeward
From the land of the Dacotahs;
When the birds sang in the thickets,
And the streamlets laughed and glistened,
And the air was full of fragrance,
And the lovely Laughing Water
Said with voice that did not tremble,
"I will follow you, my husband!"

In the wigwam with Nokomis,
With those gloomy guests that watched her,
With the Famine and the Fever,
She was lying, the Beloved,
She, the dying Minnehaha.
"Hark!" she said; "I hear a rushing,
Hear a roaring and a rushing,
Hear the Falls of Minnehaha
Calling to me from a distance!"
"No, my child!" said old Nokomis,
"'T is the night-wind in the pine-trees!"

    "Look!" she said; "I see my father
Standing lonely at his doorway,
Beckoning to me from his wigwam
In the land of the Dacotahs!"
"No, my child!" said old Nokomis.
"'T is the smoke, that waves and beckons!"

    "Ah!" said she, "the eyes of Pauguk
Glare upon me in the darkness,
I can feel his icy fingers
Clasping mine amid the darkness!
Hiawatha! Hiawatha!"

    And the desolate Hiawatha,
Far away amid the forest,
Miles away among the mountains,
Heard that sudden cry of anguish,
Heard the voice of Minnehaha
Calling to him in the darkness,
"Hiawatha! Hiawatha!"

    Over snow-fields waste and pathless,
Under snow-encumbered branches,
Homeward hurried Hiawatha,
Empty-handed, heavy-hearted,
Heard Nokomis moaning, wailing:
"Wahonowin! Wahonowin!
Would that I had perished for you,
Would that I were dead as you are!
Wahonowin! Wahonowin!"

    And he rushed into the wigwam,
Saw the old Nokomis slowly

Rocking to and fro and moaning,
Saw his lovely Minnehaha
Lying dead and cold before him,
And his bursting heart within him
Uttered such a cry of anguish,
That the forest moaned and shuddered,
That the very stars in heaven
Shook and trembled with his anguish.
     Then he sat down, still and speechless,
On the bed of Minnehaha,
At the feet of Laughing Water,
At those willing feet, that never
More would lightly run to meet him,
Never more would lightly follow.
     With both hands his face he covered,
Seven long days and nights he sat there,
As if in a swoon he sat there,
Speechless, motionless, unconscious
Of the daylight or the darkness.
     Then they buried Minnehaha;
In the snow a grave they made her
In the forest deep and darksome
Underneath the moaning hemlocks;
Clothed her in her richest garments
Wrapped her in her robes of ermine,
Covered her with snow, like ermine;
Thus they buried Minnehaha.
     And at night a fire was lighted,
On her grave four times was kindled,
For her soul upon its journey
To the Islands of the Blessed.
From his doorway Hiawatha
Saw it burning in the forest,
Lighting up the gloomy hemlocks;
From his sleepless bed uprising,
From the bed of Minnehaha,
Stood and watched it at the doorway,
That it might not be extinguished,
Might not leave her in the darkness.
     "Farewell!" said he, "Minnehaha!

Farewell, O my Laughing Water!
All my heart is buried with you,
All my thoughts go onward with you!
Come not back again to labor,
Come not back again to suffer,
Where the Famine and the Fever
Wear the heart and waste the body.
Soon my task will be completed,
Soon your footsteps I shall follow
To the Islands of the Blessed,
To the Kingdom of Ponemah,
To the Land of the Hereafter!"

XXI
The White Man's Foot

In his lodge beside a river,
Close beside a frozen river,
Sat an old man, sad and lonely.
White his hair was as a snow-drift;
Dull and low his fire was burning,
And the old man shook and trembled,
Folded in his Waubewyon,
In his tattered white-skin-wrapper,
Hearing nothing but the tempest
As it roared along the forest,
Seeing nothing but the snow-storm,
As it whirled and hissed and drifted.
    All the coals were white with ashes,
And the fire was slowly dying,
As a young man, walking lightly,
At the open doorway entered.
Red with blood of youth his cheeks were,
Soft his eyes, as stars in Spring-time,
Bound his forehead was with grasses;
Bound and plumed with scented grasses,
On his lips a smile of beauty,
Filling all the lodge with sunshine,
In his hand a bunch of blossoms

Filling all the lodge with sweetness.
    "Ah, my son!" exclaimed the old man,
"Happy are my eyes to see you.
Sit here on the mat beside me,
Sit here by the dying embers,
Let us pass the night together,
Tell me of your strange adventures,
Of the lands where you have travelled;
I will tell you of my prowess,
Of my many deeds of wonder."
    From his pouch he drew his peace-pipe,
Very old and strangely fashioned;
Made of red stone was the pipe-head,
And the stem a reed with feathers;
Filled the pipe with bark of willow,
Placed a burning coal upon it,
Gave it to his guest, the stranger,
And began to speak in this wise:
    "When I blow my breath about me,
When I breathe upon the landscape,
Motionless are all the rivers,
Hard as stone becomes the water!"
    And the young man answered, smiling:
"When I blow my breath about me,
When I breathe upon the landscape,
Flowers spring up o'er all the meadows,
Singing, onward rush the rivers!"
"When I shake my hoary tresses,"
Said the old man darkly frowning,
"All the land with snow is covered;
All the leaves from all the branches
Fall and fade and die and wither,
For I breathe, and lo! they are not.
From the waters and the marshes,
Rise the wild goose and the heron,
Fly away to distant regions,
For I speak, and lo! they are not.
And where'er my footsteps wander,
All the wild beasts of the forest
Hide themselves in holes and caverns,

And the earth becomes as flintstone!"
      "When I shake my flowing ringlets,"
Said the young man, softly laughing,
"Showers of rain fall warm and welcome,
Plants lift up their heads rejoicing,
Back Into their lakes and marshes
Come the wild goose and the heron,
Homeward shoots the arrowy swallow,
Sing the bluebird and the robin,
And where'er my footsteps wander,
All the meadows wave with blossoms,
All the woodlands ring with music,
All the trees are dark with foliage!"
      While they spake, the night departed:
From the distant realms of Wabun,
From his shining lodge of silver,
Like a warrior robed and painted,
Came the sun, and said, "Behold me
Gheezis, the great sun, behold me!"
      Then the old man's tongue was speechless
And the air grew warm and pleasant,
And upon the wigwam sweetly
Sang the bluebird and the robin,
And the stream began to murmur,
And a scent of growing grasses
Through the lodge was gently wafted.
      And Segwun, the youthful stranger,
More distinctly in the daylight
Saw the icy face before him;
It was Peboan, the Winter!
      From his eyes the tears were flowing,
As from melting lakes the streamlets,
And his body shrunk and dwindled
As the shouting sun ascended,
Till into the air it faded,
Till into the ground it vanished,
And the young man saw before him,
On the hearth-stone of the wigwam,
Where the fire had smoked and smouldered,
Saw the earliest flower of Spring-time,

Saw the Beauty of the Spring-time,
Saw the Miskodeed in blossom.
   Thus it was that in the North-land
After that unheard-of coldness,
That intolerable Winter,
Came the Spring with all its splendor,
All its birds and all its blossoms,
All its flowers and leaves and grasses.
   Sailing on the wind to northward,
Flying in great flocks, like arrows,
Like huge arrows shot through heaven,
Passed the swan, the Mahnahbezee,
Speaking almost as a man speaks;
And in long lines waving, bending
Like a bow-string snapped asunder,
Came the white goose, Waw-be-wawa;
And in pairs, or singly flying,
Mahng the loon, with clangorous pinions,
The blue heron, the Shuh-shuh-gah,
And the grouse, the Mushkodasa.
   In the thickets and the meadows
Piped the bluebird, the Owaissa,
On the summit of the lodges
Sang the robin, the Opechee,
In the covert of the pine-trees
Cooed the pigeon, the Omemee;
And the sorrowing Hiawatha,
Speechless in his infinite sorrow,
Heard their voices calling to him,
Went forth from his gloomy doorway,
Stood and gazed into the heaven,
Gazed upon the earth and waters.
   From his wanderings far to eastward,
From the regions of the morning,
From the shining land of Wabun,
Homeward now returned Iagoo,
The great traveller, the great boaster,
Full of new and strange adventures,
Marvels many and many wonders.
   And the people of the village

Listened to him as he told them
Of his marvellous adventures,
Laughing answered him in this wise:
"Ugh! it is indeed Iagoo!
No one else beholds such wonders!"

He had seen, he said, a water
Bigger than the Big-Sea-Water,
Broader than the Gitche Gumee,
Bitter so that none could drink it!
At each other looked the warriors,
Looked the women at each other,
Smiled, and said, "It cannot be so!
Kaw!" they said, "it cannot be so!"

O'er it, said he, o'er this water
Came a great canoe with pinions,
A canoe with wings came flying,
Bigger than a grove of pine-trees,
Taller than the tallest tree-tops!
And the old men and the women
Looked and tittered at each other;
"Kaw!" they said, "we don't believe it!"

From its mouth, he said, to greet him,
Came Waywassimo, the lightning,
Came the thunder, Annemeekee!
And the warriors and the women
Laughed aloud at poor Iagoo;
"Kaw!" they said, "what tales you tell us!"
In it, said he, came a people,
In the great canoe with pinions
Came, he said, a hundred warriors;
Painted white were all their faces
And with hair their chins were covered!
And the warriors and the women
Laughed and shouted in derision,
Like the ravens on the tree-tops,
Like the crows upon the hemlocks.
"Kaw!" they said, "what lies you tell us!
Do not think that we believe them!"

Only Hiawatha laughed not,
But he gravely spake and answered

To their jeering and their jesting:
"True is all Iagoo tells us;
I have seen it in a vision,
Seen the great canoe with pinions,
Seen the people with white faces,
Seen the coming of this bearded
People of the wooden vessel
From the regions of the morning,
From the shining land of Wabun.

    "Gitche Manito, the Mighty,
The Great Spirit, the Creator,
Sends them hither on his errand.
Sends them to us with his message.
Wheresoe'er they move, before them
Swarms the stinging fly, the Ahmo,
Swarms the bee, the honey-maker;
Wheresoe'er they tread, beneath them
Springs a flower unknown among us,
Springs the White-man's Foot in blossom.

    "Let us welcome, then, the strangers,
Hail them as our friends and brothers,
And the heart's right hand of friendship
Give them when they come to see us.
Gitche Manito, the Mighty,
Said this to me in my vision.

    "I beheld, too, in that vision
All the secrets of the future,
Of the distant days that shall be.
I beheld the westward marches
Of the unknown, crowded nations.
All the land was full of people,
Restless, struggling, toiling, striving,
Speaking many tongues, yet feeling
But one heart-beat in their bosoms.
In the woodlands rang their axes,
Smoked their towns in all the valleys,
Over all the lakes and rivers
Rushed their great canoes of thunder.

    "Then a darker, drearier vision
Passed before me, vague and cloud-like;

I beheld our nation scattered,
All forgetful of my counsels,
Weakened, warring with each other:
Saw the remnants of our people
Sweeping westward, wild and woful,
Like the cloud-rack of a tempest,
Like the withered leaves of Autumn!"

XXII
Hiawatha's Departure

By the shore of Gitche Gumee,
By the shining Big-Sea-Water,
At the doorway of his wigwam,
In the pleasant Summer morning,
Hiawatha stood and waited.
All the air was full of freshness,
All the earth was bright and joyous,
And before him, through the sunshine,
Westward toward the neighboring forest
Passed in golden swarms the Ahmo,
Passed the bees, the honey-makers,
Burning, singing in the sunshine.
     Bright above him shone the heavens,
Level spread the lake before him;
From its bosom leaped the sturgeon,
Sparkling, flashing in the sunshine;
On its margin the great forest
Stood reflected in the water,
Every tree-top had its shadow,
Motionless beneath the water.
     From the brow of Hiawatha
Gone was every trace of sorrow,
As the fog from off the water,
As the mist from off the meadow.
With a smile of look and triumph,
With a look of exultation,
As of one who in a vision
Sees what is to be, but is not,

Stood and waited Hiawatha.
    Toward the sun his hands were lifted,
Both the palms spread out against it,
And between the parted fingers
Fell the sunshine on his features,
Flecked with light his naked shoulders,
As it falls and flecks an oak-tree
Through the rifted leaves and branches.
    O'er the water floating, flying,
Something in the hazy distance,
Something in the mists of morning,
Loomed and lifted from the water,
Now seemed floating, now seemed flying,
Coming nearer, nearer, nearer.
    Was it Shingebis the diver?
Or the pelican, the Shada?
Or the heron, the Shuh-shuh-gah?
Or the white goose, Waw-be-wawa,
With the water dripping, flashing,
From its glossy neck and feathers?
    It was neither goose nor diver,
Neither pelican nor heron,
O'er the water floating, flying,
Through the shining mist of morning,
But a birch canoe with paddles,
Rising, sinking on the water,
Dripping, flashing in the sunshine;
And within it came a people
From the distant land of Wabun,
From the farthest realms of morning
Came the Black-Robe chief, the Prophet,
He the Priest of Prayer, the Pale-face,
With his guides and his companions.
    And the noble Hiawatha,
With his hands aloft extended,
Held aloft in sign of welcome,
Waited, full of exultation,
Till the birch canoe with paddles
Grated on the shining pebbles,
Stranded on the sandy margin,

Till the Black-Robe chief, the Pale-face,
With the cross upon his bosom,
Landed on the sandy margin.
      Then the joyous Hiawatha
Cried aloud and spake in this wise:
"Beautiful is the sun, O strangers,
When you come so far to see us!
All our town in peace awaits you,
All our doors stand open for you;
You shall enter all our wigwams,
For the heart's right hand we give you.
      "Never bloomed the earth so gayly,
Never shone the sun so brightly,
As to-day they shine and blossom
When you come so far to see us!
Never was our lake so tranquil,
Nor so free from rocks, and sand-bars;
For your birch canoe in passing
Has removed both rock and sand-bar.
      "Never before had our tobacco
Such a sweet and pleasant flavor,
Never the broad leaves of our corn-fields
Were so beautiful to look on,
As they seem to us this morning,
When you come so far to see us!'
      And the Black-Robe chief made answer,
Stammered In his speech a little,
Speaking words yet unfamiliar:
"Peace be with you, Hiawatha,
Peace be with you and your people,
Peace of prayer, and peace of pardon,
Peace of Christ, and joy of Mary!"
      Then the generous Hiawatha
Led the strangers to his wigwam,
Seated them on skins of bison,
Seated them on skins of ermine,
And the careful old Nokomis
Brought them food in bowls of basswood,
Water brought in birchen dippers,
And the calumet, the peace-pipe,

Filled and lighted for their smoking.
    All the old men of the village,
All the warriors of the nation,
All the Jossakeeds, the Prophets,
The magicians, the Wabenos,
And the Medicine-men, the Medas,
Came to bid the strangers welcome;
"It is well", they said, "O brothers,
That you come so far to see us!"
    In a circle round the doorway,
With their pipes they sat In silence,
Waiting to behold the strangers,
Waiting to receive their message;
Till the Black-Robe chief, the Pale-face,
From the wigwam came to greet them,
Stammering in his speech a little,
Speaking words yet unfamiliar;
"It is well," they said, "O brother,
That you come so far to see us!"
    Then the Black-Robe chief, the Prophet,
Told his message to the people,
Told the purport of his mission,
Told them of the Virgin Mary,
And her blessed Son, the Saviour,
How in distant lands and ages
He had lived on earth as we do;
How he fasted, prayed, and labored;
How the Jews, the tribe accursed,
Mocked him, scourged him, crucified him;
How he rose from where they laid him,
Walked again with his disciples,
And ascended into heaven.
    And the chiefs made answer, saying:
"We have listened to your message,
We have heard your words of wisdom,
We will think on what you tell us.
It is well for us, O brothers,
That you come so far to see us!"
    Then they rose up and departed
Each one homeward to his wigwam,

To the young men and the women
Told the story of the strangers
Whom the Master of Life had sent them
From the shining land of Wabun.

    Heavy with the heat and silence
Grew the afternoon of Summer;
With a drowsy sound the forest
Whispered round the sultry wigwam,
With a sound of sleep the water
Rippled on the beach below it;
From the cornfields shrill and ceaseless
Sang the grasshopper, Pah-puk-keena;
And the guests of Hiawatha,
Weary with the heat of Summer,
Slumbered in the sultry wigwam.

    Slowly o'er the simmering landscape
Fell the evening's dusk and coolness,
And the long and level sunbeams
Shot their spears into the forest,
Breaking through its shields of shadow,
Rushed into each secret ambush,
Searched each thicket, dingle, hollow;
Still the guests of Hiawatha
Slumbered In the silent wigwam.

    From his place rose Hiawatha,
Bade farewell to old Nokomis,
Spake in whispers, spake in this wise,
Did not wake the guests, that slumbered:
    "I am going, O Nokomis,
On a long and distant journey,
To the portals of the Sunset.
To the regions of the home-wind,
Of the Northwest-Wind, Keewaydin.
But these guests I leave behind me,
In your watch and ward I leave them;
See that never harm comes near them,
See that never molests them,
Never danger nor suspicion,
Never want of food or shelter,
In the lodge of Hiawatha!"

Forth into the village went he,
Bade farewell to all the warriors,
Bade farewell to all the young men,
Spake persuading, spake in this wise:
    "I am going, O my people,
On a long and distant journey;
Many moons and many winters
Will have come, and will have vanished,
Ere I come again to see you.
But my guests I leave behind me;
Listen to their words of wisdom,
Listen to the truth they tell you,
For the Master of Life has sent them
From the land of light and morning!"
    On the shore stood Hiawatha,
Turned and waved his hand at parting;
On the clear and luminous water
Launched his birch canoe for sailing,
From the pebbles of the margin
Shoved it forth into the water;
Whispered to it, "Westward! westward!"
And with speed it darted forward.
    And the evening sun descending
Set the clouds on fire with redness,
Burned the broad sky, like a prairie,
Left upon the level water
One long track and trail of splendor,
Down whose stream, as down a river,
Westward, westward Hiawatha
Sailed into the fiery sunset,
Sailed into the purple vapors,
Sailed into the dusk of evening.
    And the people from the margin
Watched him floating, rising, sinking,
Till the birch-canoe seemed lifted
High into that sea of splendor,
Till it sank into the vapors
Like the new moon slowly, slowly
Sinking in the purple distance.
    And they said, "Farewell forever!"

Said, "Farewell, O Hiawatha!"
And the forests, dark and lonely,
Moved through all their depths of darkness,
Sighed, "Farewell, O Hiawatha!"
And the waves upon the margin
Rising, rippling on the pebbles,
Sobbed, "Farewell, O Hiawatha!"
And the heron, the Shuh-shuh-gah,
From her haunts among the fen-lands,
Screamed, "Farewell, O Hiawatha!"
    Thus departed Hiawatha,
Hiawatha the Beloved,
In the glory of the sunset,
In the purple mists of evening,
To the regions of the home-wind,
Of the Northwest-Wind, Keewaydin,
To the Islands of the Blessed,
To the Kingdom of Ponemah,
To the Land of the Hereafter!